CRISIS OF GOVERNANCE

By the same author

- **US Policy Towards South Asia:** *With spl. reference to Indo-Pak relations*
- **Human Rights in India:** *Issues and Chailenges (ed.)*
- **Pakistan's Fourth Military Coup** (*ed.*)
- **US Military Aid to Pakistan and India's Security**

CRISIS OF GOVERNANCE

Edited by
Aftab Alam

Raj Publications
Delhi-110 009 (INDIA)

First Published in 2003

ISBN 81- 86208- 25- 9

Published by : **Mrs. Poonam Goel**
Raj Publications
R-115/2, Model Town - III,
Delhi - 110009
Tel. : 011- 7143321
E Mail:- rajpub@now-india.net.in.

Laser Typesetting by : Aarati Computers, Delhi-110 009

Printed at : Chawla Offset Printers, Delhi-110 052

PRINTED IN INDIA

Contents

Preface

The concept of 'governance' came into vogue only recently though the story of governance is as old as human civilization itself. The terms like governance, good governance, and crisis of governance are being increasingly used in political and academic discourse. The quest for good governance seemingly is an endless task. The search for 'goodness' in governance has been an aspiration of people and challenge to rulers since the very dawn of human civilization. It has been a romantic ideal for political thinkers round the ages. In recent years, however, there has been sudden resurrection of the study of the problems of governance or of reinventing or renewing governance. The shift of fucus from traditional concept like government and politics to the more broader concept of governance is a remarkable development.

The problem of governance emerged as a global concern in recent years when multilateral and bilateral aid agencies blessed it as a part of precondition for economic aid or a process of reform qualifying for such aid after a realisation that 'project success' depends quite substantially on conditions of governance in the aid receiving countries. The World Bank report of 1989 on Sub-Saharan Africa has been of crucial importance in stimulating this concern world wide. The report suggested that the Bank's programme of adjustment and investment in that area were being rendered ineffective by a 'crisis of governance'. In its discussion of the symptoms of such crisis the World Bank identified the following elements : the failure to make a separation between public and private, thereby facilitating the appropriation of public resources for private gain; the failure to establish a predictable framework of law and government conducive to development; excessively regulatory rules which impede the functioning of markets; misallocation of resources following from priorities not consistent with development; and non-transparent decision making. Thus insistence on 'good governance' was primarily intended to check corrupt practices and misuse of public funds adversely affecting in significant manner the resources of the borrowing countries.

The World Bank has identified three distinct aspects of governance: (i) the form of political regime; (ii) the process by which authority is exercised in the management of a country's economic and social resources for development; and (iii) the capacity of governments to design, formulate and implement policies and discharge functions. The World Bank's definition of governance has been further widened by other aid agencies to include the degree of democratisation to prove legitimacy of the state, media freedom, and transparency in administration to promote accoutability of government; individual and group rights and peoples' participation in administration to establish rule of law and respect for human rights, and finally competence of governments to formulate policies and deliver services to the people.

Simply put 'governance' means 'the act or process of governing'. Which means governance refers to a process or the act of exercising (usually legitimate) authority to regulate affairs of men in given territory, generally a state. Governance, according to one definition, is neither government nor administration, nor even the structure of the state, although all of them are important. The central focus of governance is how a society, through the nation state, handle the affairs of the state, which enables its people to lead a peaceful, orderly and reasonably prosperous and participative life in running their affairs.

The term 'governance' has more wider meaning and implication than the 'government'. Government refers to the machinery and institutional arrangement of exercising the sovereign power for serving the internal and external interests of the political community, whereas governance means the process as well as result of making authoritative decisions for the benefits of the society. Government applies to ruling the people by official machinery while governance relates to serving the people. It is a system in which exercise of the legitimate authority of the state does not become the prerogative of elected leaders or selected bureaucrats rather it seeks to ensure the active participation of people in this process in just, transparent and accountable manner.

Governance comprises the complex mechanism, processes, and institutions through which citizens and groups articulate their interests, mediate their differences, and exercise their legal rights and obligations. The Commission on Global Governance has defined it as the sum of the many individuals and institutions, public and private, to manage their common affairs. It is a continuing process through which conflicting or diverse interests may be accommodated and co-operative action may be taken. It includes formal institutions and regimes empowered to enforce compliances as well as informal arrangements that people and institutions either have agreed to or perceive to be in their interests.

The concept of 'good governance' derives its relevance in the context of misgovernance or crisis of governance which is found all around, especially in the developing countries in rampant degree. In many countries, the democratic form of government has proved to be ineffective for checking swindling of public funds for private gains by the elected leaders as well as permanent bureaucrats. Misuse of power, fraud, chicanery and embezzlement of funds are systematically perpetrated by the leaders of government and their minions. In many countries political system is characterised by arbitrary policy making, unaccountable bureaucracies, unresponsive governments, unenforced or unjust legal systems, the abuse of executive power, a civil society unengaged in public life, and widespread corruption.

The governance scenario in India is also not very satisfactory. It is a rather gloomy one, uninspiring and dismal. With regular elections, high voter participation, multi-party representative system, independent Judiciary, and free and vibrant press we proudly claim to be the largest democracy in the world. But its functioning seems to be bereft of all the canons of good governance. We have managed to retain only the form of democracy rather than its substance. Almost all institutions of governance are in shambles. Corruption has become all pervasive. Criminalization of politics has tended to acquire legitimacy. Political parties are working in most undemocratic and irresponsible manner. The civil services has been highly politicised. The executive is unresponsive and apathetic to the needs and aspirations of the people. Prevailing chaos, indiscipline, unruly behaviour, hoolingism, physical fight inside the house, forced disruption of proceedings, walkouts, deadlocks, defection etc. have characterised the working of legislatures. And there is not all well with the Judiciary - many of our laws and judicial processes are too old, colonial, defective, unjust and violative of human rights. There has been erosion of the basic principles of federalism. We have failed to eradicate abject poverty and to provide atleast the basic necessities of life such as food, safe drinking water, sanitation and access to health facilities, a minimum education and even the simplest kind of social security. Caste, communal, ethnic and sectarian divisions have assumed a serious dimension. All these suggest that the goal of good governance still eludes to the most of the people in India.

It is true that we cannot reach to a consensus on all the ingredients of good governance as it may vary for various reasons. It should, however, be agreed that good governance is committed to development oriented administration, aiming improvement of quality of life of people of a nation. It also relates to the capacity of political and administrative system to cope up with the emerging challenges of the society. Good governance implies presence of the rule of law, safeguarding of basic human rights, presence of honest and efficient government; accountability, transparency, openness and a strong civil society participating in the public affairs. In simple terms, good governance is participatory, consensus oriented accountable, transparent, responsive, efficient and effective, equitable and inclusive, and follows the rule of law. It assures that corruption is minimized, the views of minorities are taken into account and that the voices of the most vulnerable in society are heard in decision making. While all these characteristics may lay the foundation for good governance, a vigilant and active citizenry is must to its sustenance.

The World Bank's agenda of good governance has been subjected to vehement criticism ranging from encroaching upon sovereignty to spreading the gospel of capitalism. The question has, therefore, been raised: what are the real intentions of the World Bank and the western world? Is it 'democracy' concern or 'domination' concern? Further, the World Bank and other donor agencies define governance in terms of their own perceptions and interests rather than the specific local context and their needs which remain poorly understood and inadequately addressed. Good governance cannot be introduced from outside. More appropriately, the criteria and expectations about good governance should emerge from within the society, particularly from the grassroots level. These aid giving agencies, mostly under control of the west especially the USA, are trying vigorously to push through their own narrow agenda of promoting one particular model of governance - liberal democracy, free market, privatisation, deregulation, and state withdrawal from many economic spheres. There is a keen move to push the states to divert their energies towards offering securities to the corporate sector rather than the poor and marginalised. The World Bank's concern for good governance has remained narrowly focussed on only those select points which constitute power shift from state to either private or non-governmental sector. The very fact of governance agenda being handed down to aid receiving states as a part of conditionality set by aid giving agencies implies denial of a democratic choice for the former.

To conclude, a dynamic concept like good governance need not be narrowly conceived in the manner the aid giving agencies have sought to present it. There is no doubt that a more creative and indigenous approach and a lot of rethinking on the subject is called for. To be pragmatic, good governance has to be in tune with fast changing political, social and economic milieu along with international environment and conditions. The World Bank itself acknowledged that 'governance is a continuing and not necessarily unidirectional; it does not automatically improve over time. It is a plant that needs constant tending. Citizens need to demand good governance. Their ability to do so is enhanced by literacy, education, and employment opportunities. Governments need to prove responsive to those demands. Neither of these can be taken for granted'. The concept of good governance, therefore, requires periodical rethinking and even remodelling. The search for good governance has to be a continuing exercise. It is in this background, a round table on 'Governance in India: Issues and Challenges' was organised by the Department of Political Science, Aligarh Muslim University in association with the Indian Council of Social Science Research, Northern Regional Centre, Delhi on March 14-15, 2001.

The present volume contains the papers presented at the round table. Though not originally conceived to lead to a publication the quality of some of the papers presented, and the nature and importance of the subject merits their dissemination to a wider audience. Understandably some of the articles may not be comprehensive. The book itself is not carefully structured with individual authors discussing issues that they viewed as important. Yet topics raised are important enough to be seriously considered. This book is a modest attempt in developing better understanding of the concept of governance in the context of India.

Grateful acknowledgements and thanks are due to contributors and all those who helped directly or indirectly to the successful completion of this work. Vice Chancellor, of the Aligarh Muslim University Mr. Hamid Ansari, Honorary Director, ICSSR-NRC Prof. Balveer Arora and the Chairman, Department of Political Science Prof. M.A.Kishore must be specially mentioned for all the assistance, encouragement, and collaboration in organising this seminar. Lastly, I must express my gratefulness to Mrs. Poonam Goel of Raj Publications for bringing this book in a very short time but in an elegant manner.

— Aftab Alam

1

Crisis of Governance : Need for Political Reforms

Aftab Alam

More than five decades ago, after a long struggle against colonial rule, 'we the people' of India won independence and resolved to constitute India into a Sovereign, Socialist, Secualr and, Democratic Republic and to secure to all its citizens Justice, Liberty and Equality. We promised in our fundamental law of the land - a social order for the promotion of welfare of the people; social, economic and political justice for all; minimization of inequalities in income, and elimination of inequalities in status, facilities, and opportunities among individuals and groups of people; right to adequate means of livelihood for all citizens men and women equally; right to work, to education and to public assistance in cases of unemployment, old age, sickness and disablement and safeguarding of forests and wild life and; promotion of international peace and security.

We conciously chose the democratic path as the political instrument of achieving its long term goal of a modern, equitious and prosperous nation. As a democratic state India has already held 13 general elections for the Lok Sabha and hundreds of elections for Vidhan Sabhas on the basis of adult franchise and secret ballot. The judiciary is independent and vibrant so is the press. The country has made remarkable progess in many respects. India now has one of the world's biggest reservoirs of top-class specialist personnel such as scientists, technologists, engineers, software experts, doctors, surgeons, lawyers, administrators, leaders of business and industry, managers etc. It has become one of the most advanced industrialized countries of the world and now manufactures almost every conceivable item, from pins and needles to highly sophisticated machinery, ships, aircrafts, tanks and missiles. India has now become a nuclear power. India's scientific achievements have been glittering. India has successfully accomplished a 'green revolution' in agriculture and is now self-sufficient with respect to food item. It has a well-established political, administrative and judicial structure. With all these facts India legitimately claim to be well administered democratic state.

But what has been stated above is only a half truth. Our success on all these fronts should not blind us from admitting the remaining half truth. Even after 53 years of independence we sadly find that many of the promises, which we made in our constitution, still remain distant dreams. The fundamental principles of good governance ordained by the constitution are defied, defaced and debunked openly almost daily. Our *Swaraj* appears to have lacked *Suraj* or good governance as was fervently hoped for when India awoke to freedom in the midnight hour of August 15, 1947. Political freedom has not yet brought freedom from poverty, hunger, unempoloyment and other sufferings to hundreds of million of our people. Five decades of Swaraj has not yet enabled us to eradicate abject poverty and to provide at least the basic necessities of life such as food, safe drinking water, sanitation and access to health facilities, a minimum education and even the simplest kind of social security. There are many villages where animals and human beings use the same village pond for meeting all their water needs from dawn to dusk. Our developmental policies despite their rhetoric of benefiting the poor, have actually managed to marginalise the large sections of the population. We see frequent reports of death caused by starvation, while food grain is rotting in FCI godowns. Even today, there are fellow Indians who live on food grains retrieved from washing cowdung.

Caste, communal, ethnic and sectarian divisions have assumed a serious dimension. Corruption has crept into all walks of public life - polity, administration, society and business etc. Criminalization of politics has tended to acquire legitimacy. Almost all institutions of democratic governance have been weakened and rendered infructuous over the years. It is crude reality that we have managed to retain only the form of democracy rather than its substance. We have transformed democrary into mere electoralism. There is a crisis of character and values in politics and administration. Politics has become the means to power and government the manifestation of the quest of domination. In short, our democratic governance is in the throes of a serious crisis.

Reflecting on the current situation in the country, President K.R. Narayanan in his address to nation said that: "I am painfully aware of the deterioration that has taken place in our country and in our society in recent times. The traditional cultural and spiritual values which has been the mainstay of our civilization seem to be loosing their grip over society and politics. Sheer opportunism and valueless power-politics have taken over the place of principles and idealism that had been the hall-mark of our social and political life. Violence has increased in the relationship between people, groups and parties. Social evils like ill-treatment of women and the weaker sections like the scheduled castes, including atrocities against them are on the increase marring the fair name of India in the world. And corruption is corroding the vitals of our politics and our society." Against this backdrop this paper endeavoures to present an overview of the present crisis of governance. Corruption in public life, criminalization of politics, working of our political parties and electroal system and the crisis of our political institutions are some of the highlights of this paper. These issues have been presented both as symptoms as well as consequences of the present crisis of governance.

Corruption in Public Life

Corruption is presently the most alarming malady afflicting our system. It is not an exaggeration to talk about corruption in terms of a crisis or a cancer endangering our society, polity and economy. Corruption is on the rampage, depriving the people of fair governance and thwarting the process of development. Deals, scams, scandals, hawala etc. have become common words of our daily parlance. Corruption in India has become all pervasive leaving virtually no sector of life uncontaminated. Things have come to such a pass that from India's capital city to the smallest village in the country, virtually no official decision or stamp of approval can be obtained unless and until the requisite bribe has been paid. The giving and taking of bribe is now commonly accepted as a way of life. Bribes, commissions, under the table payments and gifts are no longer frowned upon, rather subtle ways have been discovered to legitimise them as a part of normal life activity. At the time of final transfer of power to India, the then British Prime Minister Winston Charchill said: "They (Indians) are all corrupt and they will not be able to run their administration". We scoffed off at Churchill's observation but his prediction has come true.

According to a study conducted in 1996 by a German NGO - Transparency International and Goettingen University about the extent of corruption in 54 countries showed India to be the 9th most corrupt country in the world.

The only solace to India : the two neighbours with whom we always seem to be in competition in some sphere or another, are worse off. Both Pakistan and China rank above India according to the indices of official corruption. Of all countries surveyed New Zealand was found as the most honest country and Nigeria as the most corrupt. The survey, however, did not find a single country to be entirely corruption free.

The effect of corruption on the economy and polity is obvious. It undermines investment and economic growth, decreases the resources available for human development goals, deepens the extent of poverty, subverts the judicial system, and undermines the legitimacy of the state. Public funds allocated for the welfare of the desperately poor are largely siphoned off into private pockets. In fact, when corruption becomes intrenched, it can devastate the entire economic, political and social fabric of a country-that is why there is an urgent and strong need to take effective punitive and corrective measures to tackle the problem.

Corruption in India is not entirely a new development. What is new, of course, is its seriousness and magnitude. Only four days before assassination Gandhiji warned his countrymen of dangerous effects of corruption. On the eve of independence Dr. S. Radhakrishnan had warned the nation against corruption in high places: 'Unless we destroy corruption in high places, root out every traces of nepotism, love of power, profiteering and black marketing, which have spoiled the good name of the country in the recent times, we will not be able to raise the standard of efficiency in administration, as well as production and distribution of necessary goods of life." He further said "from tomorrow .... from midnight today we can not lay the blame on the Britishers ...... our possibilities are great, but let me warn you, when power outstrips ability we will fall on evil days". In 1963, the then President of the Indian National Congress Sanjivayya Reddy complained publically at Indore that congressmen who were paupers in 1947 had become millionaires without have any ostensible source of such income. Gunnar Myrdal called India a 'soft state' where nothing moved unless bribe was paid. Since Myrdal's days the level of corruption has risen from leaps and bound. Today it is so widespread that the credibility of the entire political system is at stake.

The corruption in public life was noticeable even during Jawaharlal Nehru's tenure as Prime Minister. Though personally above board, corrupt politicians flourished under his protective umbrella. Krishan Menon, as India's High Commissioner in London, was allegedly involved in waht was then known as the Jeep Scandad. The sacm involved the acquisition of 2000 all terrain four wheelers for the severely handicapped, under-prepared and beleaguered Indian Army engaged in the infant nation's first military operation to prevent Pakistani occupation of Kashmir valley. The Jeep Scandal indicates that by the early 1950 corruption had begun to rear its ugly faces in India. The problem at this stage was that of recognizing, with foresight, that corruption could become a demonic problem in the years to come, spreading its tentacles to every organ of the state unless it was nipped in the bud. But unfortunately our successive governments lacked this foresight and required political will to tackle this problem.

The Jeep Scam involving Menon was not an isolated event of Nehru's era, rather many other scams also surfaced during his 17 years of rule. Pratap Singh Kairon, then Chief Minister of Punjab was guilty of abusing power and influence for his own benefit and that of his sons and relatives. K.D. Malviya the then minister of mines and fuel was indicted by a judicial commission for showing undue favours to a mining magnate of Orissa. There were reports in a section of the press that spoke of alleged gifts of jewellery worth fifty five thousand rupees to Malaviya's wife and the presentation of a car to her and another to Malviya's private secretary. In another episode, namely the Mundra deal, the then Union Finance Minister, T.T. Krishnamachari was balmed for LIC's investments in concerns controlled by Haridas Mundhra, a

Calcutta based businessman. In a severe indictment of functioning of the finance ministry and minister Krishnamachari in particular, the Chagla Committee said that the government had gambled with the savings of million of citizens, thereby abusing their trust.

This trend, unfortunately, took a nose dive during the period of Indira Gandhi who is regarded by many throughout the world as the most charismatic, most courageous and strongest prime minister India has ever had. Although there were no personal charges of corruption against her but it flourished like anything during her regime. Indira Gandhi personally was well endowed and did not need any outside support for herself. Nor did she seek to amass money for her descendants. But to finance her politial party, to reward her loyalists, to manage her political campaign throughout the country, and to ensure the success of her nominee at the coming elections, she needed money. And her economic model of development which involved enlarged state ownership as well as greater governmental control over the private sector through the mechanism of 'permits, licences and quotas' provided huge opportunities for corruption. Kickbacks were paid in several contracts entered into by public sector undertaking such as the State Trading Corporation and Mineral & Metal Trading Corporation. She also patronised politicians against whom there were proved charges of corruption and mismanagement. These included Gunddu Rao, L.N. Mishra, J.B. Patnaik, Jagannath Mishra, Kedar Pande, A.R. Antulay and a host of others. Indira Gandhi, however, had countered the mounting criticism of corruption on the ground that it was a global phenomenon. Thus the corruption which had already began to surface during Nehru era got its roots firmed during the Indira regime.

Political corruption rocked the political system in 1987 when Rajiv Gandhi was alleged to have received Kickbacks in the purchase of Bofors Guns amounting to over US $ 1.3 billion. After 1½ year long preliminary enquiry, the CBI registered a case on January 22, 1990 against several persons including Marten Ardbo, former president of Bofors, Win Chadda and G.P. Hinduja who were all reportedly linked to the deal. The case still continues and its finding may yet unravel the mystery of the Bofors payments. Bofors case received a setback on June 10, 2002 when a single judge bench of the Delhi High Court quashed the chargesheet against the Hindujas-the main accused, on the technical ground that the CBI had not obtained the central vigilance commission's consent before filing it. the supreme court, however, on July 12, 2002 stayed the Delhi High Court order and directed continuance of proceedings before the trial court. The bench significantly observed: "if such judgements are not stayed, no prosecution will succeed."

Bofors was followed by HDW Submarine deal, Airbus A-320 case, St. Kitts forgery case, Sugar Sacm, Urea Sacm, J.M.M. Bribery case, Jain Hawala Scam, Fodder Scam etc. Since the Bofors deal, the problem of corruption has assumed demonic proportion. And now we have the Tehelka Tapes which have caused tremors at the highest level and have disturbed public opinion all over the country. Not that Tehelka Tapes have revealed anything that was not known earlier. It is the audiovisual proof over the electronic media which has generated utter contempt among the people for the political masters and the bureaucrats interested in lining their pockets rather than giving the best equipment to Jawan who is expected to stake his life under the most inhospitable conditions. The shocking part is that what the tapes have shown is only the tip of the iceberg. With the disclosures of these recent scams and scandals India seems to has plunged into the worst political corruption crisis in its history.

It is high time for India to take a serious look at the question of corruption in public life. The problem of corruption cannot be solved unless prompt and effective action is taken to enquire into the allegations and guilty punished without delay. If corruption is to be eradicated, it is essential to make punishments both efficacious and certain. The certainty of punishment, even more that its severity, is a great preventive step. The conviction and punishment of a few major corrupt figures will go a long way in breaking out corruption culture. There is an urgent need to set up exclusive anti-corruption courts to tackle all the corruption related cases rapidly. These special courts should have automatic jurisdiction over all corruption related cases. Politicians, bureaucrats, military officers and other important high officials must be required to declare their assets every year after assuming office. This must be accompanied by an effective prosecution agency that can freely and fairly investigate unusual discrepancies between the living style and their asset declaration.

There are already plethora of brilliant reports of the Committees and Commissions appointed by the Government to suggest ways and means to combat corruption. But regretebly no action is taken to implement them. Even though there is growing feeling that corruption has now become incurable, things could still be improved if there is genuine desire and determination in mending matters. A bold, concrete anti-corruption agenda needs to be devised and implemented. There is an urgent need to create a zero tolerance for corruption which must be embedded in legislative frameworks, policies and local value systems. The experiences of Hong Kong, Botswana, and Singapore suggest that it is possible to end an era of corruption eruption by strong political commitment.

Criminalisation of Politics

Criminalization of Politics is rather a recent development in Indian politics. But within a very short span of time it has acquired such a dangerous proportion that it is proving deadly and eroding the very roots of democratic governance. During the early years of independence the criminals were kept subdued because those were the days when a galaxy of national leaders both at the Centre and in States as well as in the opposition steeped in moral values and personal integrity governed country. Those were the days when a person with criminal background never dared to seek election on any party tickets. As we slided downwards from the "Age of Heroes" to the "Age of Pygmies", the down hilt drift of politics and politicians was swift with disastrous consequences. Now being criminal or having criminal background is no more a taboo in electoral politics, rather it is considered to be an advantage. Criminal activities do not affect the respectability and social standing of politicians. It is, infact, here the real danger lies. The stranglehold of criminals over politics and politicians is a sad commentary on our democratic governance. Any country where elections are fought with the support of gangsters and guns, instead of ballot, can hardly describe itself as a functioning democracy.

Broadly, criminalization of politics would mean (i) the use of money and muscle power by politicians especially during elections; (ii) aiding and abetting crimes and sheltering criminals by politicians in power, if necessary, by interfering in the working of the enforcement agencies; (iii) politicization of the administration, particularly the police with the latter obliging politicians in power by permitting interference and sometimes being privy to it; (iv) persons with a record of heinous crimes such as murder, extortion, kidnapping being elected to the state legislatures and Parliament; and (v) criminals succeeding in occupying high places of honour and status in governance - becoming ministers and governors. Thus what we are facing today is not only criminalization of politics but even more sinister development - politicization of criminals.

Earlier, the criminals preferred acting as the back-room boys, they themselves remained in the background and were content to support politicians. This support was part of the larger protection deal which they needed and in practice even got. The criminals or musclemen are made to carry out multiple tasks in Indian politics, particularly during elections - to intimidate the voters, to capture polling booths, eventually to win the election; and even to eliminate the political rivals. The criminals are also used by politicians to instigate caste and communal riots to extract political benefit out of crisis situation. In return, they get protection from politicians who use their clout in this regard. Gradually, around 70s, a stage came when criminals felt that rather than helping politicians, why did they not themselves get into the legislature or Parliament and occupy ministerial position; and use these to further their criminal activities. As criminal elements began to gain experience in electoral manipulation, intimidation and fraud, it became more profitable for them to contest elections themselves. Barring few exception, almost all political parties began distributing tickets to these criminals. The irony here is that well known criminals often do not actually have to engage in electoral fraud, particularly in local and state elections, their reputation are sufficiently ferocious to terrorise the population to vote for them. Another irony is that many candidates with criminal records are hugely popular in their home regions. Thus gone are the days when the criminals were a pawn in the hand of politicians. The position is practically reversed today. It is no longer the dog that wags the tail but the tail that is wagging the dog.

The Election Commission statistics show the grip that the criminals appear to be gradually tightening over our political life and system. According to EC records of eleventh Lok Sabha elections (1996) out of 13,952 candidates who contested, nearly 1500 had criminal records of murder, dacoity, rape, theft or extortion. Of this number, atleast 40 managed to enter the Lok Sabha. And nearly 700 MLAs out of 4722 in the country were involved in criminal cases and trials were pending against them. The sight of criminals entering Parliament, Legislative Assemblies and Local bodies is now rather common. The process of criminalization of politics is going on unabated. In such a situation, voters are left with Hobson's choice; they have in many cases to choose between the scoundrels.

The Vohra Committee Report (1993) has confirmed the fact that criminalization of both the political and administrative apparatus has become all pervasive. The

Committee observed that: (i) All over India, crime syndicates had become a law unto themselves. Even in the smaller towns and rural areas, musclemen had proliferated and assassinations were common place. A nexus between the criminal gangs, police, bureaucrary and politicians was a common occurrence in various parts of the country; (ii) There has been a rapid spread and growth of criminal gangs, armed *senas*, drug mafias, smuggling gangs, drug peddlers and economic lobbies in the country, which have, over the years, developed an extensive network of contacts with the bureaucrats/government functionaries at the local level, politicians, media persons and strategically located individuals in the non-state sector. Some of these syndicates have international linkages too, including those with foreign intelligence agencies; (iii) In states like UP, Bihar and Haryana, the mafia gangs enjoy the patronage of local level politicians and the protection of government functionaries. Some politicians became leaders of these gangs and get elected to the state assemblies and parliament; (iv) The mafia network was virtually running a parallel government, making the state apparatus virtually irrelevant; (v) These syndicates have acquired substantial financial and muscle power, social respectability and wield enough influence to make the task of the investigating and prosecuting agencies extremely difficult. Even members of the Judiciary have not escaped the influence of mafia. The Vohra Committee report reminds us the gravity of situation.

The criminalisation of politics and politicization of criminals are seriously undermining our democratic traditions and polity. We need to wake up before these criminals virtually take over our entire political and representative democracy. The issue of criminalisation of politics figured prominently during the special session of the Parliament held from 26-31 August 1997. At the end, in a show of a sense of rare unanimity, they passed a resolution reiterating their commitment to rid the polity of criminalization of politics, but not many have taken this determination seriously. The Vohra Committee had recommended immediate preventive action. The Law Commission report on electoral reforms (1999) also suggested detailed measures for weeding out criminals and corrupt politicians. But there has been no follow up on these recommendations.

Is there no redress in law to stop criminals from invading representative bodies - the temples of our democratic system? The present law (Representation of People Act, 1951) purports to keep out criminals from elective bodies, but it is applicable only to those convicted by courts for serious criminal offences and sentenced to imprisonment of two years or more. Even such convict become eligible to contest five years later after release. Section 8(3) of the Act says that if a person is already a member of Parliament or legulature when the conviction is pronounced, the disqualification shall not take effect until three months have elapsed from that date or if within that period an appeal or application for revision is brought in respect of the conviction or the sentence, until that appeal or application is disposed of by the court. It means that even if a sitting member of Parliament or state legislature commits the most heinous crime he can not be disqualified till he is pronounced guilty, sometime which can take years. But even he has been pronounced by a court to be guilty he does not become disqualified; all he has to do is to file an appeal against the sentence within three months from the date of conviction. Thereafter till all the appeals, to the court of sessions, the High Court, to the Supreme Court, have run their course and that may take decades, he continues to be an MP or MLA and even minister.

In view of lacunas in existing laws to curb criminalization of politics, there is an urgent need to make necessary changes, to meet out the ground realities. Already many substantive proposals have come out from the media, eminent persons and the Election Commission. A committee headed by Justice H.R. Khanna has suggested that a person who has been convicted of criminal offence as well as those against whom a charge has been framed in a criminal court shall be liable for disqualification to contest the election for any representative bodies including Parliament and State Legislatures. The Election Commission has been pressing since 1996 elections for early changes in the electoral laws. The Commission has suggested two amendments to the Representation of the People Act (1951), which if accepted, should go a long way in weeding out criminals from electoral politics and from our legislative chambers.

The Election Commission's suggestions include : (i) Any person who is accused of an offence punishable with imprisonment for five years or more should be disqualified, even when his trial pending, provided that a competent court of law has taken congnisance of offence and framed charges against him. (2) Whoever is convicted of any offence by a court of law and sentenced to imprisonment for six months or more should be debarred from contesting election, for a period totalling sentence imposed plus an additional six years. In the commission's view, the first proposal, which seeks to debar hose facing trial for heinous crimes, constitutes a reasonable restriction which imposed in the greater public interest in order to ensure the sanctity of the supreme law making bodies in the country. The second proposal seeks to plug the loophole that currently allows a rapist or murderer serving a long jail sentence to jump into the electoral fray half-way through his incarceration.

The Election Commission has also taken a revolutionary step of defining the term 'conviction'. It declared that any person who has been convicted for an offence listed in the Representation of People Act 1951, by a trial court would attract disqualification, even if that person had appealed against the order in a higher court. This meant that those out on bait after appealing against the trial court's judgement also stood disqualified. This shut the doors on a large number of persons who use the multi-tier justice system to file appeals and to prolong litigation for decades. The Election Commission has also appealed to the conscience of political leaders to decide on their own that their party will not give ticket to a person who has a known criminal record.

Sadly, this has invoked no response. Every political party has eye only on the wining chances of a person. All other finer considerations find no place in real politics.

Some other important suggestions have been made to prevent criminals occupying seat in the Parliament and legislative bodies. Every candidate must be required to file an affidavit along with the nomination form specifying the cases in which he is involved and the present position of those cases, and this information may be printed alongwith every bit of election material which is furnished by him or on his behalf; and secondly, along with their audited account every year, political parties should be required to submit to the Election Commission and the Speaker of the Lok Sabha, a list furnishing details of the criminal cases in which their legislatures are implicated and the current position of each cases. In a very significant development the Election Commission on June 28, 2002 decided to implement the May 2, 2002 Supreme Court's directive making it mandatory for candidates to furnish personal details on assets, educational qualifications and criminal antecedents whild filing nomination papers. In case of furnishing wrong information or suppressing of a fact or refusal to file any affidavit at all, such situation may lead to rejection of the nomination paper, besides triggering legal prosecution under the Indian Penal Code. The information furnished by each candidate in the affidavit shall be disseminated by the Returning Officers. This mechanism, if implemented, will foster public verification and promote transparency.

Reforming Political Parties

Political parties are considered to be the backbone of the democratic system of governance. Democracy and political parties are indissolubly linked together. It is obvious that the negation or weakness of the party system has dangerous consequences for democracy. Unfortunately our political parties are facing a serious crisis of credibility. The functioning of political parties is severely impaired as many evils have crept into the party system over the years. A former Chief Election Commissioner, M.L. Shakdher once pointed out that: "Political parties make strong demands for the conduct of free and fair elections to legislative bodies, but choose to ignore the application of the same principles when it comes to the functioning of their own party organs. It has been revealed before me variuous cases that parties do not follow their own constitution. They hold no party elections, they function for years on an adhoc basis. Sometimes there has been a tyranny of the minority over the majority because of undemocratic functioning and other practices. A few persons in a party occupying the vantage position in the apex body, quite often strangulate the democratic functioning and aspirations of the members of the party at the grassroots and keep the party under their strict control. The voice of the majority does not find expression in important decision making process, thereby creating fissures in those organs and eventually leading to splits." Later he listed three major defects (i) non-observance of the basic provisions of the constitution of the party, (ii) failure to hold regular organisational elections, and (iii) lack of accountability.

Madhava Menon has observed that "Political parties are literally non-accountable to the people and they are free to exploit every divisive sentiment in society to advance their power game. Rule of law does not seem to apply to political parties for whom constitution becomes relevant only when they get into trouble. They have misused and abused every institution of government and have put the blame on the people and the constitution." It is because of political parties that politics has become a scramble for power. Parties do not appeal to reason of the individuals and they do not give enough importance to human values. the concept of accountability of the repre-sentatives to the people has become a sham.

There is steep decline in the working of political parties. Manifestoes of all major political parties are big on rhetoric and generalities but small on ideas, specifics and original thought, except for the Left parties to some extent. Most parties have turned out to be coalition of elites loosely tied together by personal interests and short term goals rather than by ideological or programmic commitment or long range obectives. No one speaks of providing basic needs of life-food, water, house, medical care, education and polution free environment to millions of countrymen, women and children. These are at the core of good governance. Political parties do not distribute their tickets for the Parliament and other elective bodies on the basis of qualities or qualifications of candidates rather yardstick of winnability, which more often means caste, sub-caste/community, may be in addition money and muscle power of the candidates have become the sole criterion. Political parties have made the job of our voters more difficult - they have to choose between competing evils.

Further, the vote bank politics has adulterated the basic principles of participatory democracy. Such is the cold logic of electoral politics that parties of all hues cultivate their socio-economic constituencies and nurse their vote banks only to win elections. Vote banks are sought to be created not only through caste alliances, but also through regional, linguistic and religious appeal. Caste and communal leaders have emerged as mobilisers of votes, and as brokers in politics. The vote bank politics of political parties has reduced the politics to sheer struggle for power.

It is indeed strange that despite a sublime democratic environment within the country, political parties have not developed in a healthy manner. The primary reason for this is that barring exception, all political parties in the country are personality oriented. And since the persona of the leader is many times bigger than the party, the party's policy making bodies do not develop and function in a democratic environment. The stunted growth of political parties has inevitablly had its impact on the working of parliamentary institutions in the country. It is one of the major paradox of the Indian political system that our democrary is run by political parties which are not only undemocratic but often unabashedly authoritarian.

Proliferation of political parties at large scale is another serious issue to reckon with. India has as many as seven national political parties, 33 state level and about 612 registered unrecognised parties. The present Lok Sabha includes members of as many as 40 widely differing political parties. Formation of a political party of their own has become one of the most favourable job of our political leaders. One analyst has aptly observed that: "Infact, India is probably one of the few flourishing democracy in the world in which launcing a political party is as easy an opening a paan shop." The moment a politician discover that his self-interest is not being immediately served, he quickly floats a new outfit, taking full advantage of the caste lobbies and other parochial affiliations. Even a party wresting one seat in the Lok Sabha is seen to claim a ministerial berth or an equivalent office of profit, thanks to era of coalition govts. With a plethora of parties in existence and their ever-shifting alliances and loyalties crisis of gover-nance becomes inevitable.

Any reform in the working of political parties should begin at the begining, lay down strict rules for registration of national and state level political parties, arm the registration authority in this case the Election Commission - with adequate powers to enforce the rules. It should be made compulsory for every recognised political party to annually declare and publish, along with its constitution and list of duly elected office bearers, the list of its primary members and the subscription collected from them among all other sources. Registration and renewal of such registration should be subject to a resonable verification of the facts stated. The party constitution itself must be democratic in content and spirit, quite transparent and must provide for periodic elections by the primary members. Non-compliance of these provisions should render the party disqualified from contesting election.

The Law Commission of India has suggested that only registered political parties should be entitled to contest elections to Parliament and State assemblies, and in order to secure registration from Election Commission, a party must fulfill following conditions: (a) It must swear allegiance to the Constitution of India; (b) It must have a Constitution that outlines the procedure for admission, expulsion and resignation of members; the grounds on which and the procedure according to which disciplinary action can be taken against members; the composition and powers of the Executive Committee and other organs of the party; the manner in which general body meetings can be requisitioned and conducted and the procedure for holding conventions to decide questions of continuance, merger, and other such fundamental matters; (c) It maintains regular accounts of the funds it receives and submits its audited accounts to the Election Commission; and (d) Holds election at the national and state levels in the presence of observers nominated by the Election Commission.

The Law Commission has also suggested that a party's candidates for election to Parliament and state assemblies should be selected by its executive committee "on the basis of recommendations and resolutions passed by the concerned local party units." And, mushrooming of political parties must be prevented and their number drastically reduced by law providing for a reasonably higher percentage (atleast 10%) of nation-wide or state wide vote being compulsory for recognition and registration as a national or state party. There is also a suggestion that a party must be at least two years old before it can contest any election to public office or membership of Parliament or any state legislature. Further, all political parties should make a case to unite the people or muster support on the basis of ideologies and/or their services to people. Instead of polarising the people on caste and communal lines, they should work to create harmony between various communities and social groups. Political parties should be a greater force for modernization and political development and not force of divisions in the society. All this could be achieved by the united efforts of people and politicians through proper legislation.

Funding of political parties and mounting electoral expenses of the candidates are two major issues which must be at the core of our agenda of electoral reforms. It is very unfortunate that the political parties in India have been unwilling to accept any discipline and transparency of their fund. And even more unfortunate part of the story is that those who make such huge contributions to various political parties keep the act a secret. In fact most of the money received by the political parties and candidates is black, then how can source be revealed? If any attempt to do so is made, the sources will dry up instantaneously. Also, when the elections require tonloads of money and a great deal of election expenditure has got to be on clandestine and socially unacceptable activities, how can the accounts be kept or opened for any scrutiny? The collection of illegal funds by the party organisation obliges the party as a whole to perpetuate corruption once it is in power, through suitable alteration of government policies or questionable award of contracts, to repay their patrons and keep the route of future supply of resources open.

It is quite legitimate for a political party to raise funds for its activities, and obviously no party would say no to a big donor. But to make our electoral system clean, what is now needed is that all contributions to political parties should be made public for public scrutiny. This by itself would create an atmosphere where vulger spending on elections would be curbed, and no money would be used, atleast directly, to buy votes. This will also put a check on many other electoral mal-practices which have crept into our electoral system over the years.

What is really needed is a law to provide that all recognised political parties shall take contribution only through cheque, or at least take the money that is acknowledged in some or other manner. It should also be made mandatory for all recognised political parties to get their annual statements of account audited and made public, either by placing it at the annual general session of the party, or through other means. A copy of such an audited statement of account should broadly show the receipts and expenditure during the year. A copy of the statement should also be submitted to the Election Commission, failing which the party should be derecognised.

It is really a matter of great satisfaction that the Congress party has decided that it will accept contributions from corporate bodies and individuals only through cheques. The Telegu Desham (TDP) has gone a step further in adopting the principle of transparency in contribution. The TDP recently held its General Council session, at which, its president Chandrababu Naidu presented an audited statement of account showing the receipts and expenses by the party last year. It listed the big contributions, disclosed the identity of the contributors and stated the activities for which those funds were utilised. The statement also showed a net balance or surplus of about two crore rupees in the party coffers. It was perhaps for the first time that a ruling party in a region publically accounted for its finances. Now a begining has been made. It is for the other political parties to take steps to cleanse the electoral system.

It is generally argued that since no legitimate money is available to political parties to fight elections, they have to depend on illegitimate source of money. It is against this backdrop the idea of state funding of election is often proposed and debated. The Tehelka Episode has once again revived this debate. There are well meaning and generally perceptive observers and commentators who are deeply impressed by the theory that corruption in politics can be easily tackled if politicians and parties did not need the astronomical costs of contesting elections. They, therefore, suggest about state funding of elections. One politician interestingly argued that "if parliament is part of the democratic structure, then in order to get into Parliament political parties are indispensable therefore, if running the state is the responsibility of the people, then creating these institutions, which enable you to run the state, is also the responsibility of the people. Hence, the expenses of elections must be met by the people."

Dinesh Goswami Committee and the Indrajeet Gupta Committee have gone into the proposal of state funding. The Gupta Committee proposes state funding in kind, not cash. Included in this would be rent free office accomodation with telephone, free time on DD, AIR and private networks for individuals, fuel for a specific number of vehicles, paper for printing, election materials, postage stamps, one set of loudspeakers for every assembly segment (six for parliamentary constituency), some free telephone calls, refreshments and food packets for polling agents etc. The Law Commission has also come out with a feasible recommendation in favour of limited state funding of elections, in the form of certain facilities suggested above by the Gupta Committee. But the question remains that whether the state funding of elections will end the political corruption. The idea of state funding of elections seems to be good but it suffers from many practical difficulties. In view of India's socio-economic and political realities, state funding will not necessarily eliminate all corruptions and wrong doings, instead it will put additional burden on genuine tax payers. The state funding will only encourage the proliferation of fund seeking parties or the break up of existing parties by ambitious faction leaders. This option is thus unworkable in the Indian situaion, especially when the party system is fluid. Instead of harping on state funding we should try to reduce the costs of electioneering by adopting some practical measures. This step will also address, to some extent, the issue of equality of political opportunity by lessening dependence on a small number of wealthy donors and making candidates more responsible to the grass roots.

The existing law to check the misuse of money in elections needs to be strengthened and suitably amended to meet the existing ground realities. Currently there is expenditure ceiling limit to a maximum of Rs 6 Lakhs and 15 Lakhs for Assembly and Lok Sabha constituencies respectively. But these limits are seldom followed by the candidates. In an apt remark made way back in 1967, BJP stalwart and current Prime Minister Atal Behari Vajpayee said that every M.P. elected to Lok Sabha began his parliamentry career by making a false statement the statement of account of his election expenses. Decade later, his comment remains as valid as when first made. The most often cited reason of this false statement of account is that the limit on the amount which an aspiring MLA or MP can legally spend on his election is absolutely low. The situation further worsened with the Supreme Court ruling that expenses incurred by a political party on the campaign of its nominees could be deemed to have been spent by the candidates himself and must be included in his accounts for calculating his total expenses. But this argument is not tenable as practically there is no limit at all on how much a candidate can spend through his or her supporters.

The Supreme Court ruling was later annulled through an amendment to the Representation of People Act to exclude party contribution from a candidates account of election expenses. The explanation to sub-section I of Section 77 of the R.P. Act was appended through this amendment, which says that : "Not withstanding any judgement, order or dicision of any court to the contrary, any expenditure incurred or authorised in connection with the election of a candidate by a political party or by any other association or body of persons or by any individual (other than the candidate or his election agent) shall not be deemed to be, and shall not ever be deemed to have been, expenditure in connection with the election incurred or authorised by the candidate or by his election agent ....." To put it straight there is no limit to how much the kith and kin of the candidate can spend on his or her.

The Supreme Court in the G. Yaswant Rao versus Balasaheb Vikhe Patel case (1994) also observed that : "The existing law does not measure up to the existing realities. The ceiling on expenditure is fixed only in respect of the expenditure incurred or authorised by the candidate himself but the expenditure incurred by the party or any one else in the elction campaign is solely outside the net of legal sanction ..... The prescription of ceiling on expenditure of a candidate is a mere eyewash and no practical checking on election expenses for which it was enacted to attain a meaningful democracy ... The provision has ceased to be even a big leaf to hide the reality." This is not the only loophole. Futher, the Election Commission can only demand that return of expenditure be filed. But it is court to decide whether the expenditure is in excess or not. As the record goes, till date no candidate has been disqualified for faulting the expenditure ceiling.

In a remarkable development the Election Commission, recently ordered that the total amount expended by a political party for electioneering (including costs incurred in chartering planes and helicopters for their central leaders) would be divided by the number of candidates fielded by the party, and the figure arrived at would be added to each candidate's own expenditure in order to calculate the total ammount spent by him. The Election Commission feels that the measure has become essential as candidates were getting away flouting every norm by claiming all expenses above the ceiling to have been incurred by 'others'. The EC was in fact forced to crack down on poll expenses following the Supreme Court's directive asking it to stop the naked display of black money during elections. The Election Commission also appointed observers in every constituency to check out on poll expenses and to tally their reports with the one filed by candidates.

The former Chief Election Commissioner, T.N. Seshan's solo effort to curb illegitimate election expenses and other malpractices will go down in history as one of the rare success stories in India's battle against corruption. T.N.Seshan must be given credit for pulling in full force the implementation of the code of conduct, which until now was in limbo. No poster wars, no banners, no wall smeared with ugly caricatures and scrawals, no blaring loud speakers, no Yelling, no noise and no traffic jams - all was quiet and sober. He was able to significantly curtail wasteful election expenses. Creditably, Seshan was able to notch up these remarkable achievements by insisting on the enforcement of rules that were already in the statute book but observed almost solely in their violation. Seshan's success story shows that many of the existing electoral malpractices including reducing the cost of electioneering, can easily be tackled simply by strictly implementing existing laws and in some cases by minor amendment and modifications to them.

Crisis of Institutions

Almost more than a decade ago eminent political analyst Rajni Kothari had observed that : "a process of decline and erosion of institutions places too great an emphasis on personalities, their sense of personal security and their attempt to use the public realm as an arena for resolving personal crises. In India the last several years have witnessed precisely this. There has been too much stress on leadership, too little on institutions, their integrity and autonomy. This has not only led to a sharp erosion of both effectiveness and morale in crucial segments of the state apparatus - the party system, the Parliament, the Bureaucracy, the law and order machinery, the judiciary - and corresponding increase in arbitrariness and in highly partisan and reckless interventions by political upstarts. Much worse, it has led to a systematic neglect of the public realm and a tendency to treat power as a personal aggrandisement and the state as an instrument of patronage and profit." What Kothari observed a decade ago has become even more relevant today.

Here one point needs to be emphasised that to provide good governance, democracy must be supported by stronger institutions such as representative parliament, more responsible executive, and impartial judiciary. Most importantly, ordinary people must feel that their institutions are accessible. These institutions must be transparent and accountable. Sadly in recent years India has been experiencing a steady erosion of impartant institutions of democratic governance. The independence of the judiciary has often been subverted through executive power. The civil service has been highly politicised. The executive is only overtly accountable to legislature. Our legislative institutions are in shambles. If we want good governance, we must first revive these ailing institutions otherwise our democracy may collapse any time.

In the multiple guises of a watchdog, regulator, representative, and law maker, the parliament is vital in ensuring and sustaining good governance. Unfortunately our legislative bodies suffer from a variety of ailments which have become more serious in the recent years. India has witnessed constant decline in parliamentary values, and quality of members, poor levels of participation and the defection for money and office, and the like. A certain cynicism towards parliamentary institutions and an erosion in the respect for normal parliamentary processes and the parliamentarians present a disturbing scenario.

The sanctity of Parliament demands an adherence to procedure and decorum on the part of parliamentarians. But our parliament and state legislatures have not worked with dignity and decorum expected of them. The unruly scenes in UP and Bihar assemblies are testimony to this. The nation and the world was shocked to view the roudy behaviour of our law makers when Kalyan Singh was seeking a vote of confidence in the House in 1997. House Marshals used wooden planks and files to shield themselves even as hapless ministers crawled under their desks. Indians were horrified to see the guerrilla warfare that was on between rival legislators who converted benign microphones into deadly missiles. The most unfortunate part of the episode was that not a single MLA was punished for this bout of violence even though many provisions of IPC were violated by dozen of legislators. Not only state legislatures even the Parliament is often held to ransom by the disorderly behaviour of the MPs. What was, till a few years ago, an unusual scene in the chamber of the law making bodies, has now unfortunately become a matter of common occurrence.

There were times in the history of our parliamentary democrary when Speaker was never seen standing on the podium because it was considered an affront to the Speaker to make him stand and upbraid the unruly members. It was also considered undemocratic and against the parliamentary practices. These days, however, the situation is quite the opposite - one can see the Speaker standing most of the time and only occassionaly sitting. This new parliamentary culture has made the proceeding of the House a laughing stock. There is a written code of conduct approved by Parliament, to be observed by members when inside house. Rule 349 enjoins that "a member shall not enterrupt any member while speaking by disorderly expression or noises or anything in a disorderly manner; shall maintain silence when not speaking; shall not obstruct proceedings or interrupt it; shall avoid making running commentaries when another member is speaking; shall not tear off documents in protest; shall not utter derogatory words; shall not use his right of speech for the purpose of obstructing the business of the House." But what has been prescribed in the Rule Book, is seldom observed by the members.

In the recent few years, a strange practice has developed among our parliamentarians - that of resorting to frequent adjournments of the House. The number of working hours lost owing to disturbances or adjournments in Parliament on various issues has been rising steadly. It is generally seen that on the even slightest provocation the MPs resort to well running and forcing the presiding officer to adjourn the House. The house is mostly adjourned for an hour or two but when it reassembles again the same thing is repeated by the opposition members with greater vigour, and presiding officer has to adjourn the House once again. This see-saw struggle between the Government and the Opposition goes on in the House and by the time order is restored the tantrum of our MPs have already cost the exchequer a huge amount.

Perhaps our MPs are oblivious of the fact that every minute they spend Rs 17,677 in the House when they waste several hours without transacting any business, they make the nation pay for their absence from the House, and at the end of the day the expenditure of each House comes to Rs 79.55 lakh. The total expenditure on the running of Parliament has multiplied over the years starting with Rs 27.72 crore in 1990-91 to Rs 194.89 crore in 2001-2002.

But chaos and disorder within the Parliament and the State legislatures is just one of the problems plaguing our legislative bodies. There is a perceptible decline in moral standards, parliamentary etiquette, quality of debates and in the working of parliamentary parties and parliamentary committees. Some years ago former Lok Sabha Speaker P.A. Sangma, appalled at the quality of questions being raised in Parliament, had lamented that muscle and lung power often seem to count more than intelligence and commitment to causes. Over the falling standards of Parliamentary behaviour, he had appealed for serious and enlightened debates on national and international issues. Reminiscing the time when proceedings in Parliament were marked by rudition, debating skills and members' mastery over facts and figures, he made fervent appeal to political parties to properly orient their elected members. The net effect of these trends is that they have not only weakened the role of parliament but also greatly diminished its moral authority.

But the most serious problem which afflict our parliamentary system is the defection by the MPs and members of state legislatures. Defection represents the worst form of political amorality since it is a breach of the electorate's faith. The issue of shifting loyalties in not only one of political morality but is linked with the very survival of our democracy. The statement of objectives of the 52nd Amendment Act of 1985 rightly referred to defection as an 'evil' which if not combated - is likely to undermine the very foundation of our democracy and the principles which sustain it. The Tenth Schedule was incorporated in the constitution via the 52nd Amendment Act, so as to curb this evil. This is also popularly known as Anti-Defection Law, which was passed because our elected representatives were auctioning themselves like anything before the highest bidders in legislatures. The Law provides that if a member voluntarily resigns from or votes in the House against the directives of the party on whose symbol he or she was elected, then he or she would be liable to be disqualified from membership. However, no disqualification would be incurred in cases where a split or merger of a party in another is claimed. In the event of split, atleast one third of its members decide to quit or breakaway, and in case of a merger, the decision should have the support of not less than two thirds of the party members. Thus, while anti-defection law seeks to curb defection, it allows for democratic realignment of forces in the House by way of a merger of two or more parties or a split in an existing party.

But the anti-defection law has miserably failed in eradicating the menace of defection, instead it has encouraged more defections. In fact, as per official statistics, on average more defections have taken place per year after the enactment of anti-defection law than it took in the years before the enactment of the law. In all these years defections have continued to happen with unceasing regularity. The landslide defection in UP convincingly shows that there is something seriously wrong with our representative system. Overnight change of loyality of our legislatures to grab power has become most familiar feature of our democracy. Fragmentation, permutation and combination are common affairs. In most cases the defection, merger or split are primarily either for forming a government to share power or preventing others from forming a government. Unfortunately, even after capturing power, in the absence of any shared ideology or common programme, they do not remain united for long. Infighting goes on in every combination of coalition of parties. One analyst has rightly observed that "as identity politics becomes more assertive, and as party politics enters the period of coalition formation, defection will only grow in frequency in India. As long as the capacity of the system to penalize defections is weak, and as long as the state is rent-seeking state and politicians bounty hunters, defections will be an attractive route for the political behaviour of representatives in India."

To save our democracy from the scourge of defections, we need to strengthen existing laws by blocking obvious loopholes and adding more stringent provisions for defection. As the lure of ministerial office or other remumerative political post had been generally found to be the root cause of defections, all defectors be barred from holding any remunerative political office till the life of the legislature or till his election in a fresh general polls. The Y.B Chavan report also says that a defector should not hold any office for one or two years to shield him from temptation. The clause of exemption to split and merger also needs to be suitably amended. The recognition of a split has itself legitimised defection and encouraged parties to exploit legal loopholes. One third is an imposing number in the context of big parties. With smaller outfits- the worst affected it amounts to little. No one anticipated that in less than a decade the strength of legislature parties would be reduced to two digit and even signle digit numbers. The Constitution Review Commission has suggested that protection under the provision of a split should be scrapped. In other words all defectors whether defecting individually or in group from a party (on whose ticket they have been elected) must quit their house and seek fresh election. A blanket ban on defections, as recommended by the NCRWC, is impractical and would go against the spirit of democracy and encourage bossism and authoritarianism in political parties, which are already suffering from many acute problems. The best course would be as suggested by Y.B. Chavan report, that defectors should be debarred to hold any political office for atleast the duration of the remaining term of the existing legislature or until the next election whichever is earlier. Additionally, the vote cast by a defector to topple any existing government should be treated as invalid.

The present anti-defection law gives immense discretionary powers to the Speakers of the House to decide whether a 'split' or 'defection' has occurred. The role of the presiding officers in deciding the question of disqualification has always been a tricky affair. Our experiences show that in most cases, unfortunately, presiding officers have tended to act in a partisan manner. Gone are the days when speakers used to shed their party lables soon after assuming the charge and acted impartially thereafter. In the recent years speakers have mostly decided in favour of the party to which they belong. Even the Supreme Court has observed that the presiding officer, being an authority within the House and his tenure being dependent on the pleasure of the majority therein, could in theory be seen as acting in a partisan manner. It is, therefore, time to withdraw from presiding officers, the power to decide the question of defection and rest it in the President in the case of Parliament and Governor in the case of a state Legislature; to be exercised in accordance with the opinion of the Election Commission. The record of the Election Commission in this respect is, by and large, commendable.

To ensure that the Election Commission too decides impartially, a set of procedures should be specified which constrains the scope for arbitrariness. These concern (a) the time frame within which the Election Commission will forward its advice to the Governor/President, (b) the time frame within which the Governor/President will act on advice, (c) the condition under which the Governor/President may not accept the advice, (d) the penalties that can be imposed on the legislators who have defected/split, especially with reference to holding office, and (e) the avenues for appeal. The recent experiences show that the most crucial element in the decision process is time frame which is necessary to prevent dilatory tactics on the part of all concerned including the adjudicatory authority to avoid a series of isolated defection adding up to a split by the time the decision is taken. Lastly, there is a need to raise public awareness and to popularise value-based politics, without which no law can be effective.

While lamenting the present state of affairs in the Legislature and elsewhere, one is unfortunately no more in a position to say that all is well with the judiciary. Many of our laws and judicial processes are too old, colonial and antiquated to be relevant or effective today. Citizens who had the misfortune of coming into contract with courts of law to seek justice invariably have many tales of woe. Things have come to such a pass that law abiding citizens are afraid of approaching the courts for justice. Litigants have to bear the worst lapses of a system that seems to have been designed to enmesh them in time-consuming and costly proceedings. More often than not, the ideal of justice remains as elusive, since cases fail to be resolved expeditiously, and in a manner that does not financially or otherwise cripples some of the parties. There has been an erosion of confidence particularly in the lower judiciary. Lower courts are generally perceived as being manned by an insufficient number of inadequately trained and ill-paid judges. This result in long delays, huge backlog of cases, and a generally poor quality of judgements. Justice V.R. Krishna Iyer has rightly characterised our justice delivery system as "slow motion justice, high priced legal service, long distance delivery centres, mystiques of legalise and lacunal laws and processual pyramid made up of teetering tiers and sophisticated rules and tools."

The most serious matter of concern is judicial delays. It is appalling to find many accused persons having spent in jails longer years than the maximum jail sentence prescribed for the offence they are alleged to have committed. Millions of cases are remain pending for years in courts at various stages. Justice Iyer has pointed out that delayed justice is inherent in our judicial system because most of the time of the court is now wasted on long arguments and intricate points, about court fees, bar of limitation, defects in pleadings, sufficiency of service of notice, torture some steps for simple amendments or to implead legal representatives, long-winded arguments about cause of action and jurisdiction. Justice Iyer feels that there is indefensible remissions and avoidable wastage of time at several stages of the proceedings and at several levels of the hierarchy.

One of the reasons of the judicial delay and the huge backlog of cases seems to be the lesser working days of our courts. The Supreme Court hears cases for only 165 days (approximately), which works out to nearly 50 per cent of the days in a year. The High Courts and the subordinate courts have equally long vacations. Of course, their offices work for a little longer. And all this is happening in the backdrop of over three crore cases pending in the district courts, over 30 Lakh in the High Courts and over 70,000 in the Supreme Court. Most of these cases have been pending for the last several decades. In view of millions of cases pending in various courts there is no justification for the judges continuing the luxuary of long vacations which are only a colonial hangover.

Although there has been substantial increase in the number of cases at rapid pace in past years, this has not been matched by an increase in the judicial system's capacity to deal with this rising demand. Ever since independence, little attention has been paid by the Government on improvement of infrastructure of judiciary. There is dearth of courts, judges and court buildings. In several cases, even the minimum facilities have not been given due to lack of planning and proper budgeting of the courts' requirements in consultation with the judiciary. The Constitution Review Commission has pointed out that in the last five decades, there has been no proper allocation of funds commensurate with the corresponding increase in population, legal awareness or increase in legislation. Even the vacant posts of judges are left unfilled for years. The 21 High Courts have around 187 vacancies, against the sanctioned strength of 647 judges. Similar is the case with the subordinate courts where large number of posts are laying vacant. Consequently, judges are over burdened with cases and this act as a major hindrance in the speedy delivery of justice.

To remedy the situation, vacancies need to be quickly filled, additional posts for judges created, and more courts set up. Similarly time limits for disposal of cases should be laid down and arrears cleared under a time-bound programme. Judicial processes and procedures have to be simplified and made more citizen friendly. Number of non-working days must drastically be reduced. Judges should sit for 230 days atleast and each day for longer hours. Devices like the Lok Adalats need to be used more widely.

But what disturbs the most is the charges of corruption against our judges. Recently Chief Justice S.P. Bharuch admitted that "while a good majority of judges in the country are upright and honest, there is a minority which is corrupt and should be identified and severely dealth with." In this regard, the former Chief Justice, ES Venkataramaiah, once observed: "Judiciary in India has deteriorated in standards perhaps because some of the judges are willing to be influenced by lavish parties and whisky bottles, condemning the habitual "dine and wine judges." To save the judiciary from evil of corruption and to ensure judicial accountability some institutional mechanism must immediately be divised. The said body should be empowered to entertain and examine complaints about alleged misbehaviour and charges of corruption against judges. The stream of justice should be clean, clear, and transparent. It is sullied even partly due to the misdeeds of a few. There is, therefore, an urgent need of judicial reforms and it should be undertaken before the judicial system totally collapses and loses its credibility and prestige.

Do We Need Systemic Change?

The present crisis of governance has led many politicians and political analysts to argue in favour of systemic change. They are so dissatisfied with the present parliamentary form of governance that they are inclined to throw it away and in its place opt for the Presidential form of government. It is argued that an assured and uninterrupted tenure of presidential government would give the Indian executive the necessary authority and stability to govern, to accelerate the pace of development and to set itself free from the bane of defections and corruption and would successfull arrest the process of decline and degeneration of our institutions of goverenance. This argumentation is primarily based on the premise that the present crisis of governance lies in the failures of the constitutional system per se.

But the question that becomes more pertinent is whether the systemic change by itself will cure all the maladies which have aflicted our present system of governance and be able to achieve the goal of good governance? I feel certainly not. In this debate one crucial point is generally ignored by the proponents of systemic change - it is not the provisions of the constitution which fail but it is 'we the people' or our representatives who fail the constitution. This point was very rightly raised by the former President K.R. Narayanan. Speaking at a function to commemorate the 50th anniversary of the Republic in Parliament's Central Hall, the President asked the nation to ponder over "whether it is the constitution that has failed us or whether it is we who have failed the constitution." To reinforce his formulation the President quoted his predecessor Dr. Rajendra Prasad as saying that "if elected representatives were men of character and integrity, they could make the best of a defective Constitution. If they are lacking in these, the constitution can not help the country. After all a constitution, like a machine, is a lifeless thing. It acquires life because of the men who control and operate it and India needs today nothing more than a set of honest men who will have the interest of the coutry before them."

In fact, the success or failure of a constitution depends not so much on having well drafted, nobly worded provisions of the constitution rather how they are implemented. Dr.

B.R. Ambedkar, Chairman of the Drafting Committee rightly said that: "however good a constitution may be, it is sure to turn out bad because those who are called to work it happen to be a bad lot. However bad a constitution may be, it may turn out to be good if those who are called to work it happen to be a good lot. The working of the constitution does not depend wholly upon the nature of the constitution. The constitution can only provide the organs of the state such as the legislature, the executive and the judiciary. The factors on which the working of these organs of the State depend are the people and the political parties they will set up as their instruments to carry out their wishes and their politics. Who will say how the people of India and their parties will behave ?" He said that it is "futile to pass any judgement upon the constitution without reference to the part which the people and their parties are likely to play." We have the example of the Weimar Republic of Germany, which had perhaps the finest constitution of the world in its time. It was given a burial by the people operating that constitution. Hitler come to power in a perfectly constitutional manner and wiped out the constitution. We have had the experience of Black Emergency when democracy was temporarily derailed and a form of dictatorship introduced. Thus to blame a constitution for the grave acts of commission and omission by those in power and authority is not justified. Rather, we should put the blame squarely and fully on those who deliberately defy the constitution or distort it for their narrow or political gains. In fact, there is no need to change the constitution. Instead what is needed is a change in the culture of governance.

This is, however, not to suggest that necessary and effective constitutional reforms are not required. Reforms and revitalisation of the present system is imperative. The working of the Constitution for the last 50 years confirms that it is suffering from many maladies and it is absolutely essential that it is purged of them without further twiddling and dethering. Whether it is the issue of electoral reforms, stability and accountability of the governments, or the question of discipling and democratising the political parties, reforming the judiciary or working of our legislative bodies or the issues like crime, corruption and defection, urgent necessary measures will have to be taken. But these measures do not call for a systemic change. The solution to present crisis of governance does not lie in protecting existing hegemonies through a presidental system, but in strengthening and extending parliamentary democracy to the lowest levels. Without getting too involved in the controversy about systemic change, we need to ensure that good, honest and able people are chosen to operate the constitution. Unless the right kind of people come up, nothing will work. And well informed and democratically instructed citizens are, in the end, our only hope for the success of democratic governance.

2

Crisis in Governance and the Need to Reinvent Governance

Ambrose Pinto, S.J.

Introduction

Governance means different things to different people. For the masses in India, governance means evolution of effective policies through participation and their implementation for the general welfare of the people specially the poorest and the weakest. The elite understand the term very differently. A good government is that government that satisfies the needs and desires of the class and permits the class to influence and determine state policies. They would prefer a government that promotes capital growth through privatization and competition with no state interference. The role for the State as far as elites are concerned is to provide stability, status quo, subjugation of the masses through hegemony or through brutal force. The World Bank has identified three factors as being crucial for good governance - the form of the political regime, the process by which the authority is exercised in the managment of a nation's economic and social resources for development and the capacity to government design, formulate and implement policies and discharge functions (World Bank Report 1994: XIV). Basically, the thrust of the World Bank has been on liberal democracy at the political level and liberalization, privatization and globalization in economics. What is good for the World's dominant power is considered good for all. This is not something that is acceptable. That is why, the word govenance is conflict-ridden. Its usage and definition is determined by people situated in a context of their own. The term conveys different things to different people depending on their socio-economic and cultural sitution, values and interests.

Is There A Crisis in Governance?

And yet wherever one is located, there is unanimity that the governance of the India state is in crisis. When does a crisis take place? Indian State has a Constitution. Good governance is centred on following the dictates fot the Constitution. Our Constitution speaks of equality, fraternity and justice on the one hand and secularism and pluralism on the other. The Citizens expect the government in power to remain faithful to the Constitutional ideals. When the government remains faithful to the dictates of the Constitution, one can say there is good governance. On the other hand, when there is a dichotomy between the expectations of the citizens from the state and the incapacity of the state to satisfy or meet those expectations of people, there is a crisis. That is what is witnessed all over the country. The governments in power have not been able to satisfy the aspirations of the people at large in spite of loud pronouncements and rhetoric. Though the Constitution speaks of equality, through the years inequality among social groups has increased. The SCs/STs have remained where they have been. The reservation policy has not only been not fully implemented, it has created vested interests. The literacy rate among SCs/STs has not yet come to the national level. With the increasing poverty and wide gap between the rich and the poor social tensions in the country have only increased than decreased. Equality remains a distant dream because governance has failed.

Divisive forces in the name of caste, creed and religion have damaged the polity. Instead of premising the state on a secular agenda, political parties and vested interest forces have destroyed the spirit of brotherhood. The minorities in recent years have been defined as the "other" creating and promoting insecurity among them.Christians and Muslims have been victims of the vicious hindutva hate compaign specially in the last two years of their power in governance. Crimes in the name of god and religion are committed on SCs/STs. Untouchability though abolished by law is widely practised. Women have been targeted by the regressive forces and subjected to further exploitation in the name of culture. Sati is glorified. Home science courses have been introduced in colleges exclusively for women. They have been prescribed special dress codes. Beauty pageants, Valentine day celebrations, honeymoons have all been banned. When oppression is carried on in the name of caste, religion, culture and gender there can be no fraternity. We are a divided people.

Table 01: Gap in literacy level between SCs/STs and General Population

Year	Gap(%)
1961	17.59
1971	19.13
1981	19.84
1991	17.20

Source: Eighth five year plan 1992-1999.

With the market economy we have an increasing situation of injustice. The power has shifted from nation state to transnational corporations and with that the control of natural resources too. The farmers suffer from food insecurity. While on the one hand there have been starvation deaths on the other farmers have committed suicide due to the agricultural policies of the government. With technology taking over, labour is displaced. The bargaining power of the trade unions has been destroyed by capital. Service sector has been commercialized. Ever since India took to economic reforms the number of the poor have increased. Justice, the commitment the framers of the Constitution made to the people is yet to be realized. From all pointers it is not likely to be realized with the state abdicating its responsibility and handing over the entire economic planning to corporations and financial institutions like IMF, World Bank and WTO.

The other two goals of the framers of the Constitution yet to be realized are secularism and pluralism. It is on the bedrock of secularism that India had visualized to build itself. Political parties with the objective of grabbing power have resorted to sentiments of religion and thus have divided the country into "majority" and "minority". The concept of "hindu rastra" enimical to secular India has been widely and openly championed by BJP and its saffron brigade. There is support to the construction of "hindu rastra" from certain sections of the centrist parties too besides the rightwing groups. The fact that 21 parties claiming themselves as secular could align with the communal BJP to rule the country is an indicator that commitment to secularism is not deep in India. Religion belongs to the private sphere and yet religious sentiments are made use of in large measure in the public sphere in politics. Secularism thus has suffered a set back. BJP and the Sangh Parivar have made it clear that they have no faith in India's pluralism. "Unity in diversity" is something that is foreign to the BJP ideology. Their goal and objective is to construct a nation with unity is uniformity than "unity in diversity". Their party manifesto loudly professes "one nation, one people and one culture" - opposite of what the Constitution enshrines. We are a country of many nationalities, varied people and diverse cultures. The Sangh

Parivar's goal of creating a hindu rastra has created insecurity among minorities and other secular and democratic forces. Such a nation will be against the interests of SCs/STs/OBCs/ minorities and other secular and progressive forces, the majority of Indian population.

The Real Scenario

In an effective governance, everyone has a voice, it is a governance that listen to the voices of the voiceless, the poor, the weak and the dispossessed. The vast majority of the poor are no participants in the governance at present. Their only duty is to go to the polling booth once in five years or more frequently in recent years to cast their votes. For the rest the elite decide governance to suit their tastes and fancies.

The situation is made worse by the market policies of the ruling elite. They prefer the private to the public sector. Instead of being faithful to the Constitutional norms of socialism and justice they are providing legitimacy to the neo-liberal agenda. As a result there is a shift from government provided services to market provided services. Subsidies to the poor and the marginalised no more exist. Education is getting more and more privatized. The economic sector is being fast handed over to corporations. The process is on at increasing pace but is not over. The marginalised groups have been questioning the withdrawal of the state. And yet the local and national governments in nexus with IMF, World Bank and WTO have been furthering the neo-liberal agenda of the markets, agenda of multi-national and transnational corporations. The consequence is the increasing concentration of wealth, income, economic power and dominance of the MNCs and TNCs in the domestic economy.

Not only inequality among social groups have increased but also among states. There are developed states and underdeveloped states. Several states in the south have been doing better than in the North. Due to illiteracy and lack of basic infrastructure material inequality among states has increased. If Bihar per capita is only Rs. 3835, Goa has a per capita income of Rs. 19,719.

Table 02. Per Capita Income of Some States

Per Capita Income of some States (Quick Estimates) 1996-97.

State	Rupees
Bihar	3835
Tripura	5432
Orissa	6422
Assam	6663
Uttar Pradesh	6733
Madhya Pradesh	7445
Meghalaya	8474
Rajasthan	8487
Kerala	9066
West Bengal	9441
Andhra Pradesh	9867
Karnataka	10279
Arunachal Pradesh	10887
Tamil Nadu	11708
Gujarat	13932
Haryana	16199
Maharashtra	17295
Punjab	18213
Goa	19719

Source: Economic Survey 1998-99.

Governance is also criminalised. It is estimated over 20% of our politicians have criminal cases pending against them. Politicians have protected criminals and have been running government even with their support. In the 1960's criminals remained in the background and were satisfied to support politicians to get protection to their evil deeds. Since 1970s such elements have directly entered politics. All parties have cirminal elements today. In fact, criminals and politicians are hand in gloves with each other. It is a reciprocal process and a two way traffic. Corruption too is quite high. Government have proved ineffective in checking swindling of public funds for private gains by the elected leaders and bureaucrats.

Do We Opt For Less Governance?

Because the governments have failed in securing common good the political right argues in limiting the functions of the government and handing over administration to private bodies, business houses and corporations. This is no solution. The legitimacy of the State lies in the people not in the elite or one section of the people. Those who advocate less governance see a role for civil society and NGOs too. Because the governance is in crisis, the idea should not be to get rid of governance. The test of a democratic government is its closeness to the people. At present the government is distant from the people at large. With privatization, liberalization and globalization of the economy, the state is attempting to abdicate its responsibility of social welfare.

Such an attempt to do away with its functions of welfare or common good is a unilateral decision of the governing elite. The masses have not consented to mortgage public property and sell public wealth to corporations. That the public sector was not efficient and running at a loss and hence privatization is the answer is the prescription of the governing elite that needs to be fought. What we must opt is not getting rid of public good and transfer it to private hands but to reinvent governance. The idea of less governance can lead to dele-gitimisation of governance itself. The poor, the hungry and the needy require governance. What kind and type of a government should we have, to cater to common good is a question. But less governance or getting rid of governance is no solution. Every society needs governance for common good. When the ruling elite loose sight of common good and opt for individualism, competition and consumerism, there is a betrayal of people and total lack of governance. Instead of public good what is pursued is private good.

Rethinking Governance

Governance is for common good. Government come into existence to provide good life to the members of society. It was invented at one time. To be effective, it needs to be reinvented. However, it is not easy to reinvent. There are large number of vested interests that would obstruct any change in the status quo. It is the experience of practically all African and Asian countries that the administration in all these countries have remained unresponsive, inefficient and unsympathetic.

In the situation we are in, where the governing class in nexus with the ruling class loots and plunders public wealth and corporatises the economy, it is necessary to rethink governance. No doubt, people at large have lost confidence in governance. Hundreds of protests taking place all over the country against the corporatisation of the economy is a good indicator. Tehri, Narmada and National Fishworkers movements are not the only protests. People are revolting against land alienation, industrial pollution, power projects, reckless destruction of life sustaining resources and the defence of commons of their livelihoods. Unless governance is rethought, the crisis is likely to deepen. The alienation of the people from the state has gone too far. In fact, what is happening is a revolt against governance. To add to the protests there are other groups who have taken to militancy, killings and extortion. The Peoples war groups, Naxalite movements and other groups in Kashmir, North East, Andhra, Mumbai and several other places are undermining the power of the state itself. The need is to rethink governance.

Immediate Steps To Reinvent Governance

(i) *Decentralized democracy:* 73rd and 74th Constitution amendment Acts have made grassroots democracy real in the country. And yet the Panchayati institutions have been complaining of lack of powers and financial resources. At the local level programmes of literacy, education and employment are essential to empowerment. Governance is primarily meant to cater to the basic essentials of the people. Against the present centralized and global model of governance, the need is to opt for local governance. Real issues are at the grassroots. The issues people are fighting for are for control of local community resources. To protect the local resources decentralization of power is key. People should have power to control their own resources and take their own decisions.

(ii) It is the centralising tendencies of the ruling elite that has deprived states of their legitimate rights and claims. As a result people are fighting for decentralisation. Four new states were carved out in 2000. Several other regional groups are also making demands for separte states. In a country of such variety and diversity, the need is to cater to regional aspiration instead of national goals. The nation must emerge from below. Any discrimination of people is bound to lead to resistance. The need is to be sensitive to federal aspirations.

(iii) *Abolition of Government:* Community organizations in several parts of the country have solved collective problems of the people. From the grassroots protests one gets the impression the masses as a whole want the abolition of the present kind of governance. The community organizations may be able to occupy that space if the present kind of governance is abolished. The tribal communities have functioned as self-sufficient communities for centuries with their own mode of governance. Dalit hutments or colonies too have had their communitarian organizations. Several other communities too managed their community life with their organizations. One of the challenge is how to transform community organization into units of governance. The future may lie in self-ruled communities linked to a federal system. Of course science and technology cannot be ruled out in such self-ruled communities. But they will be under the control of the people.

(iv) *Banning of anti-socials from governance:* Ambedkar observed, "I feel, however good a Constitution may be, it is sure to turn out bad because those who are called to work, happen to be a bad lot. The working of the Constitution does not depend wholly upon the nature of the Constitution. The Constitution can provide only the organs of State such as the legislature, the executive and the judiciary. The factors on which the working of those organs of the state depend are on the people and the political parties, they will set up as their instruments to carry out their wishes and their politics. Who can say how the people of India and their parties will behave?" (Constituent Assembly Debates, Vol. XI. No.11, November 25, 1949, Page 975).

We have seen the behaviour of our ruling elite. The need today is to ban all anti-social forces from entering governance right from the local level to the top central level.

Conclusion

Governance to be effective must be decentralized, community centred and should meet the basic needs of people. Ruling elite at every level should be made accountable to the people. Transparency in financial management, participation of people at every level and addressing basic needs of people is the core of all governance. The present crisis is due to the ruling class living away from the masses at the cost of the masses. Reinventing governance to meet the aspirations of the people, and to make people responsible for their lives by active participation in all matters pertaining to their lives.

3

Absence of Good Governance on the Plea of Absence of Political Stability

Akhtar Majeed

Systemic breakdowns and political instability are not the result of constitutional defects but are the consequences of changes in various balances of power. No stability is possible without the empowerment of all sections of our society. What is actually termed as instability is, in fact, a manifestation of the electorate's dissatisfaction with the performance of the power-elite, and if such a dissatisfaction is tried to be thwarted from expressing itself in frequent changes of governments then the alternative could only be dissents, protests, agitations and extremisms. The plea of desirability of stability of a government cannot over-ride the desirability of having only the government that represents people through the majority support in the Lok Sabha. Making the Lok Sabha and the State Assemblies 'stable' for fixed terms of five years would neither be in the interests of good governance nor compatible with the democratic principle. Democrary involves a dynamic interplay of socio-political forces and changes in it occur either through elections or through realignment of political forces. May be the fear of losing seat provides some deterrence to lapses of our worthy representatives. If a term is assured for five years, come what may, the stability may well transform itself into an unbridled and autocratic show of power and influence for the spoils of office. If the term of rulers is made unalterable, even when they might have ceased to represent the popular will, it would make it difficult to distinguish between this type of democracy and autocracy. Such a government would do what it likes, no matter at what cost to the nation. This would not be good governance as we have seen many a stable governments, in the past lasting and snoozing for full five years.

Making our representatives stable in their seats of power, and thus making them more unresponsive to the needs of the people, making them unaccountable for the governmental acts of omission and commission, would take away people's general empowerment. And *that* would facilitate political instability.

Since passing of no-confidence motion would not involve the ouster of the government, the executive would cease to be responsible to the legislature, and it would greatly alter the balance of power between the two wings of government. Whereas the executive would assume pervasive powers, it would result in the 'dis-empowerment' of the Parliament. And that would mean altering the basic structure of the constitution. An unaccountable executive cannot become a guarantee for stability. Political stability is not undermined by elections but by the reluctance to face the people after failing them at governance. Any election, whether a regular one after five years or a mid-term one, provides the people an occasion to give their verdict and this makes the democracy more vibrant, more strong. Any freezing of democracy would provide a premium to manipulative tactics to let a government continue in power even after losing its mandate. Taking away from the people their right to choose their government would be grossly violative of the spirit of our Constitution. And depriving people of their rights has never been a guarantee for stability.

Is this not strange that the same sections of our polity which point to the instability of the coalition government as the reason for not taking up 'contentious issues' are supporting the entire review of the constitution by the same 'unstable' coalition governments? Isn't it strange that these sections of our polity had criticised the constitution as not being framed by a truly elected and representative Constituent Assembly, but supported the review of its working not by the elected representatives of the people in Parliament but by a Commission appointed by the Government?

It would be good if an analysis is made of the reasons behind this sudden concern for stability. It is our expanding mercenary middle class, which perceives economic growth to be dependent upon political stability that is being mobilized to support the need for such stability. Economic reforms have, so far, benefited the urban middle class and, for further benefits, it perceives political stability as a protection against disorder. Apprehensions about political stability lead to apprehensions about the viability and usefulness of our parliamentary system.

This high-profile concern does not appear to be intended to enhance the quality of Indian polity, or to secure social justice, or to curb corruption, or to protect the liberal social-political system. In spite of the resilience of our existing system, the major concern seems to be protection against ministerial instability at the cost of ministerial accountability and responsibility. The obsession, that a strong central government is a pre-condition for national integration, needs a closer scrutiny. The central government is likely to be more stable and more strong if it is willing to respect regional aspirations and to accommodate the states' viewpoints. It is the concern and the bias of the privileged elite, from the Indian middle class, which is responsible for the supposed national concern for 'stability'. This concern and bias reflects the middle class apprehensions about the growing influence of regional leaders and groups/parties. The tactical demonisation of regional leaders ("likes of Rabri, Mulayam, Jayalalitha, Laloo") reflects the erosion of political privileges hitherto enjoyed by leaders representing the other end of the social strata. Now that the hegemony and privileges seem to be slipping away from the erstwhile elite, there is no option for them but to equate their stability with the political stability of the nation. It is this mindset that gets agitated over the prospect of sharing that power which was considered their divine right in the plural context of Indian politics.

It is erroneous to assume that political instability results if the government is not stable or durable. Regime stability should not be identified with political stability or constitutional stability. We have witnessed profound political instability when the central government was supposedly strong and stable, being run by one single political party: intensified militancy in Kashmir, Punjab and the North-East, communal riots and the challenge to the state's authority from different social groups. However, we have witnessed political consolidation even when the governments were being run by disparate 'unstable coalitions' and alliances of mutually fighting political parties: mitigation of militancy due to political accommodation, pacification of social unrest, economic reforms, successful global diplomacy and a resounding victory in a war. It is more than clear that as long as there is a broad political consensus and political accommodation, there is hardly any scope for political instability even if the government is not durable or stable. And if the political rulers get jittery when the going gets tough, it reflects on their nerves, on their art of governance, on their political immaturity, and not on the stability of the system.

Further, it is interesting to note that the supposed political instability, during the last decade of the past century, is held responsible for our failure to realise our potential as a nation. However, the solid political stability also, which prevailed during the preceding three decades, could not be very effective in this direction. It is an unpalatable fact, in India, that reforms and innovations have resulted from compulsions arising out of apprehensions of losing power because of instability. During the periods of political stability, the elite sees no reason to initiate any policy shift or reform, which are initiated, out of desperation, only when the status quo is challenged.

Not only is there a distinction between political stability and regime stability, the pre-condition for the latter (legislative majority) in a parliamentary system is not necessarily a pre-condition for political stability. A small majority in the legislature can provide greater stability because that forces the government to act more responsible. A large majority, on the other hand, tends to make a government complacent, too sure of it's position to bother about accommodating diverse interests, feeling too strong to pay attention to administration and governance. Since it does not feel threatened for its continuance, it becomes autocratic in nature whereas the weak strength of a small-majority government does not allow it to resort to authoritarian measures. Once it is realised that the survival of a particular government is different from the survival of the nation-state, it would be easier to accept that stability does not depend upon a large legislative majority. Even a small legislative majority, accommodating diverse interests and sharing in the power, can provide political stability.

It is the perception of non-accommodation of interests and sharing of power that erodes political legitimacy of a government. This, in turn, results in a decrease in people's identification with, and conformity to, governmental policies, a decrease in the ability of the government to mobilise support, a breakdown of policy coordination, a growth of apathy and indifference among the people. It is the absence of popular faith in the integrity and fairness of state power that delinks popular identification with governmental policies. It is the presence of major differences over what are the core national values that signifies the propensity of a state for loss of legitimacy. And it is this erosion of legitimacy that results in the erosion of political stability.

In a country like India, with the problems mentioned above, threats to stability mainly originate from socio-economic causes. Even the threat of external intervention, and the foreign-initiated political instability, is possible because of internal weaknesses arising out of socio-economic imbalances and maladies. No doubt, vital national values do get jeopardised due to such instability. No doubt, some of this instability may be initiated and encouraged by outside forces. But, many a times, in order to hide their inefficiency and mishandling, governments are apt to see an ever-convenient 'foreign-hand' in attempts to destabilise *the regime.*

In India, the modernisation process has not led to any major cracks in the traditional social organisation and there has been a blending of tradition and modernity at different stages; and this has resulted in new channels being opened for the expression of various identities in the democratic process. In the process of political accommodation, these avenues act as a democratic barrier against various forms of extremism. As the Indian political system has evolved from dominant party system to multi-party system, effective decision-making is now possible only through political bargaining and accommodation. Indian political coalitions are, thus, not manifestations of political instability but are compulsions of power-sharing and political accommodation reflect a new level of political consciousness and maturity of judgment on the part of

Indian voters. If anything, it reflects the dissatisfaction of the electorate with the dominant note of any single political party which might lead to dissents and extremism.

It is the socio-political cohesiveness that determines the degree of political stability of a state. In the absence of such cohesiveness, and in spite of formidable state power, overwhelming legislative majority and wide range of resources and capabilities, even a super power may face the problems of being a weak state (like the former Saviet Union). The best method to achieve stability is to arrive at consensus and to agree to share power. But if the consensus has been achieved through coercion, stifling political opposition, then it is of no use, in the long run, for political stability. Consensus is linked with legitimacy and loyalty which can only be achieved through an accommodative process and not forcibly imposed. If a government wants to acquire support for its legitimacy, it has to accommodate diverse interest and agree to share power with them.

Indian social diversities are reflected in our federal democracy as its social base and this pluralism has sustained our political federalism. All this is reflected in our multi-party system, in various regional and linguistic identities, in different ideological persuasions, and all of these are our social and political realities. These are the realities that nurture the roots of Indian democracy and, even if some of them are not very attractive for some of us, they cannot be just wished away.

4

Modern State and the Crisis of Institutions

Ravi P. Bhatia

Introduction

Modern state is a complex set of institutions which are integrated and hierarchically structured. It is sovereign within a space that defines its territory. The sovereignty flows from the legal authority exercised within its territory and is not subject to any external legal control or any other internal and independent source of power. The importance of territory is for instance, spelt out in the first article of the Indian Constitution itself.

The state must hold itself together and safeguard its territorial integrity. That is why the State enjoins its citizens to protect the unity and integrity of the country. Persons comprising the state are not treated as individuals but rather as citizens or voters. It distils such characteristics as economic status, religious or regional loyalties and transforms them into rights and obligations of citizens. Since the law provide them equally, all citizens are ideally speaking (and this is provided in our Constitution also) treated equal with equal rights and privileges. In the process, the state tries to discourage and dismantle the group affiliations-cultural, religious, caste and tribal, and tries to mould them into a uniform and easily governable community.

In the process of unification and homogenization of its subjects, the state does not directly intervene as long as they do not come into conflict with the established law of the state. While maintaining their independence, the state nevertheless ensures that these activities are regulated and encompassed in a framework of rights and duties.

According to Bhikhu Parekh (Parekh, 1996), whereas the earlier states used to rule, they rarely governed in the modern sense. The modern state through its various institutions: the executive, the legislature, the judiciary, comprising different courts, the ubiquitous bureaucracy, the military and police etc. whose reach is long and all pervasive, is able to put any individual or group of individuals to fall into line. It puts pressure and uses its ample machinery to educate, advertise and persuade. The state also enjoys the right to use force and does use it when necessary.

The State has built up a complex web of institutions to administer and govern. The government is composed of individuals and officials occupying these institutions who derive their authority from their office. However, one must distinguish between the state and the government. The former exists even when there is no government. Governments may come and go but the state continues to exist. The form of a government may change but the identity of a state does not alter, unless there is a revolution or war or mutual entente. There may then be a fusion of two or more states to combine into a bigger whole of fission when a bigger part gets divided into two or more fragments.

Recent examples of the above are Germany and Pakistan respectively.

Education is an important tool in the hands of a state. It is required not only to impart required skills to its citizens, but also to propagate a set of common values, a sense of national identity and loyalty to the state. Education lays stress on a common language, a common flag and national anthem and other symbols to inculcate a sense of belonging. That is why there is stress on the concept of a 'Fatherland' or "Bharat Mata" etc. The importance of education to inculcate a common sense of values and foster a homogenized behaviour is particularly important in countries like USA, Canada or Germany which welcome a large number of immigrants.

Like education, communications and modern technology are also important tools in the hands of a modern state to achieve the above objectives as well as to satisfy the multifarious demands like physical movements of people and goods. Technology is necessary for ensuring welfare of people as well as to monitor their behaviour and be ready if an emergency arises. When needed, force is permitted to ensure 'law and order'. Appropriate laws are passed through the various organs of legislature. It appears that one of the major functions of a modern state is to legislate. It sets up a structure of authority with specific duties and functions to carry out the various objectives of a modern state including quelling internal disturbance and meeting the challenge of external aggression.

The relationship of a modern state with the society is complex. Earlier the state carried out its business in an integrated manner with the society, its authority being derived from the collective life of the community. Today, the authority of the state is intrinsic to it and not directly related to the activities of the society. It is outside the life and customs of a community or a group of communities but the latter are nevertheless under the state's overall authority and jurisdiction. As long as the activities of a community do not entail any conflict with the state, the community can act independently, but as soon as a conflictual situation arises, the long arm of the state is present to ensure 'peace and harmony'.

The autority of the modern state is not a collection of discrete rights and prerogatives, but an overarching all exclusive power called sovereignty. From this follows a group of laws or legal system, which is rationalized, homogenized and centralized, into the State. This authority or sovereignty is unitary, impersonal and legally binding on all its citizens. Although customs, traditions and religious beliefs do form occasionally, the basis of formation and enactment of these laws, but once passed and enacted, these laws acquire a life of their own and a supreme authority and power and can override all the traditions and beliefs.

The modern state speaks to its citizens in a formal language— the language of law. It does not recognize any other authority or rule. For example, it will not recognize the code of conduct or customs of individual groups if they come into conflict with the sovereign law of the state. It is this rationale or argument that propels the BJP to aim at evolving a common civil code for all religious groups including the Muslims. With the system of laws enshrined in a Constitution, and an alert and pro-active judiciary to oversee and monitor the laws, it is difficult for any group or community or even the government ot escape from the clutches of law and act independently.

The Contemporary State

The above features describe a classical modern state but today we are living in a globalised environment where the sovereignty of nations and the capacity to act independently are severely affected. Although it has evolved from the modern state, the contemporary state has acquired radically different features. Thanks to multilateral agencies like the WTO, World Bank and IMF etc., most states are constrained to follow their guidelines and conditionalities and modify their policies suitably.

Whether it is in modifying interest rates or in devaluation of the currencies or in reducing the subsides in agriculture, the states are dictated to by these agencies. And at the behest of the WTO, the contemporary states, especially of the third world are compelled to allow free flow of imports and to lift quantitative restrictions on them despite the ruinous impact on their manufacturing and farming.

Samir Amin (Amin, 1996) has in a perceptive article discussed the process of democratization of the political regimes all over the world. But in the third world countries, this process remains confined to the middle or upper middle classes and the organized sectors of the urban society. Accompanying this process is another trend— the marketisation of society: the philosophy that markets are the means of liberating the third world countries from their backwardness and poverty. In fact so powerful are these concepts of democracy and markets that the two are usually equated, i.e. market = democracy and democracy = market. It was because of this that after the Soviet Union fragmented and many East European countries came out of the communist fold, many financial experts were rushed to these liberated countries with their market philosophy in order to democratise them and orient them to the market. But as Amin ' as argued the two cannot be equated. The bourgeois democracy has established equal rights and personal liberties but not true equality except in law, as already indicated earlier. Amin argues that:

> "Western democracy is restricted to the political domain, while economic management continues to be based on non-democratic principles of private ownership and competition. In other words, capitalist mode of production does not of itself require democracy but rather its characteristic oppression is hidden in economic alienation affecting the entire society..."

The above analysis of Amin helps us in understanding the inequalities of present day India: the inequalities in terms of incomes and consumption, the inequality in terms of educational opportunities and achievement, the inequalities in terms of job opportunities and wages and the inequity in terms of basic justice and dignity for all.

Working of Institutions in India

India can justifiably feel pround that our democracy is working unlike many other third world countries which after gaining independence from former imperial powers, have slipped into military rule, dictatorships or autocracies. The resilience of our decmocratic institutions is demonstrated by the fact that we have successfully held thirteen Lok Sabha elections and several more Assembly elections in our states. Our institutions — the presidency, the parliament, the judiciary and the executive, etc., are working but signs of strain and discord can be seen. Although, India is a functioning democracy, increasingly, it is not well governed. In the words of Atul Kohli (Kohli, 1990): "The evidence of eroding political order is everywhere. Personal rule has replaced party rule at all levels... and the civil and police services have been politicized..."

The rowdy and occasionally violent behaviour both inside and outside Parliament and State Assemblies is a matter of shame and disquiet. Not only is this a distressing aspect of modern democratic processes, it also prevents the legislature from carrying out its duties. Important bills like the Women's Reservation bill, the CVC bill, etc could not be tabled because of this disruption in the last (2000) winter session of parliament. In fact this session has been dubbed by observes as the most fruitless and wasteful parliamentary session ever.

Political scientists have offered different reasons for the crisis of the state in modern India (Kaviraj, 1997).

Where Rajni Kothari talks of a process of atrophy of democratic institutions, Ashish Nandi and T.N. Madan put the responsibility for this situation on the imposition of alien western institutions by the elite of India.

Constitutional Provisions regarding Welfare for the People

The Constitution of India unambiguously provides for economic and social justice in many articles listed below:

* Promotion of welfare of People (Article 38 (1))
* Minimizing the inequalities of income and of status, facilities and opportunities (Article 38(2))
* Provision of right to work, to education and public assistance (Asticle 41)
* Provision of free and compulsory education to childern up to age 14 (Article 45)
* Raising levels of nutrition and standard of living and improvement of public health (Article 47).

But the implementation of many of these articles through its various organs - the executive, the judiciary and a powerful bureaucracy, by which the state tries to administer, govern and provide economic and social justice to its citizens, is extremely unsatisfactory and there are large inequities in respect of food, nutrition, health services, education, income distribution etc.

Role of the Judiciary and the Supreme Court

Unfortunately, while the courts are seized with issues that are strictly speaking in the realm of the executive (government), they are unable to ensure that the basic features enshrined in the Constitution for the good of the common people are implemented uniformly and equitably.

Take the example of the Sardar Sarover Dam where the Supreme Court (SC) has recently removed the stay on further construction. This has been done despite the fact that the *Narbada Bachao Andolan,* which has staged massive rallies and *dharnas* under the leadership of Medha Patkar, has been stressing upon the tragic displacement of millions of people from their ancestral homelands. That there will be large-scale displacement is not in doubt, although the number of people likely to be affected is in question. The important point is that whatever be the merits of the case, the final authority has devolved to the SC. Even the government has been underlining this fact and has pronounced its intentions, in no uncertain terms, of following the decision of the SC. Unfortunately, there has hardly been any attempt at negotiation with the tribal and other affected people to minimize their suffering.

In another case, that of displacement of polluting industries from out of Delhi, the concern has been only for pollution that is likely to result in Delhi but not in the areas where these industries are to be shifted. The Supreme Court is apparently also not concerned with the loss of thousands of jobs in the process. Many industrialists would find it more economic to close down their units rather than shift them to distant and unfamiliar areas whose viability would need to be first established. Again, the question arises whether the SC is morally or ethically speaking, competent to take such far- reaching decisions that affect the welfare of thousands of people.

Another disturbing move has been the judgment of the SC to allow luxury hotels to be built in Goa in violation of the Coastal Regulation Zone Act (CRZ). Similarly, as pointed out by Harsh Sethi (*Seminar,* January 2001), efforts are under way to amend the Fifth Schedule of the Constitution legally allowing the state to acquire land in tribal areas for opening up mining and industry in their areas. The existing law does not permit non-tribals to own property rights in scheduled areas and hence the need to amend the Schedule.

We may also mention that bonded labour is illegal and unconstitutional. The SC had earlier released all bonded labour and given them freedom. But even today there exist several families who are bonded in the states of

Rajasthan and Orissa. Just a few weeks back, an NGO had filed an appeal against the existence of these bonded persons and asked for the relief of about 900 people working as bonded labour in the mines of Rajasthan. The problem with the bonded is that even after they are released, they are not rehabilitated and are compelled to again get into the clutches of their old masters for their livelihood.

While the judiciary has been more than active, it has yet to put its own house in order. There is large degree of misuse of the legal process leading to prolonged litigation and delays in getting justice. According to some estimates, there is a backlog of 3.5 crore (35 million) cases pending in various courts all over the country. The delays will result in ordinary people losing faith in the judiciary and may lead them to resort to extra-judicial measures for seeking justice. The Union minister for law, justice and company affairs, Mr. Arun Jaitley, has admitted to 3.4 million pending cases in the High Courts and 21,600 cases in the Supreme Court in the year 2000 (Jaitley, 2001). Part of the problem is the shortage of judges, but as Mr. Jaitley himslef has admitted, merely appointing additional judges will not be enough. Court procedures need to be simplified and Mr. Jaitley has suggested amendments to the Civil Procedure Code (CPC) and other measures to expedite the disposal of cases.

Atrophy of Institutions

Not only the judiciary, but also many other institutions are in peril. As the noted constitutional expert A.G. Noorani has observed (Noorani, 2000):

> 'India's federalism has suffered grievously at the hands of successive governments at the centre, regardless of their political complexion and with uniform disdain for constitutional norms and values, or scruples for political morality. The office of the Governor of the state has been systematically abused

> for political ends by those (in power) in New Delhi. The office of the Chief Minister of states is also afflicted by the same abuse. Very many Chief Ministers owe their office not so much to the confidence of their Legislature Party as to the bounty of the Party's *High Command.*'

This has also been brought out in an article which appeared in *The Hindu* (Bhatia, Singh, 2000a) where several examples of the High Command changing the Chief Minister in several States-U.P., Maharashtra, Karnataka etc., have been cited.

In the above article, the authors have also pointed out at another unhealthy trend in the political system-the rapid fragmentation of parties as a result of confederal pressure. The party maintains a facade of federal organization but finally disintegrates and fragments into separate regional parties. Not a single party has escaped this fragmentation. This has happened in the Janata Dal, the Congress, the BJP and the BSP etc. The fragmentation of the Janata Dal into Rashtriya Janata Dal (RJD), Biju Janata Dal (BJD), Janata Dal (U), Janata Dal (S) etc. in a preiod of about a decade, is truly remarkable.

A related problem is that the political parties do not hold the party elections and even if they do, it is more a ritual than a meaningful election. The example of the recent election of the President to the Congress Party, is a case in point and even when it was held last year with late Shri Jitender Prasad contesting against Sonia Gandhi, various big-wigs had tried to make Prasad withdraw from the contest. When their efforts failed, the contest became a mockery with the result a forgone conclusion. The Election Commission has often berated this fact but in the absence of a suitable law, has been unable to do anything in the matter. However, it has at least ensured that party elections according to the Partys' constitutions are held regularly.

Similarly, in many recent cases—whether it is in the protection of the minorities or in implementation of certain decisions of commissions and judicial decisions, the executive has been found to be lax and ineffective. In fact the Supreme Court has had to intervene to ensure that decisions taken are implemented. The atrophy of the executive and the judicial arms of the state is an ominous sign on the functioning of good governance (Bhatia, Singh, 2000b).

In addition, other features of the Indian Constitution are being ignored or at least, the government has been found wanting in its efforts to ensure welfare for the people at large. We can see that unfortunately for about half the population, the above provisions of the constitution are largely meaningless. If by welfare, one means good health facilities, clean drinking water, sufficient food, housing etc, then about 40% of the population is deprived of these facilities. The income inequalities and those of status and opportunities are closely related with these basic requirements and there is a large divergence in the provision of these basic facilities between the haves and the have-nots. Similarly, the right to work is jeopardised with millions of people unable to get any employment both in the rural and urban centers. The educational achievements are equally unsatisfactory in terms of access to education, enrolment, literacy levels and pupil-teacher ratio etc. The situation is worse in the so-called BIMARU states.

Education and Literacy

According to the 1991 figures, 52% of Indians were literate (64% males and 39% females). This figure has increased in 1997 to 62 % (73% males and 50% famales). Among women, the highest literacy rate in 1997 was 86% in Kerala and the lowest of 20% was in Rajasthan. Among rural areas in Rajasthan, only 11.6% were literate and among the tribal women, certain districts of Rajasthan and Orissa have a shockingly low figure of literacy of 4% only.

Education and literacy are not only important in themselves as they open up a world of opportunities and ideas to the educated, but are also instrumental in the process of economic growth, development and empowerment. Greater access to education leads to greater life expectancy and contributes to higher economic growth. In addition, it leads to improving worker efficiency and has a positive impact on agricultural growth.

Despite all these advantages the government, not only the present one but also the previous ones, have not been able to universalize elementary education. Although compulsory education is provided in the Constitution as a directive principle, the Supreme Court has recognized education as a fundamental right, in the Supreme Court ruling in the Unni-Krishnan vs. the state of Andhra Pradesh (Supreme Court, 1993). There is also a constitutional amendment bill making education a fundamental right pending in the parliament since 1997. This was to have been considered in the last session of the parliament, but as indicated earlier, it could not be because of the prolonged disruption in the parliament.

Food Producation and Nutrition

The availability of food and nutritional levels are also poor and unequal with about 40% people BPL (below the poverty line). This is bizarre and tragic when we consider the fact that the government godowns are overflowing with food grains and rats and rodents are having a picnic.

The growth of food output and population growth are shown in Table I below:

Table I: Growth of food output vs. population growth

Year	Food Output %	Population Growth %
1980-81 to 1991-92	2.92	2.14
1991-92 to 1998-99	1.8	1.85

Source: Patnaik (1996)

The growth of food has slowed down from 2.92 to 1.8% whereas the population growth has declined from 2.14 to 1.85%. Thus the growth in food output has not been able to keep pace with the population growth. This has led to disastrous consequences. On one hand, the prices of food items have increased due to withdrawal of subsidies on food and due to a general escalaton in prices; on the other hand the purchasing power of the people to buy food has decreased.

Another problem is the trend towards shifting in the pattern of agricultural production from grains especially from coarse grains to oil seeds, sugar and other exportables. The shift in area under cultivation of food grains and other products is shown below in Table II. This shows that land has been shifted from coarse grains, which is consumed by the poor to oilseeds. There has been some increase in the area of wheat and rice but this is not enough to meet the increasing population. Similarly, there has been a noticeable decrease in the area growing pulses. The shifting pattern of agriculture has resulted in increased rural poverty and despair among marginal farmers. It has also led to less availability of food to the poor.

Table II: Shifting Pattern of Agriculture in India

Agricultural Product	Percentage change from 1989 to 1995
Wheat and rice	+0.98
Coarse grains	-11.8
Pulses	-6.13
Oil seeds	+10.23

Source: (Patnaik, 1996)

The per capita consumption of food is low and due to a spurt in prices is declining further for the very poor. This is borne out by the fact that there is a surplus of about 30 million tons of food grains in the government godowns. The poor who were already malnourished are becoming greater victims of the malnourishment and there are estimates that there are about 300 million malnourished people, more so than the poor in India.

Poverty and Employment facilites

Economists have devised different methods of calculating poverty of people. One of them is the head-count poverty ratio, which is the percentage of people below the poverty line. The figures for this in the rural and urban areas are depicted in the following Table:

Table III: Head-Count Poverty Ratio

Year	Rural	Urban	Combined
1983	45.65	40.79	44.48
1987-88	39.09	38.20	38.86
1989-90	33.70	36.00	34.28
1990-91	35.04	35.29	35.11
1993-94	37.27	32.36	35.07
1994-95	38.03	34.24	36.98
1995-96	38.29	30.05	36.08
1997	38.46	33.97	37.23

Source: Mahendra Dev (2000)

As we can see the poverty ratios had declined in the 1980s, reaching the combined ratio of 34.28 in 1989-90. But since that time, the ratios are increasing especially in the rural sector. In fact, the levels of rural poverty as well as the overall poverty are higher in the post liberalisation phase of 1997 than in the pre-liberalisation phase of 1989-90 and approach the levels of 1987-88, which was a drought year.

Poverty and employment are intimately related. The greater the availability of employment, the less is the poverty level and vice-versa. The situation of employment in the 1990s in the post liberalization period is quite bad. In fact, there is clear evidence that the employment situation in 1990s was worse than during the 1980s —i.e. during the pre-liberalisation period. It can be argued that it is liberalisation itself, which is responsible for the increasing poverty of the people (Bhattacharya, 2000). The figures for number of people employed in the recent past are presented in the Table IV below:

Table IV: Employment figures in public and private organised sector.

Year	Public sector employment (Million)	Private organized sector employment (Million)	Total employment (Million)
March 1991	19.06	7.67	26.73
March 1992	19.21	7.85	27.06
March 1993	19.33	7.85	27.18
March 1994	19.45	7.93	27.38
March 1995	19.47	8.06	27.53
March 1996	19.43	8.51	27.94
March 1997	19.54	8.69	28.25
March 1998	19.42	8.75	28.17

From the above we see that the condition of employment remains bleak. The total employment in 1998 is less than in the previous year mainly because the public sector is cutting down on employment opportunities and the growth in the private sector is very small. The employment has increased in the public sector in the period 1991-98 by only 1.9% although in the private sector, it has increased by 14%. However, in the latter sector, the percentage change in employment over the previous year has been maximum (5.58%) in 1996 but has slowed down since then. The corresponding figures for the years 1997 and 1998 are 2.11 and 0.69% respectively. In addition to the huge backlog of unemployed, there is also a large annual increment of about 8 million in the labour force. To make matters worse, provisional data show a decline in real wages for unskilled farm labour by 2.12 % This is already causing social tensions and pushing a greater percentage of the population below the poverty line. Thus we see that the government is unable to address the basic welfare needs of the people.

Conclusions

We have considered some important features of a modern state and have showed that sovereignty is an essential prerequisite of it. However, in the contemporary globalised situation with the economy opening up, the freedom of most states to act independently in the interests of their citizens, is severely curtailed by the multilateral agencies like the World Bank and the WTO. These institutions have imposed serious conditionalities which are affecting the basic governance of countries and jeopardising the interests of the common man as far as job opportunities, availability of food and health services are concerned and are pushing a large number of people below the poverty line.

In the context of our country, whereas the Constitution clearly spells out the duties of the government to provide welfare for the people and eliminate inequality of income and opportunities, the government is unable to do so for about half the population. It is also unable to universalise elementary education despite the clear mandate of the Constitution and the Supreme Court to do so. The Supreme Court is taking on a very pro-active role in areas which are outside its jurisdiction, but its own house is not in order. There are legal delays leading to a backlog of several million cases pending in the various courts of the country. It is clearly that the contemporary situation calls for concerted efforts for the amelioration of the conditions of a vast majority of people. There is a crisis of governance that has been made worse by the liberalisation and globalisation of the economy.

References

Amin, Samir (1996): "Democracy in the Third World," in Sheth, D.L. and Ashis Nandy, (eds.), *The Multiverse of Democracy,* Sage Publications, New Delhi, 1996.

Bhatia, Ravi P. and M.P. Singh (2000s): "Call off this Pilgrimage—The High Command Syndrome", *The Hindu,* New Delhi March 7,2000.

Bhatia, Ravi P. and M.P. Singh (2000b): "Are We a Soft State", *The Hindu,* New Delhi, August 8, 2000.

Bhattacharya, J (2000): "Poverty and Employment under Economic Reforms", *Ruinous Reforms,* SFI Publications, New Delhi, 2000.

Dev, Mahendra (2000): "Economic Reforms, Poverty...", *Economic and Political Weekly,* March 4, 2000

Kabra, Kamal Nayan (2000): "The Indian Economy 1998-2000", *Alternate Economic Survey,* Rainbow Publishers, New Delhi, 2000.

Kaviraj, Sudipta (1997), (editor): *Politics in India,* Oxford University Press, New Delhi, 1997.

Kohli, Atul (1990), *Democracy and discontent,* Cambridge University Press, 1990.

Noorani, A.G. (2000): *Constitutional Questions in India,* Oxford Univertisy Press, New Delhi, 2000.

Parekh, Bhiku (1996): "The Nature of the Modern State", in Sheth, D.L. and Ashis Nandy, (eds.). *The Multiverse of Democracy,* Sage Publications, New Delhi, 1996.

Patnaik, U (1996): "Export Oriented Agriculture and Food Security in Developing Countries and India", *Economic and Political Weekly,* September 1996.

Sethi, Harsh (2001): "Backpage", *Seminar,* Vol. 497, January, 2001.

The Supreme Court Cases (1993), Vol. I, Eastern Book Company, New Delhi, 1993.

5

Judiciary and Governance

P.M. Bakshi

The title of this paper may perhaps provoke an initial hostile reaction in the minds of many readers. The question can be naturally raised as to what has the judiciary to do with governance. The traditional theory of political science divides the State into three branches, and correspondingly enunciates, the doctrine that it is the executive that governs and the business of the judiciary is to adjudicate disputes in public law and private law. Of course, the tripartite division of the functions of the State is never considered as representing watertight departments. Nevertheless, it is recognised that *primarily* the judiciary adjudicates and does not *execute* the laws. Similarly, policy is expected to be laid down by the legislature and not by the executive or by the judiciary. In fact, the judiciary itself has acted upon the supposition that the legislature cannot delegate to the executive any power to lay down policy.

[*Raj Narain Singh Vs. Patna Administration*, AIR 1954 SC; *Harakchand Vs. Union of India*, AIR 1970 SC 1453].

Impact of the judiciary

However, a little reflection will show that adjudications of the judiciary do often impinge upon aspects of governance. Sometimes, the impact of the judiciary upon the governance is negative, while at other times it is positive. Again, such impact of the judiciary is, in some instances, marginal while at other times it is noticeable even prominent. In other words, the impact presents variations both from the qualitative angle and from the quantitative angle. These variations will be dealt with, presently.

An analysis of the impact

Qualitatively it can be stated by way of analysis, that the judicial impact upon the process of governance can be classified into:

(a) restrictive impact on governance,

(b) ameliorative impact on governance, and

(c) positive or activist impact on governance.

Negative impact: *ultra vires*

It is elementary that executive action that violates the Constitution or a statute, or is otherwise violative of the legal limits of the power in question, has to be declared to be *ultra vires* by the judiciary, which must therefore set it aside. This power of the Judiciary rests on the doctrine of *ultra vires*.

In such cases, the Judiciary does not formulate any positive approach. One can say, that in such cases the Judiciary "destroys something, but does not construct anything".

Examples of this power of the Judiciary are legion. Here one can deal with only very few selected cases.

(a) Statutory rules provide that in order to be eligible for promotion, candidates would have put in service upto a certain period. Administrative instructions issued by the executive provided that this requirement need not be complied with. The instructions were held to be ultra vires.

[*HP Electricity Board Vs. Somdutt Uppal*, (1993) Suppl 2 SCC 415].

(b) Children cannot be compelled to sing the National Anthem, there being no law to that effect.

Bijoe Emanuel Vs. State of Kerala, (1986) 3 SCC 615.

In this case, the action of the school authorities was unjustified

(i) because there was no statutory support to it and also

(ii) because the action was in conflict with the freedom of speech and expression.

(c) It is elementary that if power given to X is exercised by Y, the exercise is invalid. Thus, where an Act of Parliament empowered *only the Central Government* to prohibit mining operations in respect of minor powers such a power cannot be exercised by the State Government. [*Chandeshwar Prasad Singh Vs. Sub-Division LR Officer*, AIR 1986 Cal. 1.]

(d) A provision in the Service Rules requiring a female employee to obtain Government's written permission before marrying is unconstitutional (as violating the equality clause of the Constitution) and therefore ultra vires. [*C. B. Muthamma Vs. Union of India*, AIR 1979 SC 1868.]

(e) Telephone rules which provided for preference to doctors, Journalists etc in the matter of allotment of telephones but not giving similar facility to lawyers is void. [*Shankar Birmiwal Vs. Union of India*, AIR 1982 Raj 187. (Article 14 of the Constitution was held to be violated).]

Arbitrariness

Apart from questions of *ultra vires* (want of power) there are cases where the power does exist but has been exercised in an arbitrary manner.

By now it is well established by a series of judicial decisions that all State action must be free from the blemish of arbitrariness, as otherwise it would violate the equality clause of the Constitution. Here are a few illustrative cases.

(a) Under the Unlawful Activities Prevention Act, Government can impose a ban on an association whose activities are unlawful. The Courts have held that before such an order can be passed, grounds must exist and must be communicated to the association. [*Mohd. Zafer Vs. Union of India,* (1994) Suppl (2) SCC 1.]

(b) Housing authorities cannot arbitrarily increase the prices of houses.

[*State of UP Vs. Maharaja Dharamdas Prasad Singh,* (1989) 2 SCC 505].

(c) Allotment of 33 percent marks for viva voce test in selections for posts in the public service may lead to arbitrariness. [*Ashok Vs. State of Karnataka,* (1992) 1 SCC 28.]

Mala fides or extraneous purpose

Discretionary power given to the executive by the Constitution or the law has to be exercised bona fide. (In French administrative law it is called *ditournement de peuvoir.* Here are a few examples:

(a) A person in service cannot be dealt with adversely and subjected to penal action to wreak vengeance of the Chief Minister.

[*Pratap Singh Vs. State of Punjab*, AIR 1964 SC 962].

(b) Allotment of petrol pump to friends and relations of the higher officers is illegal as arbitrary and also as based on extraneous considerations. [*Common Couse Vs. Union of India*, (1996) 6 SCC 530].

(c) Distribution of cement which was not in accordance with the law and the guidelines but in favour of certain builders for donations given by them to certain foundations of which the Chief Minister was a trustee was a mala fide exercise of power and void.

[*P.B. Samant Vs. State of Maharashtra,* 84 Bombay Law Reporter 427].

Non-application of the mind

Even where there are no constitutional or legal infirmities, non arbitrariness or want of bona fides, executive action can still be declared invalid by the Courts if it is found that the executive authority in question had not applied its mind. The proposition is supported by a few judicial decisions—

(a) Withdrawal of prosecution by the Public Prosecutor under section 321 of the Code of Criminal Procedure 1973, without taking all factors into consideration is bad for non-application of mind. [*Balwant Singh Vs. State of Bihar,* (1977) 4 SCC 448.]

(b) If a State Bar council refers the case of an advocate to the disciplinary committee without forming a reasonable belief about the existence of a *prima facie* case, such routine action is void for non-application of the mind. [*Nandlal Khodidas Barot Vs. Bar Council of Gujarat,* AIR 1981 SC 477.]

It will be seen that in all these cases, i.e. the situations of *ultra vires* acts, arbitrary action, mala fide orders and decisions pronounced or taken without applying the mind — the judiciary plays only a restrictive role. It sets aside the order or decision in question but without substituting anything in its place. The impact of judicial action on governance is negative in such cases.

Ameliorative relief

Sometimes, the courts perform an ameliorative role by affording positive relief in individual litigation. Thus, where the widow of a freedom fighter was denied pension for four decades, the court gave direction to the Government to settle the amount of pension payable to her. [*Ram Piari Vs. Union of India,* AIR 1988 Raj. 124].

Public interest litigation

It is in the context of public interest litigation that the impact of the judiciary on the process of governance is seen at its best. Here, in public interest litigation as it was evolved in India, courts have granted relief of a positive nature and have issued far-reaching directions to be implemented by the Government or other public authority. Obviously, these directions regulate the manner in which executive power is to be exercised and thus enable the judiciary to cast a shadow on what the Government is doing.

Let us examine the special characteristics of public interest litigation. There have been evolved special modes of initiation and conduct of such litigation and novel types of relief granted by the courts. Such litigation is commenced by a person on behalf of the public. He does not institute the proceeding for his own purpose. Further, courts have permitted institution of such proceedings through letters. Again, interim relief, such as appointment of an expert by the court to investigate certain facts is now common in sush litigation. When one comes to the final relief grated by the court, one comes to see the positive, constructive and active approach of the court.

For example, the court has entertained petitions regarding the practice of changing the inmates of a mental hospital.

[*Supreme Court Legal Aid Committee Vs. State of MP,* AIR 1995 SC 204].

It has also issued directions as to the *administrative* set-up of a mental asylum. [*Rakesh Chandra Vs. State of Bihar,* AIR 1989 SC 348]. It has entertained a petition against telephone tapping. [*People's Union for Civil Liberties Vs. Union of India,* AIR 1997 SC 568]. It has given various directions regarding the interest of the tribals in forests. [*Banwasi Seva Ashram Vs. State of UP*, AIR 1987 SC 374].

What is more pertinent to note is that the courts have been giving positive directions to the Government on many matters. Thus, it has issued detailed guidelines as to inter-country adoptions. [*Laxmikant Pandey Vs. Union of India,* AIR 1987 SC 232].

It has issued directions in detail as to how the authorities should deal with complaints of sexual harassment. [*Visakha Vs. State of Rajasthan,* (1997) 6 SCC 541].

Similarly, it has issued various directions to prevent water and air pollution. [*Vellore Citizens' Welfare Forum Vs. Union of India,* AIR 1996 SC 2715].

It has issued directions for protecting forest and wildlife. [*M. C. Mehta Vs. Union of India,* (1997) 3 SCC 32 and 715].

Many of these directions obviously require the Government to take positive action and the impact on governance is manifest.

Directions as legislation

The most interesting question is raised by judicial directions modulating executive action for the future on various matters. The traditional distinction beween judicial functions and legislative or executive functions gets blurred by such directions. Of course, the directions are intended to enforce fundamental or other rights or to promote public welfare in various sectors. But the question is whether such directions do not amount to indirect legislation. It is to be noted that while judiciary looks to the past, legislation generally looks to the future. Again, while legislation is framed in general propositions not confined to individual controversies, judicial adjudication is expected to deal with individual controversies and is, therefore, highly coloured by the concrete setting in which the controversy arises. Moreover, the legislature comes to its decisions after a debate in which a number of persons participate and is often enacted after due consultation with mass of organisations. Finally, legislation is drafted with great care by persons who have acquired expertise in the nuances of legal language and statutory vocabulary. A court, when issuing general directions, practically comes to act as a legislature but does not have the advantage of previous consultation, expert assistance, drafting talent and the like.

Enforceability

Another important question that arises is, how are the directions of the court to be enforced? It is true that the court can exercise its contempt jurisdiction. But such jurisdiction cannot be exercised too frequently and, really speaking, it is not meant for violation of general directions. In the past, the threat of such action has brought out the intended result. Even so, in the long run, it is better if formal legislation is enacted on a problem which the court has come to deal with. It is to be mentioned that the constitutional prohibition in article 20(1) which prohibits punishment of a person for an act which does not violate any law in meant to ensure that the citizen knows the law in advance and 'law' here means statutory law. The makers of the Constitution were aware that statute law has certain advantages of definiteness, precise language, expert draftsmanship, due consultation and so on. These are lacking in judicial activism.

6

Need for Electoral Reforms

S.S.H. Azmi

1. Introduction

One of the most fundamental principles of democracy-government of the people for the people and by the people-is that parliamentary and State Legislature elections should be free and fair. People should be able to exercise their franchise without any fear or favour. The polling should be free from booth capturing, rigging, violence etc. The issue of electoral reform has been of immense interest to political parties, Election Commission and leaders of the public to make the election free from electoral malpractices reduce the influence of money power and minimize criminalisation of politics.[1] India has the world's largest electorate of over 600.5 million, which went on poll in September 1998 entailing an expenditure of about 1000 crores on State exchequer and few thousand crore on private parties and candidates. Nearly nine lac polling booths had to be established and about 50 lac central and State government officers deployed to carry out the duties in the election work. Several lac police personnel and paramilitary forces were also engaged to ensure safety security and orderly organization and management of election.[2]

The election was conducted in five phases this time, as military men were engaged in Kargil, and they cound not be deployed in adequate numbers. Hence elections took place after a gap of one week[3] spread over a period of more than a month through out India. Many problems are being faced in conducting free and fair election. Hence electoral reform is one of the most pressing issues before us. Some of those are mentioned hereunder for discussion before this august body of academicians and politicians to find a lasting solution for them. The solutions offered in the paper are open to modification and correction.

2. Election System

(a) Issues for Electoral Reforms

In democracy decisions are based on majority rule. While electing an M.P. or M.L.A, this principle is not followed in its spirit but only in letter. In an interview, Dr. M.S. Gill, Chief Election Commissioner suggested electoral reform in the areas vote of no-confidence, stability of parliament ands placing neutral government under governors of State going to elections.[4] He observed:

> That we should introduce in our system Run-off election instead of present type. The first-past-the-post system. At present if there are 6 presons contesting the election the voting may be 40%. The candidate who gets 10% votes is declared elected. In run-off election the top two condidates will have to re-contest the next day after declaration of result. Out of two the one who gets maximum vote should be declared as elected. It is submitted that this is much better system. CEC observed that "This can be done without incurring any extra cost[5]."

This will ensure that the winning candidate has the majority vote, and will change the ideological position of different political parties. This will go a long way in diluting the ideological differences of political parties based on caste ridden ethnic groups. Influences by parochial consideration, without bothering about long turn national/ public interest. Every political party will be concerned with the welfare of other communities and castes, thus reconciling their conflicting interest with each other. The editor Hindustan Times, while mentioning about two tier elections, where only two contenders remain in the fray in the second round observes that "....it wouid considerably raise that cost of conducting elections for the exchequers and possibly generate indifference among voters who tend to get bored by recurrent elections.[6]" The apprehension of the editor appears to be justified to some extent. This may be feeling of an ordinary citizen. However Dr. M.S. Gill is in favour of this system and he has been quoted above as saying that no extra expenditure is involved in this exercise. He means to say the increase may be negligible and this being a new exercise, intra party discipline and reconciliation in the attitude of the parties may reign supreme. Hence it is worth putting it into practice for experimentation.

(b) Security Money

In the 1996 parliamentary election 13886 candidates contested the election. There was a long list of symbols which was mind boggling to the poor voters. All non serious types of persons with much black money are to be found in the fray. The security money is so small that no one bothers to loose it in case of his defeat. It is suggested that there should be steep hike in this amount so that in case of defeat of a candidate for-feited security may have deterrent effect.

(c) No Confidence Motion

The Law Commission in its report to the Government submitted in June 1999 is of the view that the proposers of no confidence motion may propose a credible alternative to the government which is proposed to be voted out.[7] This proposal is modelled on the basis of German Constitution where the term of parliament is seven years. It is submitted that the suggestion is laudable keeping in view the larger interest of the country as a whole. The game of toppling the government is very easy but it retards the national development, creates uncertainty about the future of governments and entails heavy loss on the exchequer which could be avoided. Hence it is suggested that the constitution may be amended to this effect and it is worth trying. The last general election was third in a short span of time of three years.

(d) Keeping Independents Out of Poll Fray

Last Lok Sabha had only 6 independents when a few thousands had contested the election.[8] The Commission recommendation is proper taking into consideration the long list of all types of contestants. The argument forwarded is that it is the fundamental right of every citizen to fight election. But Article 19 of the Constitution which confers such right puts the rider of reasonable restriction. When every one wants to become MP & MLA then how is it possible to accommodate. The entry of independents is also not desirable on the ground that they change sides easily. The law of defection has nothing to do with them. The parties intending to form government if short of majority have to pay a heavy price to get the support of the independents. Hence ban on independents will have salutary effect. R. Venkataraman, the former president of India touching on this issues observed that ban on frivolous candidates was "Worst than the disease". The ban would be a contravention of the fundamental right of the citizen.[9] However he suggested that the condidates fighting election should secure 20% of the votes polled to save his deposit. The candidate forfeiting the deposit should be debarred from contesting the election to any statutory body from panchayat level onwards to president of India for six years.[10] It is submitted that such person may not be debarred from contesting to low position but may be debarred to contest for others. However this submission is open to correction.

(e) Recognition of Political Parties

There are political parties who have no meaningful ideology and public support but the craze for power comples them to form a new party. In the last parliamentary election 177 parties contested the election. Out of them, 139 parties could not win even a single seat and 94 parties "had got less than 0.005 per cent of the votes polled". Some mechanism or criteria should be evolved so as to enable the Election Commission to put restriction on recognition of the political parties. Their number must be reduced to bare minimum. It is submitted that the parties which did not win any seat should be derecognised and those candidates who could not secure more than 20% of the total votes polled should be debarred for 6 years to contest such election as per the suggestion of R. Venkataraman.

(f) Implementation of Code of Conduct

The code of Conduct was formulated by political parties voluntarily and unanimously in 1967 and all of them agreed with Election Commission (EC) to abide by that. In the present context, the code of conduct means that the party in power should not utilize its power and position to gain advantage by misuse or abuse of state machinary in any way so as to cause loss to the interest of the parties out of power or in opposition. It has been observed that the Election Commission in its anxiety to fulfill the commitment under code of conduct rule, some times exceeds its limit in its enforcement and does not concentrate towards curbing booth capturing, controlling the incident of recovery of 1600 duplicate bullot boxes from strong rooms of Bihar[11] and other gory incidents taking place. However, the government (the party in power) is also taking undue advantage of its position, knowing well that Election Commission can do nothing to desperate persons like Kalyan Singh, who violated the Election

Commissions guidelines relating to Independence day speech on Decentralization of power.[12] However the Election Commission successfully prevented the the media person to accompany him on his election tour and directed prasar Bharty and Doordarshan to be neutral in election matter.[13]

(g) Over Exercise of Power By Election Commission To Enforce Code of Conduct

In a complaint by Election Commission to the Supreme Court for violating guideline issued by it, it was held that its issuing guidelines was not based on legitimate authority. The Court was logical in its argument when it observed that if it has power to do certain thing then it should exercise that power to execute it also and should not come before the court for enforcement. It was really absurd that the life Insurance Corporation of India was prohibited for holding its general body meeting openly and not to announce its decisions and benefits accruing to the policy holder. True, the LIC is owned by government but it is a statutory body doing business. Its normal functioning should not be disturbed.[14]

(h) Time Consuming Polling Process

It is really a wastage of time, energy, and loss of national wealth by involving the people in polling process for almost three months and the elections were conducted in four or five phases spread over a period of one month. It is better to hold them all at a time as it used to be earlier. If police force is engaged in holding election the party candidates are also engaged in the Job. But when election are held in phases. The party candidates in one area more to another and thus there is sufficient time to manipulate and subvert the electoral process.

(i) Private Armies in Bihar and Andhra Pradesh Menace of Fair & Free Election

While talking about conducting fair and free election in Bihar, the Editor Hindustan Times says that it is a "difficult proposition." "often the polling personnel are the hand maidens of the dominant political parties in the area", Though there is no intimidation but poll process is vitiated despite the presence of para military forces.[15] The Maoist Communist Centre and Ranveer Sena is a great menace for law and order situation in Bihar. The peoples war group hinders the poll process in Andhra Pradesh.[16] Police administration has no control over them.

(j) Election of Criminals

Election Commission is really concerned with fair and free election. it has urged media during election period to highlight the criminal records of persons contesting elections, so that adverse public opinion may help in defeating them in election.[17] There was a time when criminals were financing the politicians. However, now they are themselves contesting elections. The law breakers are replacing law makers. This as a sorry state of affairs.

(k) Governors/President's Rules During Election

M.S. Gill chief Election commissioner had suggested and advocated that after the notification of the dates of the dates of election, the State governments should be dismissed and they should come under central rule of governors of States. It is submitted that the governors these days are no more neutral but are more political than active politicians and much is desirable about their style of functioning.[19] However, as this recommendations has been made by a large number of individuals and committees submitting their report on electoral reform, it could be put into practice for experimental purposes and if found suitable may be enforced through legislation. It is crystal clear that the party in power does influence the polling process and takes undue advantage of its dominant position.

(l) Democratic Functioning of Political Parties

For a meaningful democracy, the political parties have to be democratic in their internal functioning. The party High Command decides as to who shall be the Chief Minister and the Chief Minister runs to Delhi for every small and big problem. There is no appreciation for meritorious. It is more often than not, the persons with criminal back ground occupy seats in august elected bodies. The Law Commission has made several sensible suggestions which are as follows:

> All political parties as a pre requisite to be qualified and recognized to contest election must have democratic Constitution with compulsory periodic elections. Election should be held from grass roots to the top bodies of every party. Sometimes secret ballot many be used to avoid under enfluence.
>
> N.M. Ghatate suggestes that elections may be held once in two years. Presidents/Chairman of the party should not be elected for more than two consecutive terms as in America. This practice should apply to other office bears. We will see that this will curb the emergence of vested interest and will facilitate the development of a new leadership. The parties should nominate only those candidate for contesting elections who are elected by party members. This procedure is more democratic and a better method to get potetial candidate who can win election and corrupt in the process will be weeded out.
>
> The party elections could be supervised by Election Commission. To curb the menace of black money, there is a need to enact law requiring all political parties to maintain account disclosing their sources of income and expenditure R. Venkataraman in his address on electoral reform observed that discloures of assets and liabilities of the candidate and their dependents should be made obligatory at the time of filing of nomination as it would help in determing the wealth accumulated by then if inquires are instituted in corruption cases against them.[21]

(m) Maintenance of Proper Account

The Apex Court in *Gajanan Bapat's Case* (1995) observed with displeasure that political parties were not maintaining accounts of their income and expenditure and suggested that the Election Commission or the legislature should frame rules in this respect. It is an irony of fate that inspite of repeated demands by many Committees and Commission since 1970's for proper maintenance of account and audit by political parties no mandatory provisions exist in law to force them to do so. The main reason is that the executive (ministers) and the legislators belong to certain parties and if any rules will be made by them, then they will also be bound by it. Hence no one is seriourly interested in eradicating these evils but rather they relish its non existence with a certain amount of amusement, though politician may in public denounce such measures. The Supreme Court has observed that "unless this was done the possibility of the purity of an election, soiled by money power could not really be ruled out."

(n) Collection of Fund From Foreign Sources

No political party should be allowed to collect and accept donations from foreign sources as this will have the effect of further complicating the issues by involving foreign elements ignoring national interest.

(o) Furnishing Detail of Criminal Cases Pending against Candidate

Any person contesting election must be legally required to furnish the details of criminal cases pending against him. One who offers himself for public service must have noble stainless pure and perfect record of his personal life. Then only he can do selfless service to the people. So if a persons furnishes information on a false affidavit he should be disqualified to contest election and that should attract penalty under Representation of Peoples Act.

(p) Absence of Upto Date Electorals Roll

The EC is yet to provide a perfect uptodate electoral rool for the country. It is the right of every citizen that when he attains the age of 18, he becomes entitled to vote. The EC must make proper arrangement to secure the name of the individual in the voters list. The use of computer alongwith easy accessibility to the electoral rolls at municipal wards or panchayats for verification at any time the voter needs will go a longway in preparation of perfect electoral roll.[22]

(q) Compaign Timing

Some constituencies have below 10 lac voters, others betwen 10-15 lac, others between 15-20 lacks and still others upto 30 lac: Is it fair and equitable that 15 days time for Compaigning is sufficient for all? For some it may be adequate. But for other where number is large it may be insufficient. This is inequitable. It has been calculated that in Delhi a constituency has 6 lac votes. Other out of Delhi has 30 lacs votes. For 6 lacs, the expenditure per person comes to Rs. 2.50 where as for 30 lacs, it comes to merely 50 paise. It will be more equitable, just and proper, if the expenditure is calculated per voter and not per constituency. In such a situation with increased amount, proper publicity can be made by spending more and thus the deficiency of time can be made up this way.

(r) State Funding of Election

It is said for fair and free election, there should be provision for the state to bear election expenses. It is necessary to improve the health of the electoral system and eliminate the role of black money in electoral politics. It is submitted that a poor state like India where elections are held every year for Parliament instead of five years will not be able to afford such heavy burden of money. Further, it is a mere surmise to think that better honest and conscionrsous persons will enter politics. The criminalization of politics has reached to such an extent that any honest dedicated sincers person doing selfness service will hardly get any chance to get the ticket itself. Even if he gets the ticket people will never allow him to win the poll. As he will have no muscle power, who will protect him from totting guns of the goons. Now a days a new trend is emerging that parties nominating candidates from their platform demand lacks of rupees for doing so. My apprehension are that it may give more incentive to non serious and undesirable elements to fight election with more vigour and strength due to the fact that they will have white money and black both put together for booth capturing, bribing, intimidating their rivals and furnish a fake and fabricated account about the expenses incurred in election. If any official may rise abjection, bis mouth may be shut with huge amount of money as the bribery is the order of the day. So to talk of government financing the poll expenses is unwise in India. R.Venkataraman, the former president of India observed that state funding would only add to the administratve costs and to the already proliferating functions of the government, the reality in India was that such funding would only serve to augment the resources of the affluents. Candidates.[23] Hence Prime Minister's call for State Funding of Elections[24] is, it submitted neither feasible nor affordable by government and hence rightly rejected by the Finance Minister.

(s) Anti-difection Law

Anti-defection law has been made to curb the practice of changing from one party of another. But the law has no teeth and hence the purpose of its enactment is totally defeated. A person is elected on ticket from certain party. The party has its own ideology. People give vote on the basis of the ideology of the party. When one person defects and Joins another party, he defames the party by changing sides and makes it weaker also. He deceives the people who have voted in his favour. He looses respect in the eyes of the people. When a group of persons defects from a certain party and joins another, its ramifications are for greater and serious. His action may lead to toppling one government and installing another. The same exercise is repeated every now and then which results into unstable government. This instability brings doom to economic development of the country in relation to International trade and commerce. International Financial institutions become hesitant to invest money due to uncertainty in political condition and business policy of the country. Every one waits and watches the development helplessly. The government of the day is on cruches. It can not give any assurance about future policy and political development in the country. R. Venkataraman, the former president of India observed in his address on Electoral Reform that a defection from a party is an affront to the electorate and the law should be amended to deprive the defector of the membership of the elected body and any other political party in future. The defector should not be eligible for admission to any political party including the party to which he originally belonged. Action should also be taken against members for not abiding by the whip or direction's of the party.[25]

3. Conclusion and Suggestion

Electoral reforms which relate to election of people's representative to the highest and most significant organs of the government are imperative in nature and are over due. However there is an apathy and lake warm response to the whole idea because those who are concerned with this reform are the most adversely affected people. No one is interested in any thing like reform. This is a dangerous tendering and if not checked in time, it may lead to further anarchy, choose and confusion all over the Union of India. Self interest should he sacrificed for larger national and public interest. Bharat can not become Mahaan (great and grand) by mere slogans but it will definitely become so by selfless service, sincerely and devotion to make India attain the pride of place in the comity of democratic nations.

References

1. For historical background of electoral reform and efforts made by different joint Parliamentary Committees and individuals *see*: L.K. Advani Electoral Reform: Imperative & Urgent' *Journal of Constitutional Studies*, Vol. XXIII Nos 1-2, 1984. and N.S. Gahlot, *Election and Electoral Administration in India* (1992)

C. Rajgopalachari "Rescue Democracy from Money Power (1977) *Report of Jai Prakash Narayan on Electoral Reform as President of Citizens for Democracy*, (1975)."

2. Subash C Kashyap "Polls in Time of War " *Hindustan Times* p. 13, 6th July, 1999. For similar statement refer inerview with Dr. M.S. Gill. Akshay Mukul "The first - Past - the - Post system should be abolished" *Hindustan Times*, August 15, 1999 at 14.
3. Akshay Mukul, Ibid.
4. Akshay Mukul. "The First-past-the post system should be abolished" *Supra* Note 2.
5. *Ibid.*
6. *Hindustan Times Editorial* "Symbolic Problem" September 14, 1999, at 13.
7. "Vote out, Vote in" *Hindustan Times* July 12, 1999, at 13.
8. *Ibid.*
9. "Need to amend Anti-defection Law" *Hindustan Times*, 10-4-2001.
10. *Ibid.*
11. *Hindustan Times Report*, August 21, 1999, at 12.
12. *Hindustan Times Report*, "Kalyan Makes Mockery of E.C. Code" August 16, 1999 at 1.
13. Kallyani Shankar E.C. Warning. Journalists Can't accompany Vajpayee, *Hindustan Times*, August, 19, 1999, at 12.
14. Read "Well Deserved Snub" Editorial *Hindustan Times* 16.9.1999.
15. *Hindustan Times*, Editorial "The Difficult States" September 13, 1999 at 11.
16. *Ibid*. "Bad Old Days Again" Sept., 20, 1999 at 13.
17. Similar opinion was also expressed by R. Vekataraman, the former President of India. *Hindustan Times* 10-4-2001.

18. E.C. Urges Media to High light the Criminal Records of candidates *Hindustan Times* Correspondent. August, 8, 1999. at. 10.
19. See "Un Workable Idea" Editorial *Hindustan Times*, July 21, 1999. at 11.
20. N.M. Ghatate "Towards a Cleaner Poll", December 1, 1999.
21. *Supra* Note 9.
22. Jana Krishna Murte "A Bule print for Electoral Reform" *Hindustan Times* 19-12-1999. at 17.
23. *Supra* Note 9.
24. "P.M. Finds The Culprit: High Poll Expenses". *Hindustan Times* 26.03.2001.
25. *Supra* Note 9.

7

Electoral Reforms: Soft Democracy and the Political Class

M.M. Sankhdher

Inspite of tall claims that democracy has taken firm roots in our soil and that we have succeeded in operating this most difficult form of governance, there is a widespread concern about the electoral process, the political system and the constitutional provisions. A subtle and healthy democracy seems a far cry in the face of serious distortions created by the "soft state" and a corrupt political class.

The setting up of a Constitutional Review Commission mandated to recommend, among others, electoral reforms, is a step to restore legitimacy and purity in the eyes of the people. The terms of reference of this Commission headed by the most reputed retired judge of the Supreme Court, Justice Venkatachalliah and distinguished members, prohibit it from touching the "basic structure." Within a limited timeframe, the commission is supposed to make it's recommendations to the Government of India and then to be placed before Parliament for discussion and for the President's approval, and then, finally for implementation.

Pious intentions, indeed!!

In exploring this theme, I am struck by the role of the political actors, comprising the political class of power-weilders and the voters, the latter at the receiving end of the power game.

The political process implying the electoral process is increasingly been vitiated by the corruption that has seeped into the vitals of democratic functioning. No empirical evidence is needed to prove the role of an ingrained mafia in polluting the political culture for grabbing the wealth and privilege. Elections are the easy means for filling the coffers and getting away by criminal means and dreadful gangsterism. The plasticity in governance provides illegitimate license to unscruplous politicians to loot the country and escape any penalty.

The root problem is the depravity of the political class and very little can be achieved by structural-functional reforms.

Prime Minister Atal Behari Vajpayee has expressed his anguish in the context of election reforms, thus: "Indian democracy exhibits a worrying parabox. While India is the world's largest democracy, yet....its manifest weaknesses in our electoral system that have impaired our democracy the most. Removal of this paradox is the greatest task before us," he concludes. The Review Commission, on its part, unfolds not only the gigantic and expensive aspects of the poll exercise, but more importantly, the serious distortios that have crept in to the conduct of elections causing deep concern.

Of common anxiety is the fallout of the exercise over the last 50 years in terms of "3MPs, viz., money power, muscle power, and mafia power, and 4 Cs, viz,. criminalization, corruption, communalism, and casteism." The farcical nature of the representative character of the polity where majority of our legislators are elected by a minority of votes making their democratic creadentials suspect. With no educational qualifications prescribed for lawmakers, the legitimacy of the electoral process is jeopardised. The cirminal-political nexus, on the one hand, and funding of political activity and compaigns with the use of black money and concealment of extravagence, on the other, democracy is reduced to a sham. The reform agenda is under severe test.

The politician seems to have a vested interest in corruption and, perhaps, that is why all previous attempts to reform and the reports of expert bodies, recommendations of the Election Commission, research outputs have failed to impact on improving the functional system. Institutions have degenerated and a decline has set in everywhere. The whole ramshackle structure and mechanism of elections is in disarray because of the corrupt practices at all levels engineered by the key-actor, the politician. Unless we convince ourselves of the need to raise the level of moral awareness and the indispensability of ethical support of the human character involved in the political process, mere institutional/structural/systemic reforms will not do.

The political class, as a whole, regardless of party affiliations, blindly pursuing power indulge in flagrant violation of norms through democratic devices of manipulation of the voter who, in turn, is vulnerable to promises, polemics, propaganda, publicity and the temptations of money and pressures in a polluted environment of power-politics. There seems to be an unholy alliance between the ruling class and the fractured Opposition that revels in strategies and tactics of siezing power and privilege by fair or foul means, mostly foul.

Electoral machinery and the Election Commission have turned victims of the deliberate or hidden designs of party leaders to perpetuate self-preservaion under the garb of a "illusory democracy." This makes a mockery of the claim that they are strengthening "the government of the people, by the people, and for the people." Ironically, in this wholly manoeuvred system, where do "the people," operate?

Apparently although, the elections are free and fair, there are constitutional safeguards, legal provisions, judicial interventions and activism, administrative and financial checks and balances, amendments for removing discrepancies, vigilance commissions and a plethora of enquiries to probe corruptions and malpractices in elections, and yet the results are far from satisfactory. While the voter is insecure, the political class is the most secure — physically, financially and socially! As a taxpayer and also as below the poverty line, in both cases, he stands exploited and fleeced. The Marxist dictum of the capitalist class as "exploiters" and the basic cause of all social evils, has been falsified by the political class grabbing that role.

Whether we like it or not, over the decades, vote-bank power-politics results in flagrant violation of norms in the election process. The unscruplous political class mercilessly squanders public money on briberies, own security, five star comforts, ostentation, patronage, travel, telephones, residences and hospitalities, hospitalizations, property deals, getting licenses and permits, petrol pumps and contracts of various sorts, criminals contesting elections from jails etc. Democracy comes handy to these polluters of the electoral machinery by encouraging bogus-voting, booth-capturing, blackmailing and distributing money and purchasing votes.

Paradoxically, while the common voter is most insecure, his political master is the most secure, physically, economically and socially!! Security guards, black cat commandoes, special security guards have become status symbols for former as well as current politicians and also those politicians on whom no one will waste a bullet are covered by the security and intelligence network. On security of the political class alone, Rs. 4000 crores are spent on 10,000 persons per year! This is just a tip of the iceberg! No politician has ever opposed the frequent raise in their allowances and privileges!

Reduction on governmental expenditure remains a far cry!!

Their bank balances, open and secret, properties, and farm-houses escalate at a fast pace. Talk of economising, frugality, and austerity looks hollow.

It is common knowledge what proportion of development fund is really spent on self development and how the budgets are manipulated and resources pocketed surreptitiously? Ironically, the poor class is pauperised, the political class becoming the new princes.

When the top politicians, exceptions apart, are corrupt the bureaucracy too shares the booty.

Elections have become increasingly divisive. The electoral system is failing to remedy itself. The electoral process is gradually derailed by mafia. The three are inextricably linked in mal performance. The basic course seems to be the unclarity of concepts on the part of those working the system. Even conceding that after Independence, a transition required some constitutional continuity by adopting the Government of India Act-1935 as the bedrock of our political system, in the last 50 years we have remained tied down to the colonial structure. Only the political masters have changed, but not its mindset! We are unconsciously suffering from information complex and the self-imposed western stereotype!

Even understanding the dilemma of our Constitution-makers, their successors, the new political class, blindly followed the superstition that, "democracy is the best form of government" and, therefore, inferred that there is no alternative to it. After adopting the foster child, democracy, we have religiously nursed and strengthened it. The results are obvious!

Ploto derided democracy as a perverted form with a strong tendency towards mobocracy. It suits the vile politician who has a vested interest in pelf and power and resists all efforts for reform. Exercises in electoral reforms in the last 50 years have gone waste. Committees-Goswamy, Inderjit Gupta, Law Commission Reports, Election Commission's recommendations, L.K. Advani's Resolution is the Lok Sabha, suggestions of voluntary bodies, editorials, individual researches, all have gathered dust!

India inheriting the wisdom of the Ages, immense capacity and genius, has been hampered by westernisd elites. India has failed to articulate a Swadeshi Constitution suited to our cultural unity and basic needs. Even the judicial doctrine of preserving "the basic structure," without clearly knowing it, impedes our traditional "Shastrarthic" open debates! an free and open society.

We keep our fingures crossed!!

8

Governing A Stratified Society Development, Conflict and Change

Abdul Matin and P.K. Mathur

I. Introduction

This arlicle revolves around the concept of social stratification in India as a problem for good governance. We consider unequal access to power as the most important dimension of social stratification, which is detrimental to development because it creates conflict. Good governance requires resolution of conflicts due to social stratification and unjust developmental strategies.

Social stratification system in India is based upon the caste system, which has been traditionally maintained by the power of the dominant caste over the deprived caste. However, the caste system is in the process of cultural as well as structural change. The former is due to social reforms, which have given rise to the process of *sanskritization, westernization,* and *secularization.* The latter through state intervention by legislation (e.g. *Panchayati* Raj Act, Land Reforms measures, etc. These have brought about a change from cumulative inequality to dispersed inequality. We have analyzed this process as a change from concentration of power to dispersion of power. All these changes have challenged the power of the dominant caste.

Relations between the dominant and deprived caste have traditionally been explained within the three fold dimensions of discrimination, exploitation and oppression (subsequently referred to as the DEO model). The DEO by the dominant caste in modern India against the deprived caste creates conflict. It has enhanced due to developmental programmes especially after Independence. In order to prevent these conflicts from erupting into violence, the state/civil society is required to intervence. It has been argued that good governance requires intervention through legislative and administrative measures for an empowerment of the deprived castes.

II. Social Stratification in India

Sociologists used the term 'Social Stratification' to refer to the ranking of groups on the basis of unequal amount of wealth, prestige or power (Tumin, 1987: 1). The term is derived from stratum and is analogous to the geological use of the term to mean layers of rocks in the earth. Sociologists conceive of society as consisting of groups that are arranged in layers one on top of the other and societies vary in the kind of groups and the degree to which they are stratified. Indian society has been characterized by stratification of groups that are called castes and it is one of the oldest systems of stratification. The caste system was also an extreme form of stratification because in it all the statuses were entitled to unequal amount of wealth, prestige and power (Tumin, 1987: 5). Thus, an individuals' caste status controlled and defined all the aspects of his life --- economic, social and political. This made the caste system an all pervasive system in which an individual's economic and political status could be identified on the basis of his caste. All the individuals belong to upper castes also had wealth and power just as all the individuals belonging to lower castes were deprived of them.

The caste system has been a complex phenomenon and sociologists/ social anthropologists have provided broadly two views about its characteristics. Singh (1977:7) has made a broad distinction between the cultural and structural view of the characteristics of the caste. The cultural view stems from the Hindu ideas and values. It emphasizes caste as something unique to Indian society because these ideas and values are found only among the Hindus (Weber, 1952; Ghurye, 1961; Dumont, 1988). The structural view regards caste as a pattern of relations which may be found with some variations in other societies as well (Barth, 1960; Bailey, 1963; Berreman, 1967). The caste system may be understood as an ascriptive and rigid system of stratification consisting of status groups, which differ, in prestige according to their occupation. These status groups have some cultural characteristics such as hierarchy, purity and impurity and *karma* and *dharma* and some structural characteristics such as institutional restrictions on social interaction and unequal distribution of power (Singh, 1973: 162). The caste system is sanctioned by the power of the dominant caste over the deprived caste and Srinivas (1987: 97) defines dominance in terms of numerical strength as well as wealth and relatively higher ritual status. The caste system is an elaborate form of stratification and sociologists/ social anthropologists have distinguished between two context of the system. The first context is that of the *varnas* consisting of the four *varnas: viz.* the *brahmins* (priests), the *kashtriyas* (warriors), the *vashiyas* (merchants), and the *shudras* (servants) along with the untouchable castes now called scheduled castes, which are all India categories and form the theoretical and ideological context of the caste system. The second is context of the *jatis,* which are innumerable local groups that effectively function in different regions and form the existential and empirical context (Singh, 1973: 161). The ideological basis of the caste system has been emphasized by Dumont (1988: 71). He says that the *varna* theory subordinates the *kashtriyas* (warriors), symbolizing power and the *vashiyas* (merchants) symbolizing wealth, to the *brahmins* symbolizing ritual status. This is the principle of hierarchy of *varna* is based upon ritual status and opposes the pure and impure irrespective of economic and political considerations. This opposition is expressed most clearly in the two extremes of the *varna* hierarchy *viz.* the pure *brahmins* and the impure untouchables (Dumont, 1988: 47). Ritual status is not as clear in the middle regions of the hierarchy where wealth and power have to be considered. The ranking of *jatis* in the middle regions is subject to change if one moves from the ideological to the empirical context.

The importance of wealth and power for ritual status becomes clear in the case of those *jatis* who are able to acquire it because then can they lay claim to a higher ritual status than the one traditionally accorded to them. Such *jatis* claim membership of the *brahmin* of *kashtriya varna* by changing their customs, manners, rituals and life style in the process which Srinivas (1966: 41-45) calls *sanskritization.* This change of position traditionally occurred, more in the middle regions of the hierarchy where ranking was unclear and so subject to change. Recently, the importance of wealth and power as determinants of ritual status has increased and so the process of *sanskritization* has become more frequent and widespread. *Sanskritization* is a a process of cultural change brought about by reforms within Hinduism. Srinivas has given importance to two other processes of cultural change brought about by social reforms of Hinduism due to outside impact. These are the processes of *westernization* (Srinivas, 1966: 46-88) and *secularization* (Srinivas, 1966: 118-146). Both W*esternization* and *secularization* have weakened the Hindu ideas and values underlying the caste systems and owe their origin to British rule in India.

The caste system is in the process of cultural as well as structural change. While cultural change is due to reforms in Hinduism, structural changes have been brought about by state intervention (viz. Cooperative Movements, Land Reforms, Community Development Programmes, Panchayati Raj). These changes have brought changes in the status of individuals. Earlier, an individual's caste status defined all aspects of life so that there was status summation between ritual, economic and political status. Recently, sociologists have observed a discrepancy between caste on the one hand and economic and political status on the other. The upper castes are not necessarily having wealth and power and the lower castes are not necessarily without them (Bailey, 1957; Beteille, 1965; Chakravarti, 1975; Matin, 1990). Sociologists (Bhatt, 1975; Jayaraman, 1981: 27) have characterized this as a shift from status summation to status incongruence. This may also be expressed as a shift from power concentration to power dispersion.

The caste system was maintained by the power of the dominant caste but cultural and structural changes have led to deprived caste challenging the power of the dominant caste. A considerable amount of social conflict has therefore been generated by these changes and this process has been summarized in figure-1. Thus social stratification in India requires intervention by state in the form of legislative and administrative measures in order to prevent conflict between the dominant and deprived caste from eruptine into violence. This should be the guideline for good governance.

III. Governance, Development and Conflict

The concept of "governance" is not new. It means different things to different people. The actual meaning of the concept depends on the level of governance we are talking about, the goals to be achieved and the approach being followed. The concept has been around in both political and academic discourse for a long time, referring in a generic sense to the task of running a government, or any other appropriate entity for that matter. In this background, the lexicographical meaning provided by Webster's Third New International Dictionary (1986: 982) is a relevant one. It refers governance as a synonym for government, or "the act or process of governing, specifically authoritative direction and control." This interpretation specifically focuses on the effectiveness of the executive branch of government. The working definition used by the British Council, however, emphasizes that "governance" is a broader notion than government (and for that matter also related concepts like the state, good government and regime), and goes on to state: "Governance involves interaction between the formal institutions and those in civil society. Governance refers to a process whereby elements in society wield power, authority and influence and enact policies and decisions concerning public life and social upliftment." "Governance", therefore, not only encompasses but transcends the collective meaning of related concepts like the state, government, regime and good government. Many of the elements and principles underlying "good government" have become an integral part of the meaning of "governance". John Healey and Mark Robinson define "good government" as follows: "It implies a high level of organizational effectiveness in relation to policy-formulation and the policies actually pursued, especially in the conduct of economic policy and its contribution to growth, stability and popular welfare. Good government also implies accountability, transparency, participation, openness and the rule of law. It does not necessarily presuppose a value judgment, for example, a healthy respect for civil and political liberties, although good government tends to be a prerequisite for political legitimacy." According to the World Bank 'Good governance is epitomized by predictable, open and enlightened policy-making, a bureaucracy imbued with a professional ethos acting in furtherance of the public good, the rule of law, transparent processes, and strong civil society participating in public affairs. Poor governance (on the other hand) is characterized by arbitrary policy making, unaccountable bureaucracies, unenforced or unjust legal systems, the abuse of executive power, a civil society unengaged in public life, and widespread corruption.' The World Bank's focus on governance reflects the worldwide thrust toward political and economic liberalization. Such a governance approach highlights issues of greater state responsiveness and accountability, and the impact of these factors on political stability and economic development. In its 1989 report, from crisis to Sustainable Growth, the World Bank expressed this notion as follows: Efforts to create an enabling environment and to build capacities will be wasted if the political context is not favorable. Ultimately, better governance requires political renewal. This means a concerted attack on corruption from the highest to lowest level. This can be done by setting a good example, by strengthening accountability, by encouraging public debate, and by nurturing a free press. In this background, a working definition of governance may be outlined as follows:

* Governance refers to the process whereby elements in society wield power and authority, and influence and enact policies and decisions concerning public life, and economic and social development.
* Governance is a broader notion than government, whose principal elements include the constitution, legislature, executive and judiciary. Governance involves interaction between these formal institutions and those of civil society.
* Governance has no automatic normative connotation. However, typical criteria for assessing governance in a particular context might include the degree of legitimacy, representativeness, popular accountability and efficiency with which public affairs are conducted (IIAS: 1996).

It may be pointed out that after the World War II, many third world countries initiated systematic plans and strategies for development. These developmental measures have been necessary to meet the aspirations of the people as well as for ensuring good governance. After Independence, India has systematized the plans for development. But the development concept has constantly been changing. The concept *development* has been rightly distinguished from that of mere growth. The term 'growth' refers to only an increment to the gross national product (Dubhashi, 1987: 11). Up to the first decade of development (i.e. up to 1970) the GNP growth was considered a natural indicator of development. There were at least two major assumptions about this growth strategy: (1) It was assumed that if a country was able to attain an annual growth rate of 6 to 8 percent, it could reach the take-off stage. For this a net investible saving of 18-21 percent per annum was necessary (Harrod-Domar model) If this was not possible through domestic savings, the balance required could be met through foreign and or MNC (Multi National Corporation) investments. (2) The second assumption was that the GNP growth will automatically 'trickle down' to the lower income groups. Both these assumptions proved fallacious and the theory that the development path will proceed from initial inequality to greater equality proved unfounded (Lebenstein-Galenson model). In order to counter the failure of the GNP growth strategy, the 'basic needs' approach was evolved in order to (1) "relieve as quickly as is possible absolute poverty through intensive direct assistance to those in desperate circumstances; (2) meeting the 'basic needs' of all in terms of material wants such as food, clothing, shelter, and fuel, and also, as some argue, social needs such as education, human rights and what is called 'participation' in social life through employment and political involvement (Webster, 1984: 34). However, interestingly the 'enthronement of basic needs' did not imply the 'dethronement of GNP, for the new strategy of redistribution with growth could only take place within an expanding economy. It is pointed out that such' "incremental redistribution will encounter much less political resistance than would be the case if redistribution has to make the upper income groups worse off in absolute terms" (Singer, 1979: 37). Thus, growth does not ensure equal distribution. It is evident from the above discussion that availability of food does not ensure accessibility of food to every one. Production and distribution are inconsistently related and poverty coexists with self-sufficiency in food grains. The rate of growth of agriculture based on food crops production has averaged around 2.5% per annum. Corresponding growth of the production registers approximately 2.3% per annum. Production of food grains has increased from about 50 m tons in the 1950s to a phenomenal 150 m tons of food grains. And yet rural poverty is abounding with 40.4% of the rural population below the poverty line (C.S.O. Statistical Abstracts, 1984).

One the other hand, development connotes a qualitative and structural change (Dubhashi, 1987: 11). Development may be understood in terms of attainment of equality and liberty. It may be noted here that relationship between development at the one hand and equality, social groups and power relations on the other hand is a highly complex phenomenon. It may be added that social groups and power relations may be taken into consideration within the development framework for a proper understanding. In this context, Mukherji (1989: 37-38) has rightly pointed out the development is a process. Whether or how much a society is able to achieve development, is a resultant function of the constellation of social categories and their relative power to do so. The problem for the sociologist is: how does one go about analyzing this process concretely?

According to Mukherji (1989) equality and liberty are two main criteria for evaluating development. He further observers:

These diffuse value terms are subject to varied interpretations, hence there is need to specify them in concrete structural terms. I think these values can be better comprehended by their structural counter concepts, viz. ... Discrimination, Exploitation and Oppession (DEO) which require operationalisation with reference to the cultures and structures of specific societies. Thus it can be argued with conviction that a progressive dimunition in DEO would indicate a commensurate increase in equality and freedom, and hence in societal development.

Each of these counter-concepts refers to sets of asymmetrical relationships between groups, such that one or more exercise conveys the content of a social relationship which is asymmetrical and legitimated by societal norms. It operates at the levl of groups identified by ascriptive criteria such as kinship, caste (our emphasis added), religion, race, language, sex and so on ... identifications into which individuals are born. If groups identified by ascriptive criteria are not in an asymmetrical relationship with each other, there is no discrimination between them. Exploitation is best applied to the content of economic exchanges emanating from within a normatively defined system of exchange and market. The extent of freedom from exploitation would refer to the degree of access to the available economic resources by existing groups and individuals and also to their capacity to resist or withstand unequal exchange. Oppression is clearly a political concept, which defines the relationship between the dominant and the dominated. It is the means by which the dominant group is able to improve its conditions on those who are weak or unwilling or are deviants. More simple, oppression is overt behavioural manifestation of power, which is conceptualised as force. Oppression operates when the institutionalised asymmetries of discrimination and exploitation are sought to be subverted by 'deviant' groups (Mukherji, 1989: 37-38).

DEO model is extremely useful in understanding the failures of the cooperative movement, Land reforms, Community Development Programmes, Panchayati Raj. Because of highly unequal access to power, dominant castes have been discriminating, exploiting and oppressing the deprived castes. Dubhashi (1987: 38-84) has rightly pointed out that the concept of popular participation in development has however, undergone a change over the last three decades of planning in our country. In the 1950s, in the context of newly introduced community development programs, popular participation meant that the rural people would bear a share of the cost of local community development projects like approach roads, school buildings or drinking water well. The popular participation would be in the shape of voluntary labor called *shramdan,* provision of local material like stones and seveices like cartage. However, while in the initial years of the program of community development, there was a great deal of enthusiasm for *shramdan.* Slowly it fell into disfavor for a variety of reasons. It was found that only the deprived caste provided labor while the dominant caste only supervised. Thus the participation of all the castes was not ensured.

In the 1960s, popular participation came to be associated with the participation of the rural people in the institutions such as *Panchayati Raj* and Cooperative institutions. While the village *panchayat* was the political democracy, the village co-operative constituted the economic democracy at the grass root. However, this attempt towards political and economic decentralization was centralized in the hands of the dominant caste. It prevented the participation of the deprived caste.

In the 1970s, there was a change in the approach to development. It was realized that the benefits of development in the past accrued to the more well-to-do sections of the community. A large majority of the underprivileged, like the small and marginal farmers, landless laborers and artisans were not able to participate either in the development programs or in the institutions and benefits of development did not accrue to them. This led to disparities between the well-to-do and underprivileged. Hence attention was focussed on formulating programs which directly benefit the rural people of the downtrodden section of the society. For example programs like SFDA (Small Farmer Development Agency) and MFLA (Marginal Farmer and Agricultural Labor Agency) were efforts in this direction. These measures have been partially beneficial to the deprived castes. However, dominant caste continued wielding power.

Grassroot institutions like *Panchayati Raj* and Co-operative institutions and voluntary associations are of course excellent media for popular participation. But it can ensure only when there is a reduction in discrimination, exploitation and oppression of the deprived caste by the dominant caste. Grass root institutions become an instrument in the hands of the dominant caste, which prevents the participation of the deprived caste in the development process. It results into social conflict between the dominant and the deprived caste. Backward class movement and inter-caste violence are some of the manifestations of this conflict. In order to contain these conflicts, role of the state as well as civil society is crucial.

The state is required to empower the deprived caste so that centralization of power by the dominant caste is prevented. The lexicographical meaning of empowerment is to give official authority or legal power; to enable to promote the self-actualization. Empowerment may be defined as "focusing ... energy in ... [one's] Circle of Influence. ... it's acting with integrity to create the environment in which we and others can develop character and competence and synergy (Covery, Merrill, & Merrill, 1994: 238). And the ultimate outcome of empowerment is a community "worthy of the best we humans have to offer" (Terry, 1993: 275). Thus, Empowerment may be defined as a process by which a group/community becomes aware of their rights and use it for enhancing their quality of life. For an attainment of this goal, the state has taken few legislative and administrative measures. Some of these measures are in the direction of reservation of seats for the deprived castes, provisions for adequate representations in administration, effective redistribution of land to the deprived castes, priority in providing loans for enterpreneurship for their economic betterment.

No doubt, the above measures have empowered the deprived caste, but this empowerment has not been able to reduce substantially their deprivation, exploitation and oppression. At this juncture, special attention must be paid towards the literacy of the deprived caste to take full advantage or legislative and administrative measures of the state. A literacy drive for the deprived caste must provide priority to the youth and women so that they can play crucial role in development.

Education and empowerment of youth and women of the deprived castes may accelerate the process of social development. Indian youth constitute about 35% of the total population and in terms of number they are more than 291 million in the year 1991. By the year 2000 A.D., they will be more than 358 million (Matin, 1995: 214). This substantial number may be properly utilized as an instrument for development. Since youth are more receptive to the new egalitarian and liberal values, they should be more involved in the developmental programs. Similarly, women constitute little more than 48 per cent of the total population of India since Independence. It has been rightly pointed out by Gandhiji that education of a man is the education of an individual, the education of a woman is the education of an entire family. Since women play more positive and significant role in the socialization in the family, they should be made an important instrument for inculcating and transmitting the new egalitarian and liberal values. These broad guidelines may by adopted in evolving various measures for governing a stratified society. 73rd Amendment Act is the right step in this direction.

V. Conclusion

We have examined unequal access to power and resultant social conflict in a stratified society as a problem for good governance. The instrument of the DEO, in the hand of the dominant caste in modern India against the deprived caste creates conflict. It has deepened due to developmental measures especially after Independence. In order to contain these conflicts from eruption into violence, state and civil society is required to intervene through legislative and administrative measures for an empowerment of the deprived castes. The concept development has a varied meaning. But we have used in terms of just development for the attainment of equality and liberty. For an attainment of these two goals, we have suggested broad guidelines, in which potentials of youth and women of the deprived castes should be utilized for the governance of the stratified Indian society.

References

Bailey, F.G. 1963. 'Closed Social Stratification in India', *European Journal of Sociology,* 4 (1).

Bailey, F.G. 1957. *Caste and the Economic Frontier.* London: Butler and Tonner Ltd.

Barth, F. 1960. 'The System of Social Stratification in Swat, North Pakistan', in E.R. Leach (ed.) *Aspect of Caste in South India, Ceylon and North West Pakistan.* Cambridge: Cambridge University Press.

Berreman, G.D. 1967. 'Stratification, Pluralism and Interaction: A Compartive Analysis of Caste', in Anthony de Reuck and Julie Knight (eds.) *Caste and Race.* London.

Beteille, Andre. 1965. *Caste, Class and Power: Changing Patterns of Stratification in a Tanjore Village.* Bombay: Oxford University Press.

Bhatt, Anil. 1975. Caste, Class and Politics: An Empirical Profile of Social Stratification in Modern India. Delhi: Manohar Book Service.

Brass, Paul R. 1984. *Caste Faction and Party in Indian Politics.* (Vol. I). Delhi: Chanakya Publications.

Central Statistical Organization (C.S.O.). 1984. *Statistical Abstract.* (New Series No. 27). New Delhi: Government of India.

Chakravarti, Anand. 1975. *Contradiction and Change: Emerging Patterns of Authority in a Rajasthan Village.* Delhi: Oxford University Press.

Covey, S. R., Merrill, A. R., & Merrill, R. R. 1994. *First things first.* New York: Simon and Schuster.

Desai, A.R. 1984. *India's Path of Development: A Marxist Approach.* Bombay: Popular Prakashan.

Dubhashi, P.R. 1987. *Essays in Development Administration.* New Delhi: Archives Publishers, Distributors.

Dumont, Louis. 1988. *Homo Hierarchichus: The Caste System and Its Implications.* Delhi: Oxford University Press.

Ghurye: G.S. 1961. *Caste, Class and Occupation.* Bombay: Popular Book Depot.

IIAS. 1996. The Governance Working Group of the International Institute of Administrative Sciences.

Jayaraman, R. 1981. *Caste and Class: Dynamics of Inequality in Indian Society.* Delhi: Hindustan Publishing Corporation (India).

Matin, Abdul. 1995. 'Indian Youth: Size and Transformational Role', in Noor Mohammad and Abdul Matin (eds.) *Indian Youth: Problems and Prospects.* New Delhi: Ashish Publishing House, pp. 212-223.

Matin, Abdul. 1996. 'In Quest of Indigenous Approach to Women Studies in India', in A. J. Qaiser and S.P. Verma (eds.) *Art and Culture.*

Matin, Abdul. 1990. *Changing Agrarian Relations in Mithila, North India.* Unpublished Ph.D. thesis, University of Toronto.

Mukherji, P.N. 1989. 'Development Dilemmas: Towards a Conceptualization of Social Development' in P.N. Pimpley, K.P. Singh and A. Mahajan (eds.) Social Development: Processes and Consequences. Jaipur: Rawat Publications, pp. 27-39.

Pimpley, P.N., K.P. Singh and A. Mahajan (eds.). 1989. *Social Development: Processes and Consequences.* Jaipur: Rawat Publications.

Singer, H.W. 1979. 'Poverty, Income Distribution and Levels of Living: Thirty Years of Changing Thought on Development Problems' in C.H. Hanumantha Rao and P.C. Joshi (eds.). *Reflections on Economic Development and Social Change*. New Delhi: Allied Publishers Pvt. Ltd.

Singh, Yogendra. 1973. *Modernization of Indian Tradition*. Delhi: Thomson Press.

Singh, Yogender. 1977. *Social Stratification and Change in India*. New Delhi: Manohar Publications.

Srinivas, M.N. 1966. *Social Change in Modern Inaia*. New Delhi: Allied Publishers.

Srinivas, M.N. 1964. *Caste in Modern India and Other Essays*. Bombay: Asia Publishing House.

Terry, R. 1993. *Authentic leadership*. San Francisco: Jassey-Bass.

Tumin, Melvin M. 1987. *Social Stratification: The Forms and Functions of Inequality*. New Delhi: Prentice-Hall of India Pvt. Ltd.

Weber, Max. 1952. *Essays in Sociology*. London: Routledge and Kegan Paul Ltd.

Webster, A. 1984. *Introduction to the Sociology of Development*. London.

9

Minorities and Federal Nation Building: Issues and Challenges

Arshi Khan

The issue of minority rights and locating democratic space for minorities in the power structure in plural societies need to be discussed to determine rights and duties of State and Society. Both are required to work in harmony by guaranteeing the process of mutual coordination and constructive bargaining. Success of their coordinating efforts depends more upon their constructive roles towards ensuring shared rule and secularism in the context of democracy and modernisation. In other words, the issue of governance seems to determine political process which sets national goal and determine the identity of the country. Democratic governance of plural society can hardly overlook the issue of participation and power-sharing vis-à-vis deprived segments of society.

Democratic governance and nation-state

Particularly in the post World War II era the issue

of governance, both at the national and international levels, has been the epicenter of debate and discussion. At the international level, the issue of governance, emerging conflicts between normative and alternative international laws, growing menace of American global irredentism and demands for UN reforms can be contextualised towards emerging consensus for balanced international relations based on shared system of international governance. Demands for such reforms can be justified on the basis of the fact that the world community is full of diversities—thus federal in character.

Similarly at the national level, most of the polities in plural societies have been undergoing the difficult phase of transitions towards locating system of governance in more constructive manner. Problems and issues of creating judicious system of governance based on 'self rule' and 'shared rule' can hardly be overlooked in multicommunal and bi-communal societies, most of them situated in non-western world. Even in Western Europe, which is the hub of liberal democracies, its political construct of nation-state has been facing continuing dilemma between its system of governance and multiculturalism. Algerians and immigrants in France, 2.5 million Turks and other minorities in Germany and Turks in Greece are some of those issues, which certainly expose negative aspects of nation-State system. Even federal liberal democracies of the West-Canada and the United States are facing the dilemma of accommodation vis-à-vis Francophones and Blacks respectively. In most of Western liberal democracies particularly in Europe, minorities are described as settlers and immigrants. Western Europe which is the hub of liberal democracies has not been comfortable with the words 'minority rights'. Minorities distinct identities have neither been tolerated nor recognised as democratic attributes.

This so happened because the nation-state and/ western liberal democracy stress upon creating national society which provided powers and privileges to homogenous groups identified with majority segments. The nation-State is institutionally ill equipped to deal with federal society. Modern European state was historically grafted on the culturally homogeneous and politically self-aware ethno-religious or ethno-linguistic entities called nations. This transition from ethno-cultural to political cultural conception of 'nation' was largely facilitated by the state enforcing linguistic homogeneity within its territory, but this also made possible the growth of legal and political institutions of citizenship[1]. This is to note that citizenship rights were found insufficient for protecting even cultural identity and secular interests of the minorities.

In the post-World War II, Third World countries, which were newer and much weaker, adopted the European nation-State model more as an administrative framework for the purpose of control and stability. On the other hand, the West European countries had created a 'national' society based on homogeneity factor. In case of post-colonial countries, nation-state model created ground for majoritarianism. The process of nation building based on majoritarianism led to majority-minority dichotomy vis-à-vis democratic governance.

The ruthless policy of majoritarianism and nation-state have evolved through a long struggle between the two contradictory forces, one-enforcing uniformity and the other focussing on the socio-cultural realities. In hegemonic polities, where the state apparatus controls all spheres of life, the normal interaction of social groups, ideas, opinions and culture is forbidden. It creates a fixed national identity, which the state attempts to protect from outside influences. This theory of governance stems from the Jacobian tradition of the French Revolution and is also inherent in a corporatist system where the state directly or indirectly maintains control over the social sphere and tries to shape society in concentric circles around the state. The over-arching role of the state has led to an elitist definition of nation and citizenry. In many ways, the communications between civil society and state institutions that democracy requires remain uni-dimensional, flowing from the state to society. Because of this, the formation and expression of different opinions are suppressed.

Minorities and Indian Polity

Minorities are socio-political realities of Indian plural society. Some have attempted to categorize minorities in India on the linguistic basis but religion seems to be the most authentic factor for such categorization. Therefore, the word 'community' can preferably be used to identify social segments as minority and majority in Indian context. Though the Indian Society is multi-cultural, multi-lingual and multi-religious but about 95 percent of the Indian population consist of the two larger communities-Hindus and Muslims. So the Indian society can be described both as plural and bio-communal society in which muslims are second largest community. It is true that both these largest segments are multi-lingual and multi-ethnic and multi-regional in character. Within its territory live one billion people, speaking 18 major languages. Over 1600 mother tongues were listed in 1971 census of India.

Besides, there are other smaller communities dispersed all over India. Some of them are also multi-lingual and multi-ethnic. However, it is important to point out that both smaller minorities and the single largest minorities do not face common threats or challenges in the country. At one level both have been facing threats to their identities and cultures. But on the other, Muslims' situation is extremely deplorable at the representation level. Smaller minorities are comparatively better off. Sikhs are well-employed in private and government sectors. Christians dominate the field of education, health and service sectors. Similarly Zoroastrians and Jains are placed in privileged positions. Only recently some Christian minority's institutions became the targets of Hindu militant groups. On the contrary the whole Muslim community stands today as the most deprived and marginalised segment of Indian society. It is, however, important to raise the question that who has been left behind in the field of human development, public employments, industrial sectors and participation in elected bodies?

The minority status of Muslims in India is further complicated and painfully stressed by the militant sections of the majority who look towards patriotism in exclusive manner. Violence against Muslims and their dwindling trust in police and administrative agencies have made them vulnerable. Available data and sources indicate deplorable position of Mulsims in education, employment and elected bodies. The 1999 election manifesto of the Samajwadi Party clearly says that their share in services has gone down and their number in police and army is negligible. It also says that there is dearth of educational institutions in Muslim majority areas because of which Muslim children, especially girls are unable to go to schools and colleges. The CPI (M) manifesto of 1999 maintains that "the Muslim community and some other minorities suffer from various forms of deprivation and discrimination".

The dawn of the new Millennium has even added new dimensions to international law. Democracy (priority to people's sovereignty over state sovereignty) and human rights are becoming considered as the legitimate ground for 'UN enforcement'. In other words both principle and people are becoming unavoidable areas of serious concern. At the national level, the basic purpose of India's polity can be said to be creating vibrant and strong federal democracy. This is possible when minority rights are not usurped and exploited. This requires a new thinking for building Federal India.

If we look at the Indian Constitution, it fails to provide adequate safeguard to minorities. The Indian Constitution has placed the Union Government in a unique position in which it has attributes of a "Leviathan". The Union Government has almost been made as powerful as it was under the imperial arrangements as envisaged in the Government of India Act, 1935[2], which was the foundation document[3].

In the preparation of the Draft Constitution, the Constituent Assembly, its various committees and the Drafting Committee have borrowed a great deal from the Constitutions of USA, the Dominion of Canada, the Commonwealth of Australia, the Irish Free State and above all the Government of India Act of 1935. Of these the most important place has to be given to the Government of India Act 1935. It is not merely the ideas that have been borrowed from it but its very wording has been adopted in almost all clauses and articles. No other Constituent Assembly or Drafting Committee known to history has so blindly copied a previous model to the same extent as the Indian Constituent Assembly and its Drafting Committee has done. The Constitution is in the main a western product[4].

It is the opinion of many people that we should not have drawn upon so heavily on the Government of India Act for preparing the Draft of the Constitution[5]. With the exception of responsibility at the Centre it is essentially the Act of 1935. The Governors are there, the name of the Governor-General has been altered to the President, but essentialy the whole structure of the Constitution of 1935 remains intact. There is one important change, which will bring about, I hope a radical change in the social and political status and composition of the people in the country and that is adult franchise. Excepting for this there is very little in the Constitution to enthuse over[6].

Indian Constitution basically differs with some of the noble aims and objects of the Resolution introduced by Pandit Nehru in December 1946. Para 3 of the Resolution said that Indian State and territories "shall possess and retain the status of autonomous units, together with residuary powers." Para 6 dealt with "adequate safeguards for minorities, backward and tribal areas, and depressed and other backward classes." These were the fundamentals of the Constitution. But finally the Constitution abandoned them on the pretexts of national unity and secularism. It was not a mere of Resolution, Pandit Nehru told the Assembly, "it was a firm resolve, a pledge and undertaking[7] or as Munshi called it a political horoscope[8]". In the final third Reading of the Draft Constitution in November 1949, there were many members of the Constituent Assembly who pointed out flaws in constitutional engineering. When the Government of India Act 1935 was in force, there was a convention that the unpresented communities must be given a choice to be ministers but that has been taken away[9] by the present Constitution.

Special Provisions and Minority Rights

The Indian Constitution has, however, provided certain safeguards for Backward Class of citizens and socio-cultural rights for minorities. These statutory safeguards certainly resulted in the relative advancement of marginalised sections of the majority. The Constitution has some special provisions such as Articles 15 (4), 16 (4), 46, and Part XVI which has 13 articles. On the other hand, all minorities' rights include freedom of religion, and cultural and educational rights. Articles 25 to 30 deal with the rights of maintaining socio-cultural identities. Marginalised representation of minorities particularly Muslims in elected bodies and governmental agencies has made above-mentioned rights more vulnerable to the majoritarian encroachment. If any community or group in a plural society is deprived of sharing power with other partners, it is bound to be subjected by those controlling the levers of governance.

The Indian polity is, of course, the world's largest democracy but it has remained as a majoritarian in character. Thus the existing inequality in the spheres of power-sharing and decision-making between the majority and minority also affect the federal fabric of Indian Society which are reflected in the growing level of insecurity, disappointment and disenchantment in the minority. Those tendencies can be found in the frequency of communal flare-ups, communal tensions, prejudiced role of police and administration and militarisation of communal groups.

As a result, a question can be asked that what does really constitute minority rights in a plural society like India? Are they limited to the their freedom of religion, culture, education and language? They are fundamentally required to encompass those constitutional rights, which could guarantee minorities share in governance. It is always positive to claim that India is a federal nation particularly at the societal level where groups maintain their distinct identities together with their consensus to coexist with one another. Such a federal social pattern can only be maintained as our civilisational heritage by our collective participation in federal nation building.

It is also true that the Constitution of India was framed more on the basis of western constitutional experiences. But one can also argue that views expressed by the leading members of the Constitutional Assembly of India (1946-49) rejected the menace of majoritarianism. Perhaps they relied more on 'responsible leadership' than on their constitutional engineering. So it can be said that the Western notion of 'nation-state' was followed more as an 'strategy' to keep India united and strong. But such a notion of governance was supposed to be handed over to responsible leaders who were supposedly in favour of power sharing. The Constituent Assembly Debates and popular declarations of political parties in post-colonial India always promised federal governance but at the end the western construct of nation-state helped majority to dominate over the minorities.

Over five decades of our constitutional implementation, minority situation has relatively been disappointing. Now with the dawn of the new Millennium, minorities' demand for minority rights need to be taken seriously as a necessary part of political process to federal national building. Participation in governance on collective basis would herald a new era of federal democracy. What is striking is that safeguards provided under Articles 25-30 are 'negative', applicable to a police state but not applicable to welfare state or participatory state. According to K.V. Rao, "It is not merely religious interference that a Muslim or a Christian is afraid of, but his inability to get fair deal from the majority in matters of political gains such as employment, getting trade permits and a thousand and one benefits that the Welfare State today showers on the citizens.[10]"

One of the challenges before Indian polity is to be more viable and acceptable to all segments. In the words of Pranab Bardhan (*Democracy and Development,* 1999, p.108): "Rentsharing, regional autonomy and devolution of power, and political and constitutional ways of curbing the excesses of majoritarian democracy (where some groups are in danger of being perpetually excluded from power) are extremely important for social peace and preservation of the minimum underpinnings of economic development. While democracy in general can diffuse some ethnic tensions, certain forms of democracy may be more conducive to compromise, coalition building and coordination than other forms."

Debates on Minorities in the Constituent Assembly of India

The members of the Constituent Assembly had taken keen interests in protecting minority rights in the initial phase of the framing of the Constitution. But later they turned back. It is also true that thousands of amendment proposal were not even taken up by the Assembly.

The framers of the Indian Constitution took the rights of minorities in sharing power as a threat to secularism and nationalism. At the time of independence, minorities were identified as vulnerable and backward communities. Despite repeated pleas of some eminent Muslim Members of the Constituent Assembly of India for their safeguards, the majority leaders stressed upon following the majoritarian policies. Advocates of minorities safeguards believed that only community members can best represent interest of the minority community. But after a period of over five decades, it is now proved that the majority community has not only failed to represent the interest of minorities but also misused them as mere vote banks. Moreover, the chauvinist parties and groups raised the issue of "minorityism" (favour to Muslims).

Political Safeguards

Fear of under representation and deprivation of a minority community and backwardness always manifest itself in the form of protest and demand for its legitimate share in governance. As a result, the issue of political safeguards for minorities comes into question. The policy of ensuring political safeguards is always assessed on the basis of communitarian approach in bi-communal or plural societies. The majoritarian approach takes this policy as the mechanism of divide and rule but the minority approach considers it as safeguards against majoritarian take-over or dominance.

But the fact is that the British rulers agreed to this kind of policy after tremendous pressures and demands from the minorities. As a result, community and caste representation came into existence in some municipalities since the 1870s. On 1 October 1906, Minto, the Viceroy received a deputation of 35 Muslims from all the provinces of British India except the North West Frontier Province. In their address, they claimed for Muslims a 'fair share' to be computed not merely by reference to the numerical strength of Muslims in India, but also by reference to their political importance...[11] The address proposed for adequate Muslims representation in municipal and district boards, provincial councils and Imperial Legislative Council.[12] Ever since the introduction of Morley-Minto Reforms (1909), Indian minorities were provided with some political safeguards.

This is to note that all the members of the Constituent Assembly of India (CAI) had been elected under separate electorates. Member of the CAI, Mohamed Ismail Sahib said: "This separate electorate is not separatism at all; it means the recognition of differences between one group of people and another; it means that this difference should be recognised and wherever those differences come into play the real representatives of the group of people who are subject to that difference ought to be heard by the authorities; that is what it means.[13]"

In constitutional drafts and deliberations, political safeguards included provisions for reserved seats in legislatures, quotas in government employment, reserved posts in the Cabinet and the creation of administrative machinery to ensure supervision and protection of minorities' rights.

It is a very wrong notion that political safeguards envisaged for Muslims were withdrawn mainly due to the partition factor. The partition took place on 14 August 1947. The proposal of the Advisory Committee on Minorities was passed by the Constituent Assembly of India on August 27. It was also published in the first constitutional draft (1948). But what led to its withdrawal in May 1949 was not the partition factor but a political strategy to deny Muslims share in the governance of Federal India.

Assurances for Safeguards

On 14 August 1947 when the Constituent Assembly of India celebrated the day as historic for taking over the governance of this country and sent "greetings and good wishes for success and the best of luck" to Pakistan, its President Dr. Rajendra Prasad said categorically: "To all the minorities in India we give the assurance that they will receive fair and just treatment and there will be no discrimination in any form against them. Their religion, their culture and their language are safe and they will enjoy all the rights and privileges of citizenship, and will be expected in turn to renew loyalty to the country in which they live and to its constitution[14].

Partition factor should not be held responsible for diverting the issue of political safeguards for minorities. Cabinet Mission Plan became controversial soon after its acceptance by the Congress and the League. Its controversial interpretations had finally solidified disagreements between the parties, which gave the message that they were heading for partition.

This is to recall the inaugural address of Dr. Sachchidananda Sinha, temporary Chairman of the Constituent Assembly of India, on 9 December 1946 where he said that reasonable agreements and judicious compromises are no where called for than in framing a new constitution for a conutry like India.[15] Dr. Rajendra Prasad, elected permanent Chairman of the Assembly said on December 11 that the Constitution "will satisfy all over people, all groups, all communities, all religions inhabiting this vast land, and which will ensure to everyone freedom of action, freedom of thought, freedom of belief and freedom of worship, which will guarantee to everyone opportunities for rising to his highest, and which will guarantee to everyone freedom in all respect.[16]" The historic objectives 'Resolutions' in the nature of pledge, was placed in the Assembly on December 13 by Pandit Jawaharlal Nehru. Sixth out of eight aims and objectives clearly mentioned: "Wherein adequate safeguards shall be provided for minorities, backward and tribal areas, and depressed and other backward classes."[17]

Two weeks after the partition, Sardar Vallabhabhai J. Patel, Chairman of the Advisory Committee on Minority Rights, said in the Assembly that "this House will also be able to dispose of this question (Report on Minority Rights) in a friendly spirit and in an atmosphere of goodwill. Let us hope that we will leave the legacy of bitterness behind and forget past and begin with the clean slate."[18]

Sardar Vallabhabhai J. Patel placed the Report of the Advisory Committee on Minorities in the Constituent

Assembly of India on 27th August 1947 which was drafted after considering the report of the Minority Committee and after considering all the points raised with regards to the safeguards for diffeent minorities in the country. He said: "An attempt has been made in this report to enumerate those safeguards which are matters of common knowledge such as representation in legislatures, that is, joint versus separate electorates.... Then we have thoughts fit to agree to reservation in proportion to the population of the minorities. Then we have also provided for some sort of administrative machinery to see that whatever safeguards are provided are given effect to, so that it may not be felt by the communities concerned that these are paper safeguards."[19] Regarding their representation in Services, Sardar Patel mentioned that "it is necessary for the State to pay due regards to the claims of minorities in making appointments to public services. We recommend, therefore, that, as in the case of appointment to Cabinets, there should be in some part of the constitution or the schedule and exhortation to the Central and Provincial Governments to keep in view the claims of all the minorities in making appointments to public services ..."[20] In his words, "... it is a fundamental duty of the State to take special steps to bring up those minorities which are backward to the level of the general community."[21] The Minority Report also included in Clause 11 which said: "An officer shall be appointed by the President at the Centre and by the Governors in the Provinces to report to the Union and Provincial Legislatures respectively about the working of safeguards provided for the minorities."[22]

The Report, however, rejected separate electorates and the weightage system. Dr. P.S. Deshmukh described their rejection as 'a great achievements'. He further said "the representatives of these minorities have taken a long and nationalistic view of the whole matter... I would like to assure them on behalf of us all that they will never have any occasion to repent what they have conceded."[23]

Shri. V.I. Muniswami Pillai said in the Assembly that "any constitution that is made for the 300 millions (out of 400)[24] of this country must have proper safeguards." Dr. H.C. Mookherjee, Chairman of the Minorities Sub-Committee of the Assembly said that "it was necessary for the sake of the future progress of our country, that every attempt should be made to meet the wishes of the minorities."[25] Again Sardar Patel described this report as almost unanimous and gave 'general satisfaction.'[26]

The Constituent Assembly of India thus adopted the Advisory Committee Report on Minority Rights on 27 and 28 August 1947. The Draft Constitution (Pat XIV) mentioned these safeguards under the title - 'Special Provisions relating to Minorities' in February 1948. Draft articles 292, 294, 296 and 299 ensured safeguards for minorities.

Amazingly in May 1949 Sardar Patel backed down on political safeguards for Muslims. The Advisory Committee on Minorities, etc., was dissolved in May 1949. After the massive effort of the Congress nationalists to divert the issue of political safeguards for Muslims from December 1948 to May 1949, Mr. Tajamul Husain and Begum Aizaz Rasul, members of the Constituent Assembly, were encouraged to reject the proposal for safeguards. Whereas the whole Constituent Assembly of India had voted for political safeguards for Muslims in August 1947. As a result Sardar Patel said to drop the 'reservations' for the Scheduled Castes of Hindu community.... In two Provinces the right of the Indian Christians and the Anglo-Indian Community for political safeguards were retained.

Conspiracy against the minorities thus started in December 1948 when Sardar Patel used the words that "conditions have vastly changed" since India became free in 1947 and "it was no longer appropriate in the context of free India and of present conditions that there should be reservations ..." In his opinion. "the reservation ... did lead to a certain degree of separatism and was to that extent contrary to the conception of a secular democratic state."[27] When the Advisory Committee met on May 11 after a long adjournment under Dr. H.C. Mookherjee, it passed the following resolution: "That the system of reservation for minorities other than Scheduled Castes in Legislatures be abolished."[28] Sardar Patel mentioned in his letter (11 May 1949, para.2) to the President of the CAI: ".... that minorities were by no means unanimous as to the necessity, in their own interests, of statutory reservation of seats in the legislatures."[29] "the reservation of seats for religious communities, it was felt, would lead to a certain degree of separatism and was to that extent contrary to the conception of secular democratic state." Dr. H.C. Mookerjee, Mr. Tajamul Husain, Shri Lakshmi Kant Maitra and certain other members gave notices of resolutions[30] for abolishing reservation of seats in legislatures for any community in the country. On 11 May 1949 the resolution of Dr. H.C. Mookerjee found wholehearted support of an overwhelming majority of the members of the Advisory Committee.

On 25th May 1949 he said in the Constituent Assembly that "it is upto the majority community to create by its generosity a sense of confidence in the minorities ...."[31] He further said that "... it is in the interest of all to lay down real and genuine foundations of a secular state, then nothing is better for the minorities than to trust the good-sense and sense of fairness of the majority, and to place confidence in them."[32] Stressing upon the resolution for eleminating political safeguards for minorities Dr. H.C. Mookerjee said: "The majority community has been very generous to every one of the minority communities that is my firm belief."[33] This was a personal statement and views which he used on behalf of the minorities.

Mr. Mohamed Ismail Sahib, a member of the Constituent Assembly opposed this move. In his words: "Now, if the majority or the party in power wants to do away with any of these safeguards, that is one thing. But I submit that it is not fair to place responsibility for doing away with such safeguards on the shoulders of the minority."[34] Another member from Assam, Syed Muhammad Sadulla said: "the Minorities Advisory Committee in its sitting on 11th May came to a momentous conclusion—I am afraid according to me on very insufficient material or data. The report which the Honourable President of the Minorities Advisory Committee has submitted to the Constituent Assembly is full of very sound maxims of politics."[35]

On 26th May Prime Minister Pandit Jawaharlal Nehru said that "it is a historic motion that my colleague, the Deputy Prime Minister has put before this House."[36] Regarding the Constituent Assembly's pledge of August 1947 for political safeguards, he said: "Reluctantly we agreed to carry on with some measure of reservation."[37] He further said: "Therefore, I think that doing away with this reservation business is not only a good thing in itself - good for all concerned and more especially for the minorities ...."[38]

It now becomes very clear that the minorities' fundamental rights of share in governance was well recognised in 1947 itself but the notions of nationalism, democracy, secularism and unity were misinterpreted to do away with the rights of participation. Muslim members of the Constituent Assembly Begum Aizaz Rasul, Naziruddin Ahmad, and Muhammad Ismail Khan, who were persuaded by Sardar Patel to support Dr. H.C. Mookherjee's resolution for the abolition of such safeguards, had nevertheless expressed their trust in the majority for a better turn out. In the words of Begum Aizaz Rasul: "... when we put the majority community on its honour, it will be up to it to retain its prestige and honour and return members of the minority community, not only in numbers to which they are entitled on a population basis but perhaps in greater numbers. I do not visualise any political party in the future putting up candidates for election ignoring the Muslim."[39] All such expectations and imagined welfare of the Muslims soon collapsed on its own. Over five decades not a single nationalist, secular or democratic national political party ever thought over the rights of minorities in a federal democracy.

Therefore, the Muslim community should be given some constitutional safeguards for ensuring their adequate representation in all socio-political institutions of democracy. It is a necessity because the constitution is always obliged to be balanced and just towards all sections and communities in bi-communal and plural societies. If this obligation, in case of India, is left on the good will of the self-proclaimed majority (Upper Castes), nothing would happen. This obligation was taken up by Sardar Patel on behalf of empowered people in 1949 but nothing happened. So it is now the turn of the Constitution which should undertake the responsibility of upholding the rights of the Muslim community in services, elected bodies and other areas of participation and power-sharing. But the BJP-led coalition Government has not shown any interest in those areas where the dominance of few could be challenged. Priorities are clear before us to create a federal polity and federal society. This needs a new thinking and rational perception of problems.

Minorities in plural societies can play a key role in federal nation building. In case of India, this can be achieved by practicing a type of representative government in which power sharing is institutionalised. Consociational democracy have developed in countries that are deeply divided and identified by clear cut religious, ethnic or linguistic differences. The aim of Constitution is to ensure that all the major cleavages or segments got their due rights in proportion to their size in the society. Policy is produced as a result of negotiations between the leaders of the segments in a process known as "elite accommodation." The system of power sharing may also extend to the allocation of civil service posts (senior and middle levels) or positions in significant public authorities. In consociational democracy, the organisations representing each segment of society are guaranteed considerable autonomy in determining which issues affect that particular grouping. Each may also possess rights of veto over matters that affect their vital issues such as religious or linguistic schooling. Such power-sharing devices enable plural but deeply divided societies to hold together.

We can choose some or more vital characteristics of consociational democracy to bridge gap between minorities and nation building. In this regard, we also need to reform our election system. Majoritarian systems of election exist in France, Austria, Brazil, Peru, Poland, Finland etc. On the other hand, plurality system (first past the post) in which the winner is the candidate who receives the most votes or to win an election without winning a majority, exist in proportion to the vote they received in the election. What we really need today is to guarantee proportional representation which is designed to ensure that all parties receive representation in proportion to the votes they received in the election. Arendt Lijphart believes that propotional representation system and consensus forms of democracy provide more accurate representation and better minority representation than the majoritarian systems. The consensus democracy restrains majority rule by sharing, dispersing and limiting political power.

Thus it can be said that minority rights need to be reassessed in the specific cantext of demands, democratic inspirations and national need for federal nation building. Minority rights include all those rights, which not only provide call for various freedoms but also enact laws or provide mechanisms to ensure safeguards of minority rights in governance and society. Such safeguards would certainly encourage and strengthen minorities in federal nation building process.

References

1. D.L. Seth, "The Nation-State and Minority Rights", in D.L. Seth and G. Mahajan, eds., *Minority Identities*

and the Nation-State (New Delhi: Oxford University Press, 1999), p.23.

2. Arshi Khan "The importance of Article 356 in Centre State Relations in India: A Critical Review of its Use and Misuse", in Rasheeduddin Khan, ed., *Rethinking Indian Federalism* (New Delhi: IIAS, 1997), p.103.
3. Granville Austin, *Working A Democratic Constitution: The Indian Experience* (New Delhi: Oxford University Press, 1999), p.5.
4. M. Venkataranjagaiya, *Draft Constitution of India* (Bombay: Hind Kitabs Limited, July 1948), p.18.
5. Shri Lakshminaryan Sahu said in the Constituent Assembly (on 17 November 1949), mentioned in CAD Book No.5 (New Delhi: Lok Sabha Secretariat, 1999) p. 615.
6. Dr. P.S. Deshmukh said in CA on 22 November 1949, mentioned in CAD, Book No.5, p.776.
7. *CAD* (Vol.I) Book No. 1, p.59.
8. Cited in K.V. Rao, *Parliamentary Democracy of India* (Calcutta: The World Press, Pvt. Ltd.) p.349.
9. Shri V.I. Muniswamy Pillai said in the CA on 17 November 1949, mentioned in CAD, Book No.5. p. 609.
10. K.V. Rao, *Parliamentary Democracy in India: A Critical Commentary* (Calcutta: the World Press Private Ltd., 1965), p. 231.
11. Frazana Shaikh, *Community and Consensus in Islam-Muslim Representation in Colonial India,* 1860-1947 (Bombay, 1991), p.65.
12. P. Hardy, The Muslims of British India (London: Cambridge University Press, 1972), pp. 154-155.
13. *CAD,* Book No.3, p.279.
14. *CAD,* (vol. I), Book No. 1, p.2.
15. *CAD,* (vol. I), Book No.1, p.4.
16. *ibid.*, p.52.
17. *ibid.*, p.59.

18. *CAD* (vol.V) Book No. 1., p. 198.
19. *ibid.*
20. *ibid.*, p. 198-199.
21. *ibid.*, p. 247.
22. *inid.*, p. 281.
23. *ibid.*, p. 201.
24. *ibid.*, p. 202.
25. *ibid.*, p. 208.
26. *ibid.*, p. 210.
27. *CAD,* Vol.III, p.311, mentioned in Iqbal Ansari, "The Politics of Constitution Making in India", in D.L. Seth and G. Mahajan, eds., *Minority Identities and Nation-State,* p.118.
28. *CAD,* Book No.3, p.311.
29. *ibid.*, p. 310.
30. *ibid.*, p. 311.
31. *CAD,* Book No.3., p. 272.
32. *ibid.*
33. *ibid.*, p. 300.
34. *ibid.*, p. 278.
35. *ibid.*, p. 304.
36. *ibid.*, p. 329.
37. *ibid.*
38. *ibid.*, p. 332.
39. *ibid.*, p. 301.

10

Environmental Governance in India: From Crises to Prognosis

Md. Zafar Mahfooz Nomani

I. Discontentment Saga

Environmental governance in India suffers from policing sickness[1] and often remains bereft of democratic and participatory spirits[2]. During the past few decades a number of ecological controversies have engaged our attention towards the hierarchy and effectivity of environmental governance and conflict resolution[3]. The Narmada debate has changed the complexion of environmental battles from being fought over the fact of river valley to raise doubt about entire political system and nature of democracy[4]. The torrential increase in population, subsistence economy of survival on natural resources, massive industrialization, alarming level of pollution, incidence and severity of ecological disasters necessitated an appraisal of environmental law, policy and governance. The leakage of mythyl isocynites and oleum gas from Union

Carbide and Shri Ram industries generated serious dabate about the environmental security and economic sustainability of the state[5]. The enigma of compensation, eupheria of rehabilitation and resettlement and gradual extermination due to menacing pollution have resulted into simmering discontentment in society. The flood of litigation, insurmountable pressure on courts and delicacies of environmental conflict resolution enjoined for radical overhauling of environmental dispute redressal system[6].

On the other hand the project affected people of Narmada, Tehri, Maheshwar, Dhabol and Dhanua under popular public pressure made a strong case for refurbishing of environmental governance in India. In the context of Narmada project Arundhati Ray has poignantly paused that who owns this land river forest and fish.? These are answered unambiguously bitterly and brutaly in one voice because most of the governmental institutions squeeze natural resources for the relentless pursuits of unsustainable development[7]. Over the last fifty years India has spent Rs. 80,000 crores on the irrigation project yet there are more drought and flood-prone areas. Two hundred million citizens have no access to safe drinking water and no single river in plain has potable water. Ten million hectares of irrigated land are currently saline and water logged[8]. Despite the disturbing evidence of irrigation disaster, dam - inducted flood and rapid disenchantment with green revolution, the government has not commissioned a post-project valuation of a single one of its 3600 dams to gauge whether or not it has achieved the desired goals. The government has detailed figure for how many million tones of food grain or edible oil the country produces. It is possible to access minute to minute information about the stock exchange or the value of rupees in the world market. We know how many cricket matches we have lost on a Friday in Sharjah. But the government does not have figure for the number of people that have been displaced by dams at the altar of national progress[9]. According to an estimate there are thirty three million people displaced by big dams in the last fifty years which is more than three time the number refugees that partition created in India and ten time the number of Palestinian refugees. The million of displaced people are nothing but refugees of an unacknowledged war[10]. The Indian State has ruthlessly appropriated natural resources and re-distributed to favored cadre of paid-up elite. In fact poorest people are subsidizing the life style of richest[11].

That is why no body in India respect the highly centralized, non-participatory and autocratic governance system, which political party try to sustain not by promoting good governance but by building strong patron-client relationships and creating a facade of serving the clientele through the official loot of the treasure - subsidies, special allocation of projects and natural resources. The environmental problems only get solved when democracy enters governance systems - when *Janshakti* (peoples power) prevails over *Rajshakti* (government's power). During serious drought and electioneerring compaign in Gujrat in September 2000 people raised slogan like *"Pehle Pani Phir Advani"*[12]. Thus an inquiry into the role of governments as a neutral and autonomous institution in liberal- democratic tradition in natural resource building, bears legitimacy in view of national commitment towards growth, equity and sustainability. Since laws are the language and expressions of state power environmental law can not be read only from statute book but an articulating process in societal and governmental conflicts. The content and metaphor of environmental law is deeply embedded into conflict between union-state, legislature - executive, judiciary and citizens. The constitutional concern for protection and improvement of natural environment should, therefore, be appraised in the context of interaction and conflicts among law, society, state and institutions of the governance.[13] The present paper subsumes the genesis and crises of environmental governance to tune the operational and the managerial strategies of sustainable development.

II. Deepaning Crisis

In order to have a subtle comprehension of crisis of environmental governance one must have and overview of the diversity of perceptions prevalent among our planners stakeholders and experts regarding development and environment. Even the most enlightened community considers environment cosmetic and antiquity. The academics and professionals are aware of environmental hazards in narrow spectral context. What is not perceived is the totalities and inter linkages. The deepening crises also lies in bureaucratic perversity and inertia towards any innovative thinking. Even the well intentioned planner and technocrat use to think environmental protection as a new sector of governance for which fresh allocation of men, money, material, would have to be found amidst other competing demands of traditional sector like industries, agriculture transport, health, energy and education. It is not perceived as a dimension having direct bearing with judicious management of physical and human resource in each sector of economical growth[14]. No body seriously realizes that if environment goes wrong and planet is wounded nothing else in the economy and society will have a chance to go right. The World Bank has come out with some startling revelations. The water and air pollution imposes a heavy health cost of Rs. 24,500 crores every year of Indians. The total health cost of borne by Indians due to the effect of environmental degradation is Rs. 34,000 crores. The figure for annual economic loss (Rs. 34,000 crores) is about 4.5 percent of gross domestic product. This means the entire economic growth for the year was wiped out and that development has taken place solely at the expense of environment[15].

The environmental problem in India can be divided into three broad categories. In the first category are problems arising out of lack of development such as deforestation, fuel wood extraction, unhygienic slums, soil erosion, poor sanitation and contaminated water supply.

The second category problems are those caused by lack of environmental safeguards in development projects such as air and water pollution, hazardous waste disposal, water logging in irrigation projects, pesticide pollution, fertilizer run off into streams, etc[16]. This can be offset by sufficient investment in development projects to compensate for environmental degradation. Under the third category are global environmental problems such as global warming, ozone depletion marine pollution loss of genetic diversity, automobile pollution etc. These are created by the current pattern of development life style and energy consumption. Unfortunately we do not have enough captial to control the existence of the first two types of paradoxical environmental problems, one arising out of lack of development and the other arising out of developmental projects. If we do not develop rapidly, the slow pace of development will intensify the depletion of resources and environmental degradation. On the other hand excessive environmental circumspection will arrest economic growth.

To come out of this up impasse there are four options open to India the one which entails pursue high levels of economics growth and low degree environmental protection. This option is highly undesirable since it will result in high levels of pollution and pollution related disease. The second option is to have a low level of economic growth and low degree of environmental protection. This option will result in high level of poverty and pollution both. The third option is to have a low level of economic growth and high degree of environmental protection. This is not feasible since we will not have enough resources to pursue this option. The fourth option is to have high levels of economic growth and a high degree of environmental protection. If we have to raise the income levels of the poor and protect our environmental resources, we have to pursue this last option[17]. In other words, in a liberal democratic context, only this can sustain development with environmental protection. The economic growth agenda and environmental governance reform have to be seen in this perspective.

III. Legislative Context

Environmental governance in India is the *continuum* of the colonial legacy of *Government of India Act,* 1935 which in terms of its political thrust favors a pan-Indian centralized governance and adversarial method of conflicts regulation[18]. Under the Act one finds incidental enumeration of some related aspects of the environment. Through these were reconsidered by the Constituent Assembly yet it did not suggest any more items on environment and ecology. This status quoist trend has been a major factor for the lackadaisical approach to environmental governance. The ontological status of environmental governance under the *Government of India Act,* 1935, Draft Constitution and *Constitution of India,* 1950 received sporadic attention[19]. This phenomenon was described by Upendra Baxi as 'constitutional blindness', permeated into the regime of environmental governance till seventies. It was only after Stockholm Conference, 1992 and *Forty - Second Constitutional Amendment Act,* 1976 that a ferment for the massive codification of laws on the environment began. The state was enjoined 'to protect and improve the environment and to safe guard the forest and wild life'. Concurrently citizens are put under obligation not only 'to protect and improve natural environment but to have compassion for living creatures.'[20] The Seventh Schedule of the Constitution which serves as a catalogue and ready reckoner of subject matters within the legislative competency of the Union and State enumerates 97 items under Union List, 66 items under State List and 47 items under Concurrent List. Articles 246, 248, 249, 252 and 253 determine the ambit of legislative governance between union and state[21]. A cursory glance over the entries to Seventh Schedule and legislative framework clearly spells that natural resource conservation strategy and governance are generally the prerogative of the center with federal role limited to maintenance of common standard, research assistance, estab-lishment of administrative machinery and enforcement[22]. Entries mentioned under the Union List manifest the country's resolve to implement programs for massive industrialization and development of infra-structure to strengthen the economy with scant regard to protection and improvement of envi-ronment. The regulation and development of water resources under *Inter-State Water dispute Act* and *River Board Act,* 1956 provide a machinery for settlement of disputes and estab-lishment of board for regulation and development of inter-state river basin for consensual environmental governance among state[23].

Empirically examined most of the disputes are for from settlement and rumblings of discontentment often put state to throes of governance. Most of the agreements reached amicably in such disputes basically owes their credit to the copperation of states where the center's role has been that of facilitator of negotiation[24]. It thus questioned the very efficacy of central sponsored module of environmental governance. Forest and wildlife were moved from state list to concurrent list led to the enactment of *Wildlife Protection Act,* 1972 and *Forest Conservation Act,* 1980. The *National Wild Life Action Plan,* 1982 *Forest Policy,* 1988 and *National Bio-diversity Policy,* 1997[25] strive for the maintenance of environmental sustainability and ecological balance but most often blinker symbiotic relationship between forest dwellers, indigenous community in development process[26]. India's concern for environment basically rotates around underdevelopment, galloping population, mass poverty and industrialization[27]. To balance the imperatives of development and environment Parliament has passed a large number of legislation such as *Water (Prevention and Control of Pollution) Act,* 1974; *Forest (Conservation) Act,* 1980; The Air (Prevention and control of Pollution) Act 1981; *Environment (Protection) Act,* 1986, *Public Liability Insurance Act,* 1991; *National Environment Tribunal Act,* 1995; and *National Environment Appellate Authority Act,* 1997 and cluster of rules and notifications. These environmental statues, though impressive in range and coverage are more often observed in breach than in practice. The deterrent theory of Punishment employed under strict and absolute liability principle has achieved partial success[28]. This logically leads to the conclusion that investigation of alternative modes of environmental governances which is socially equitable, people friendly and democratically viable is the need of hour.

IV. Governing Norms

It was only after the Bhopal catastrophe a greater awareness of environmental safety, review of environmental regulations and adoption of command and control approach are vociferously articulated. The *Environment Protection Act,* 1986 inspired from 1972 Stockholm Conference and the constitutional mandate has thus become the fountain head and original source of enviro-legal activism in India. For the first time the Act encompassed water, air, land and their interrelationship with human being and other living creatures, plants, micro organism and property[29]. It recognized the omnibus role of central government as the public trustee of the environment resources of India by empowering to to take all such measures, as it deems necessary or expedient for the purpose of protecting and improving the quality of environment and preventing, controlling and abating environmental pullution[30]. The central government has also been enjoined to frame rules orders or directions under the Act[31] and the rules so made will be at par with the Act. These delegated environmental laws have also overriding effect on all other laws, if contrary, to the other spectral environmental enactment[32]. The Rules make the central government or its delegate a state Government, the statutory environmental decision making authority [environment impact assessment (EIA) agency] for assessing the potential adverse impact[33], which the new industry, operation or process or project or any modernization or expansion activity of an existing industry, operation or process or project, may have on the environment in any area of the country[34]. It can refuse to grant any environmental clearance order for the purpose if project proponent fails to comply with safeguards[35]. The central government is also required to take into consideration all the relevant factors such as material collected in the public enquiry, opinions of expert committees, materials gathered at local inspection, while assessing the potential adverse impact of the new project on the environment[36].

Any person aggrieved from governmental decisions may file an appeal before the National Environment Appellate Authority established under the *National Environment Appellate Authority Act,* 1997[37]. When an order granting environmental clearance by the concerned government is subjected to judicial review by an independent quasi-judicial body, the highest National Environment Appellate Authority, possibility of any new industries, with pollution potentiality adversely affecting the area becomes remote. But, the Central government, has yet to empower itself through the Rules which it has to make, as an environmental decision-making authority, for assessing the adverse impact which the existing industries, projects on the environment so the appropriate remedial action could be taken[38]. It must be conceded that the EPA is sensitive, comprehensive and suggestive of serious concern, although it does not empower the people to start court action to abate noxious operations and save the biosphere. Nor is there any a independent power to audit the dysfunction of the Authority. Its fatal flaws is cornering of power to take preemptive and punitive action by the central Government and its minions; and so, if the officialdom is indifferent, purchased by the proprietariat the law's hands will hang limp[39].

The Supreme Court and High Courts in India which have taken note of this deficiency, are unhesitatingly directing the central government, to take remedial action, by way of ordering closure or regulation of existing polluting industries, operations or processes or projects, wherever they are found to be polluting the areas concerned, on consideration of evidence placed before any of them or collected by any of them in the public interest litigation cases. Indeed, in such cases, when environmental decision making is done by the Supreme Court, it has even said, compelled to do so, as the central Government had not discharged such statutory responsibility under the EP Act, and it is high time that the central Government, should relieve the courts from discharging such responsibilities implying thereby that it should become an environmental decision making authority is such matters and its decision shall be subjected to judicial review by specialized appellate authorities. Even then, the Supreme Court had directed all the High Court in the country, to have their own green benches, for deciding upon such matters[40].

V. Institutional Mechanism

The Central Pollution Control Board (CPCB), State Pollution Control Boards (SPCBs) and Environmental Protection Authourities are the prominent governmental institutions made in change of prevention and control of pollution and protection of environment. In order to lend appropriate credence a study of institutional mechanism under spectral environmental statutes is quite germane. No doubt, under the Water Act, the CPB and SPCBc could prevent, control and abate water pollution from the trade effluents, or sewage effluents to be discharged into streams, wells or on land within their respective jurisdictional areas, in exercise of their environmental decision making, as statutory authorities, thereunder but prevention of such pollution is seen, when they refuse to grant consent for starting new industries, operations or processes which are likely to discharge trade and sewage effluents into streams, wells or on land in the concerned state as could result in contamination of its waters[41]. But the same is not happening as regards trade and sewage effluents discharged from existing industries, operations and processes[42], for they appear to have neither the will to do so on their own nor, are they forced to do so, by the central government, in exercise of its powers under the EP Act. by the central government, in exercise of its poweres under the EP Act. However, the orders made by the SPCBs or the CPCB being appealable under the Act, at the instance of an aggrieved party, before an appellate authority[43] to be constituted for the purpose by the concerned state government with a High Court Judge and Two technical members, which could reassess the evidence in the matter, after hearing the parties concerned the orders to be made in appeals by such appellate authority, could be regarded as those subjected to judicial review, by an independent highest environmental decision making authority in the state and could be regarded as orders made in the interests of protection and improvement of country's environment in as much as, such orders could also become the subject of judicial review by the state High Court under its writ jurisdiction or of the Supreme Court under its special leave to appeal jurisdiction.

Similar is the position in respect to matters of air pollution to be caused by the pollutants to be emitted industries, operations or processes in any air pollution control areas of the State under the Air Act[44]. Even the motor and vehicular pollution[45] and noise pollution could be controlled under the Air Act. The Impact assessment to be made on air pollution by the concerned SPCB or CPCB or the appellate authority[46], which sits in judgment over such orders, would be environmental decision making, by those original or appellate Authorities under the Air Act. Such orders are also amenable to review by High Courts under their writ jurisdictions or by the Supreme Court under its special leave jurisdiction.

When it comes to death of or injury to any person or damage to any property or environment, due to any environmental pollution, claims for compensation may be made in courts of ordinary civil jurisdiction against the persons responsible for such pollution. As the Supreme Court of India has recognized the internationally accepted juristic environmental principles, such as, 'polluter pays principle', 'absolute liability principle' and 'reversal of burden of proof principle' and 'doctrine of public trust principle', as those applicable to domestic laws of India, the courts of ordinary civil jurisdiction of the country, can award compensation for the death of or injury to any person or damage to any property or environment, unless they are barred to entertain such claims under the PLI Act. 1991[47] which is in the force or the NETA, 1995[48], which is yet to come into force. The NETA is allegedly rich with global rhetoric, profound humanism and national passion for implementation of the commitment to defend human environment. However, it needs some fundamental changes and democratization. We should facus on tribunals and their people-oriented remedial potential with elements of easy access, least expense facile process early finality and, above all, the availability of independent *pro bono publico* organizations or individuals and specialized mobile delivery system of environmental adjudication. When a bureaucratic elite reluctantly sponsors legislation its allergy to democratic access and processual facility is natural[49].

VI. Judicial Strain

The crisis of environmental governance was severely encountered by the judicial organs of the country. More than a decade ago the Supreme Court of India expressed deep sense of reluctance in resolving complex enviro-legal dispute. Justice P.N. Bhagwati observed that since cases involving issues of environmental pollution, ecological destruction and conflicts over national resources are increasingly coming up for adjudication and these cases involve assessment and evolution of scientific and technical data, it might be desirable to set up environmental court on the regional basis with the professional judge and two experts drawn from the ecological sciences research group[50]. The Court, therefore, urged upon government to set up an ecological science research group consisting of independent professionally competent experts in different branches of science and technology, who would act as an information bank for the court and government department and generate new information according to the particular requirement of the court[51]. In view of proliferation of litigation and intricacies involved in environmental dispute resolution the court in *Indian Council for Enviro-legal Action V. Union of India*[52] experienced great deal of strain in upholding the transparency of environmental governance and confidence of people in the judiciary. The Court's narration to this effect runs as under :

> The experience shows that the prosecutions launched in ordinary Criminal Court under the provisions of the Water Act, Air and Environment Act never reach their conclusion either because of *work-load in those courts or because there is no proper appreciation of the significance of environment matters on the part of those in charge of conducting of these cases*[53]. [emphasis added]

In *Vellore Citizen Welfare Forum V. Union of India*[54], the Court broad based the concept of environmental governance. Speaking through the Court Justice Kuldip Singh emphatically held:

> *The work which is required to be done by an authority in terms of section 3 (3) of Environment Protection Act, 1986 is being done by the apex court and the other courts in the country.* It is high time that the Central Government realizes its responsibility and statutory duty to protect the environment in the country[55]. [emphasis added].

The judicial exhortation regarding fine tuning of environmental governance reached to its culminating point in *A.P. Pollution Control Board* V. *M.V. Nayudu*[56]. The Supreme Court was called upon to adjudicate the scientific and technological opeinion of PCB and other specialized authorities in refusing the approval of location of a hazardous industry in the vicinity of Himyat and Osman Sagar Lakes of Hyderbad[57].

VII. Juristic Exhortation

The Supreme Court in Nayudu's case subscribed to the view that the scientific problems because of increasing specialization of in environmental law and traditional rule of detached wednesbury review needs through appraisal. While environmental law is a permanent feature of the legal science it still defies clear precincts and ought to be developed by judicial decisions and pragmatic approach[58]. The Court is quite conscious about widespread allegations about handling complex science rich cases. A judicial confession of this kind is found with utmost rarity. To quote:

> The expert witnesses on whom the system relies are mercenaries whose biased testimony frequently produces erroneous and inconsistent determinations. If these claims go unanswered, or are not dealt with, confidence in the judiciary will be undermined as the public becomes convinced that the courts as now constituted are incapable of correctly resolving some of the more pressing legal issues of our day[59].

Brian Wynne has rightly remarked that uncertainty inadequancy and indeterminacy are inherent in science[60]. This uncertainty becomes a problem for environmental governance when scientific knowledge is institutionalized in policy making or used as a basis for decision making by agencies and courts. Scientists may refine, modify or discard variable or models when more information is available. However, agencies and courts must make choices based on existing scientific knowledge[61]. The inadequacies of science result from identification of adverse effects of a hazard and then working back wards to find the causes. Secondly, clinical tests are performed, particularly where toxins are involved, on animals and not on humans, that is to day, are based on animals studies or short-term cell testing. Thirdly conclusion based on epidemiological studies are flawed by the scientist's inability to control or even accurately assess past exposure of the subjects[62]. The Indian courts in order to come out of uncertainty syndrome identified polluter-pays principle, doctrine of public trust and adverse burden of proof theory. But it was firmly realized that different environmental statutes provide appeals to appellate authorities but most of them still fall short of a combination of judicial and scientific needs. For example, the qualification of the persons to be appointed as appellate authorities under Section 28 of the *Water Act*, 1974, Section 31 of the *Air Act*, 1981, under Rule 12 of the *Hazardous Wastes (Management and Handing) Rules*, 1989 are not clearly spelled out[63]. In this context, of significant is subtle delineation of principle of environment governance. According to Justice M. Jagannadha Rao:

> Good governance is an accepted principle of international and domestic law. It comprises of the rule of law, effective state institutions, transparency and accountability in public affairs, respect for human rights and the meaningful participation of citizens - (including scientists) - in the political processes of their countries and in decisions affecting their lives[64].

The state is, therefore, implored upon for legislative administrative and institutional revamping by appropriating amendments in the constitution and composition of environmental governing institutions. The judicial sensitivity towards development of principle of environmental governance is also premised on the tender concern to human rights to environment and ecological balance. The Court was of the view that in the context of emerging environmental jurisprudence it is the benign duty of the court to render justice by taking conflicting interests of the society and danger to environmental ecology to promote sustainable development[65]. After all environmental pollution is a public wrong and constitutional tort. The doors of justice must be ajar for any public spirited person, a human rights activists or service minded organisation, to challenge a polluter, secure a remedy for the victim community and even request the setting up of a governing agencies. Sometimes, remedial pluralism, beyond mere money compensation, may be prayed for so that complete environmental justice may be given to the valiant victims and aggrieved persons[66]. When an inspectorate and governing machinery is set up by a special statute for effective and expeditious conflict resolution a broader vision must illumine the law.

VIII. Prognosistic Precept

The woefully under staffed enviro-governing inspectorate and institutional and infrastructural inadequacies resulted into massive deviane and low compliance. In spite of stringent prosecutorial strategies environmental quality has not improved because of many constraints such as a financial squeeze, basic infrastructure, over reliance on litigation, lopsided industrial location policy, inadequate use of economic instruments, poor commitment of corporate sector and absence of relevant technology. The regulaions *per se* have clear objectives, but the economic basis of regulations has been weak[67]. The success rate of compliance of environmental laws is very poor and pendency of cases in extremely high[69]. Secondly, approach of command and control requires a large staff, regulatory expense burden and comprehensive environmental monitoring and inspection system. In an economy which is rapidly expanding, the command and control approach will have a higher cost compared to the market based instrument approach. Environment damage-related charges or emission taxes provide a more effective route to the same ambient quality and also a system of pollution permits. Market-based instruments like proportional emission or discharges provide a more effective alternative to command and control by changing their behaviour through a reduction in the private cost of pollution. The environmental quality can be improved through variety of policy instruments level at national state and the firm level[69].

In view of precipitating crises under liberalization privatization and globalization the crises of environmental governance may spell into horrendous disaster. Since the new economic policy entails high rate of economic growth, the need for greater degree of environmental circumspection and control can hardly be emphasized. To come out of this morass, the major policy and statutory initiative such as environmental quality and auditing report, digitization of natural and pollution generation, environment Impact assessment environmental zoning and atlasing, renovation of environmental liability principles, epidemiological - environmental analyses and pollution source inventory and inculcation of environmental values and education, are generally advanced for effective environmental governance.

Every State should prepare an 'annual environmental quality report' covering current as well as changing status through a network of existing institutions and experts. Preparation and dissemination of such report will help in identifying major environmental concerns in terms of air quality changes, water quality status (stream as well as groundwater), solid wastes, hazardous wastes, loss of sensitive ecosystem, etc. This will also induce awareness among various interest groups. Digitization and inventorisation of natural resources environmental quality and pollution effluents right from the grass root democratic institutions should be carried out through the instrumentality of geographic information systems (GIS).

Environmental impact assessment should be done to assess the variety of environmental options of environmental governance, lifecycle emission assessment, and post project environmental improvement. Internal environmental discipline and self-regulation, preparation of environmental audit statements should cover plant by plant information of compliance of environmental parameters on a monthly basis. This will induce social auditing by public and increase self-regulation. PCBs and industrial enforcement should be asked to prepare a perspective plan to indicate industrial location sites from a long term perspective based on environmental conditions, environmental compatibility, infrastructure support and resource availability consent fee and cess have to be progessively internalized. The resource depletion costs will not only help society to move over to marginal opportunity costs as the preferred resource costing principle but also reducing resource wastage, development of clean technologies. Detailed epidemiological studies may also be undertaken to illustrate the link between environmental quality and disease burden in an objective manner for public scrutiny. Pollution source inventorisation should be followed by the identification of critical locations preparation of compliance schedule, siting procedures reduction of emissions at source through the use of environmental management plans[70]. The rule of law and environmental governance will remain rope of sand and ideally phrased statutes writ in water unless we have the people-oriented, rurally pervasive, public interest propelled justice delivery system and *suo motu* jurisdiction. There is urgent need for deepening democratization of environmental governance pollution control inspectorate and legal regime for the fulfillment of constitutional goal of equity justice and sustainable development of India.

References

1. *See*: Chhatrapati Singh, 'Legal Policy For Environment Protection in India' : in P. Leelakrishnan (ed.) *Law And Environment,* (1992).
2. Upendra Baxi, 'Environmental Law : Limitation And Potential For Liberation' in J. Bandhyopadhyay et al. (ed.) *India's Environment : Crises and Responses,* 307 (1985).
3. Madhva Gadgil and Ram Chandra Guha, 'Towards A Perspective On Environment Movements in India' LIX (1) *Indian Journal of Social Work* 453 (1998).

4. Arundhati Roy, 'The Greater Common Good', XVI (II) *The Frontline,* 4-29 (1999) at 5.
5. Md. Zafar Mahfooz Nomani, 'Law Relating To Environmental Liability & Dispute Redressal : Emergence & Dimension', XI *Aligarh Law Journal,* 85-126 (1996) at 87.
6. Md. Zafar Mahfooz Nomani, 'Environmental Insurance Liability and Industrial Disaster in India: A Study of Therapeutic Perception of Compensatory Justice', XXVII (I) *Indian Bar Review,* 77-102 (2000).
7. *Supra* note 4.
8. Arundhati Roy, The People Vs The Good of Big Dams, *The Times of India,* New Delhi, Oct. 25, 2000 p. 15.
9. *Id* at 8.
10. *Id* at 89.
11. *Id* at 9.
12. Anil Agrawal, 'Whose Government is it Anyway?' *The Hindu Daily : Sunday Magazine,* April 16, 2000 p. 12.
13. Akhileshwar Pathak, 'State, Environment And Law', *The Economic and Political Weekly,* 3138-41 (Dec. 10 1994) at 3141.
14. R. B. Jain and Kanchan Sharma, 'Implementation Machinery For Environmental Protection in India', XXXV (3) *The Journal of Public Administration : Special Number on Environment & Administration,* 405-21 (1989).
15. The analysis of World Bank Study undertaken by Cafer Brandon and Kristen Hommann originally appeared in *Down To Earth Magazine* and reported in *The Pioneer Daily : New Delhi Edition,* Oct. 1, 1996 p.2.
16. Ministry of Environment and Forest, *Policy Statement on Environment and Development,* Para. 1 (1992).
17. B. Bowonder, 'Environmental Management: Redefining Perspectives', *The Hindu Survey of the Environment,* 157-161 (1995) at 157.
18. MD. Zafar Mahfooz Nomani, 'Federalism under Indian

Constitution: A Study of Environmental Law' XXIV (1 & 2) *Indian Bar Review* 203-22 (1997).

19. Md. Zafar Mahfooz Nomani, 'Environmental Protection Under Indian Federalism: A Review of Legal and Institutional Mechanism', XXI (1 & 2) *The Academy Law Review* 145-73 (1997) at 152.

20. Md. Zafar Mahfooz Nomani, 'Enviro-Constitutional Ethos in Right Duty Discourse: Towards The Creation of An Equitable And Sustainable Socio-Legal Order', I (1) *Indian Journal of Environmental Law,* 60-9 (2000) at 63.

21. *Supra* note 25 at 151.

22. *Id* at 154.

23. *Id* at 155.

24. *Id* at 156.

25. Md. Zafar Mahfooz Nomani, 'Laws and Flaws Relating To Conservation of Biological Diversity: A Kaleidoscopic View', 2000 (2) *The Company Law Journal,* J, 20.

26. *Supra* note 19 at 158.

27. Md. Zafar Mahfooz Nomani, 'Environment Poverty And Law: The Symbiotic Relationship' XL VII (2) *The Caratis India Quarterly : Special Issue on Law And Poor,* 24 (1997).

28. *Supra* note 5 at 99-103.

29. Section 2 (a), *The Environment Protection Act,* 1986.

30. *Id* Section 3.

31. *Id* Section 6.

32. *Id* Section 24.

33. *Id* Section 25.

34. *Id* Section 7.

35. *Id* Section 8.

36. *Id* Section 9.

37. Section 11, *The National Environment Appellate Authority Act,* 1997.

38. Justice V. Venkatchalliah, 'Environment Courts And

Authorities—The Indian and Australian Experience', Key Note Address Delivered As ILS Law College, Pune.

39. V.R. Krishna Iyer, 'Environmental Tribunal - II', *The Hindu Daily: New Delhi Education* Feb. 6, (1998) p. 10.

40. *Supra* note 146.

41. Section 24, *The Water (Prevention and Control of Pollution) Act,* 1974.

42. *Id* Section 23.

43. *Id* Section 27 & 28.

44. Section 19, *The Air (Prevention and Control of Pollution) Act,* 1981.

45. *Id* Section 20.

46. *Id* Section 31.

47. Md. Zafar Mahfooz Nomani, 'Towards Creating Mandatory Insurance Liability For Environmental Catastrophe: A Case of Public Liability Insurance Act, 1999 in M.G. Chitkara, XII *Encylopaedia of Ecology, Environment And Pollution,* 121-41 (1998).

48. Md. Zafar Mahfooz Nomani, 'National Environment Tribunal Act: Retrospect And Prospect', 2000 (2) The *Supreme Court Journal,* 53-60.

49. V. R. Krishna Iyer, 'Environmental Tribunal - I', *The Hindu Daily*: *New Delhi Edition,* Feb. 5, (1998) p.10.

50. *M.C. Mehta. V. Union of India,* AIR 1987 SC 965 at 982.

51. *Id* at 981-82.

52. AIR 1996 SC 1446.

53. *Id* at 1469.

54. AIR 1996 SC 2715.

55. *Ibid.*

56. AIR 1999 SC 812.

57. P. Leelakrishnan and N.S. Chandrasekharan, 'Environmental Expertise And Judicial Review : Need For Strategy Shift And Law Reform', LIX (3 & 4) *The Journal of The Indian Law Institute,* 357-67 (1999).

58. Loard Woolf, 'Are The Judiciary Environmentally Myopic?' IV (1) *Journal of Environmental Law,* 1 (1992).
59. *Supra* note 64 at 819.
60. Brian Wynne 'Uncertainty And Environmental Learning', II *Global Environmental Change,* 111 (1992).
61. Charmian Bartor, 'The Status of the Precautionary Principle in Australia', XXII *Harvard Environment Law Review,* 510-11 (1998).
62. *See* : Alyson C. Flournay, 'Scientific Uncertainty in Protective Environmental Decision Making', XV *Harvard Environmental Law Review* 333-35.
63. *Supra* note 64 at 822.
64. Para 22, *Report of the Secretary General on the Work of the Organization,* Official Records of the UN General Assembly, 52 Seesion, Suppl. 1 (A/52/1).
65. *Supra* note 64 at 825.
66. Md. Zafar Mahfooz Nomani, 'The Human Right to Environment in India: Legal Precepts and Judicial Doctrines in Critical Perspective', V (2) *The Asia Pacific Journal of Environmental Law,* 113-134 (2000).
67. *Supra* note 23 at 159.
68. Kailash Thakur, *Environmental Protection Law and Policy in India,* 391 (1994).
69. *Id* 23 at 160.
70. *Id* at 161.

11

Human Rights, Development, and Governance

M.A. Kishore

There is no necessary correlation between development and human rights. Some of the most oppressive regimes have maintained impressive growth rates, while economically stagnant countries have retained an effective social assistance net. Yet the consensus is that a combination of both is a desirable policy objective even if not always implementable.

1. Dimensions of Development

Boutros Boutros-Ghali explores the multiple dimensions of development in his *Agenda for Development* (1994) thus: Peace, the Economy, the Environment, Society and Democracy are interlinked dimensions of development. Peace provides the most secure context for lasting development. A growing economy generates the resources for progress. A protected environment makes development sustainable. Healthy social conditions strengthen the social fabric, reinforcing peace and development. Democracy fosters creativity, good governance and the stability that can maintain progress towards development over time.

The original aims expressed in the UN Charter — Peace, Justice, Human Rights and Development — can all be pursued most effectively within a comprehensive vision, a vision that incorporates, integrates and facilitates progress all along the entire range of development issues.

Development as a Human Right

The right to development is an inalienable human right by virtue of which every human person and all peoples are entitled to participate in, contribute to, and enjoy economic, social, cultural and political development, in which all human rights and fundamental freedoms can by fully realized. The human right to development also implies the full realization of the right of peoples to self-determination, which includes, subject to the relevant provisions of both International Covenants on Human Rights, the exercise of their inalienable right to full sovereignty over all their natural wealth and resources. (Art-1 of the Declaration on the Right to Development).

The human person is the central subject of development and should be the active participant and beneficiary of the right to development. All human beings have a responsibility for development, individually and collectively, taking into account the need for full respect for their human rights and fundamental freedoms as well as their duties to the community, which alone can ensure the free and complete fulfillment of the human being, and they should therefore promote and protect an appropriate political, social and economic order for development. States have the right and the duty to formulate appropriate national development policies that aim at the constant improvement of the well-being of the entire population and of all individuals, on the basis of their active, free and meaningful participation in development and in the fair distribution of the benefits resulting therefrom.

The UN Declaration on the Right to Development was adopted in 1986. In 1993, the World Conference on Human Rights reaffirmed by consensus that the right to development is an integral part of human rights and fundamental freedoms. The adoption of the Declaration marked a turning-point in that it expressed a new way of regarding the very concept of "development" following the failure of national and international development policies, a failure attested to, on the one hand, by the growing poverty of most human beings and, on the other hand, by the increasing concentration of wealth and power in the hands of a few.

In fact, with the adoption of the Declaration on the Right to Development, the international community for the first time questioned the idea that the primary objective of economic activity was to improve economic and financial indicators. Instead it placed human beings, individually and collectively, at the centre of all economic activity, making them both the central subject and principal beneficiary of development. In that connection the Declaration defined development as a comprehensive economic, social, cultural and political process, which aims at the constant improvement of the well-being of the entire population and of all individuals on the basis of their active, free and meaningful participation in development and in the fair distribution of benefits resulting therefrom.

The Declaration on the Right to Development redefined the objective of economic activity, which was no longer geared towards the attainment of human and social objectives through the improvement of the social, economic, political and cultural well-being of individuals, groups and peoples. It also provided that those objectives must be determined by people themselves and that their benefits must be equally distributed. The meaning of development was thus subjective and required effective participation by all in the decisions affecting people's lives. The Declaration insists on a certain number of fundamental human rights principles on which development must be based, including non-discrimination, equality, social justice, self-sufficiency and solidarity.

Mutual Assistance Among States and Collective Responsibility

The right to development implicitly supposes that States will mutually assist each other when external factors impede the effective implementation of human rights. The Declaration stresses that States have the duty to cooperate in order to ensure development and to eliminate obstacles to its realization. They must exercise their rights and discharge their duties in such a way as to promote a new international economic order based on sovereign equality, interdependence, mutual interest and cooperation. The principle of self-determination requires democratization and the establishment of equitable and appropriate international structures open to effective and significant participation by all peoples and all States. This is particularly important in the case of decision-making structures dealing with economic, financial and monetary issues.

In the context of increasing globalization, developed countries have a particular responsibility to create a world economic environment conducive to accelerated and sustainable development. The most powerful States and international agencies bear the primary responsibility for the coordination of macroeconomic policies the create a stable and predictable international environment and to encourage, stimulate and promote viable human development. The multidimensional nature of a concept of development mindful of human rights also implies collective responsibility on the part of the United Nations system as a whole, which demands greater coordination of strategies and programmes, more effective cooperation in the field, ongoing consultation between specialized agencies and improved circulation of information between them.

2. Human Development, Human Rights, and Human Deprivation

The ultimate goal of development is to build human capabilities and enlarge human choices: to create a safe and secure environment where citizens can live with dignity and equality. Until recently the critical links between governance and human development were not sufficiently understood. Increasing a country's GNP is but one of the essential means towards achieving human development. It is now accepted that the main reasons for colossal human deprivation are not just economic. These problems go hand in hand with social and political factors rooted in poor governance.

Human Development in South Asia

The challenge of human development in South Asia continues against the backdrop of rapid political change, large-scale natural disasters, expanding nuclear capabilities, and global economic slow-down. The unfolding consequences of these events have raised fears of the poorest region in the world slipping into even greater poverty, with worsening nutritional, health, and educational outcomes. It is these human development issues which must be at the core of regional policies and actions. Ultimately, the real victims of economic and social turmoil are ordinary people, not governments. (Human Development in South Asia, 1999)

The sheer scale of human deprivation in South Asia is underpinned by the absolute number of people afflicted by poverty. Accounting for nearly half of the total world population living in poverty, over 500 million people in the region suffer from severe deprivation, with little or no access to adequate nutrition, health, housing, water, sanitation, education, and employment. South Asia is the world's poorest, the most illiterate, the most malnourished, the least sensitive to the needs of women and at the same time, the one region where military spending as a proportion of GNP has actually risen since 1987.

Human Deprivation and Crisis of Governance in South Asia

Much has been written about good governance, yet the concept of good governance has so far failed to match the notion of human development. Governance must enable the State, the civil society, and the private sector to further broad-based economic growth and social development.

The World Bank defined Governance as the manner in which power is exercised in the management of a country's economic and social resources. The WB has identified three distinct aspects of governance: 1. The form of political regime, 2. The process by which authority is exercised in the management of a country's economic and social resources for development, and 3. The capacity of governments to design, formulate, and implement policies and discharge functions.

The UNDP views Governance as the exercise of economic, political and administrative authority to manage a country's affairs at all levels. It comprises mechanisms, processes, and institutions through which citizens and groups articulate their interests, exercise their legal rights, meet their obligations, and mediate their differences.

Governance, if it is to promote human development, has to be not just pro-people or people-centered. It has to be owned by the people. Good governance cannot be handed down from above by the elite, however well-meaning, to the people. The people have to shape their own governance. Vulnerable people have to be protected; they have to be saved from humiliation in their daily life. Humane governance promotes a decent society in which the worst off can preserve dignity. Government has to be accountable to people. Every branch of government— executive, legislative, judiciary, bureaucracy, forces of law and order, employees of public services — have to be civil as well as servants.

In South Asia, political democracy has taken root, but the distance between the rulers and the people remains vast. At all levels, those who have public authority, fail to meet the double criteria of civility and service, which the expression, "civil servant", implies. The malaise is due to many causes, low levels of education, bias against women, and minorities, the oppressive legacy of an imperial past, persistence of feudalism and superstition, and the weakness or total absence of institutions which can interpose themselves between the people and their rulers.

Humane Governance

Humane governance is governance, indeed good governance, which is dedicated to securing human development. It requires effective participation of people in state, civil society and, private sector to help build capacities which will meet the basic needs of all people, particularly women, children, and the poor. Humane governance will also ensure that human development is sustainable.

Humane governance is conceptualized in three interlocking dimensions: 1. Good political governance; 2. Good economic governance; and 3. Good civic governance. It is a powerful concept which, if implemented, can help enrich the life of the common people and lay the basis for fairer and more just societies in which human, political, and economic rights of all people are protected and their freedom of choice expanded.

Humane governance is a norm appropriate to all countries, not just to South Asia. It remains an ideal even in mature democracies of the developed countries. But the need for humane governance is most acute in the poor populous democracies of South Asia. Fifty years ago, many countries of South Asia were born in the hope of a better tomorrow. Fifty years later, that tomorrow is yet to come. The challenge to South Asia is the challenge to humane governance.

In terms of purposes, good governance should be judged, above all by success in advancing human development in the broadest sense. The state, or its immediate realization, the government the market, or the society ultimately can have only one purpose—to enhance the well-being of the people who are members of the society citizens of the state or participants in the market. The upsurge of democratic demands in civil societies across the world has clarified the fundamental principles of humane governance. Governance must be a) Seen by people as participatory and in their own interest; b) Conducive to building of a society in which none feel humiliated; and c) Embodied in structures which are transparent and accountable to the people.

South Asia is facing a crisis of governance which if left unchecked could halt the region's democratic progress and economic and social well-being of the teeming millions. The signs of crisis are everywhere. South Asia has emerged by now as one of the most poorly governed regions in the world, with exclusion of the voiceless majority, unstable political regimes and poor economic management. The systems of governance have become unresponsive and irrelevant to the needs and concerns of people. Formal institutions of governance have often bypassed the voiceless majority. These are the unfortunate many who suffer from multiple deprivations on account of their income, creed, gender, or religion. They have not only been excluded from the benefits of growth but have failed to gain political empowerment.

Income disparities in South Asia are one of the largest in the world. All the countries in the region have a dramatic concentration of wealth and power among their richest members. All the groups in society are not equally represented. Women are worst off, contending with exclusionary practices embedded in social structures from the time they are born. In individual countries other groups also feel excluded or even targeted for persecution by governments.

In many South Asian states, democracy is fast turning into an empty rituals; elections are often the only bridge between the state and society. People continually feel excluded from the larger political process through which decisions that directly affect their livelihoods are made. Despite the existence of local governments, the state remains distant. Often, there are no local government elections, local bodies remain under the direct administrative and financial control of higher levels of government, and the scope of local government activities is severely limited.

The concentration and personalization of state power has coincided with a parallel erosion of institutions. The sanctity of the political system rests upon the prevention of individual domination and the separation of power among state institutions that follow the law. South Asia violates both of these conditions. Institutional decay is evident in parliaments that cannot protect peoples' interests, in a civil service that is heavily politicized and unable to provide basic public services, and in a judiciary that fails to deliver social justice to all.

South Asia is replete with examples of poor governance that erodes the capacity of communities and individuals, especially the poor and disadvantaged, to meet their basic human needs. From an inefficient deployment of sources and crippling debt burdens to social divisions drawn on ethnic and sectarian lines, arbitrary law enforcement, and failed political leadership, few regions shoulder governance challenge with the scope and intensity of those found in the south Asian region.

The governments in South Asia need to pursue a set of policies to bring the people back into the process of governance:

States in South Asia need to redirect their priorities. They must refocus their efforts towards the core human developments concerns;

Governments should provide a major stimulus to economic growth; increased role for the private sector; an economy well integrated with the world;

- State institutions have to be revitalized; fair representation to all sections;
- New partnerships between the state and society have to be forged;
- Civil service should be made more efficient by reducing size; Judiciary needs to be independent as well as accessible to people; and
- A concrete plan to combat corruption.

The above reforms cannot take place in the absence of political will, which in turn cannot exist without a combination of a pragmatic understanding of South Asia's needs and an idealistic vision of what the region, which has become so synonymous with deprivation and suffering, could be.

12

e-Governance in India: Genesis and Prognosis

Abdul Matin

I. Introduction

Any discussion on e-Governance entails an understanding of governance in general and good governance in particular. The word 'governance' has multiple meanings. Matin and Mathur (2002), Alam (2002) have attempted in explaining some aspects of its meanings[1]. It may be added that *Good Governance* is a concept that has recently come into regular use in political science, public administration in general and development management in particular. This concept revolves around such concepts as democracy, civil society, popular participation, human rights and social and sustainable development. The 1991 Harare Commonwealth Declaration has committed to the democratic process and institutions which reflect national circumstances, the *rule of law* and the independence of the judiciary, just and honest government, fundamental human rights, including equal rights and opportunities for all citizens, regardless of race, colour, creed or political belief. As a goal and vision to be achieved in time, these intentions remain a fundamental milestone in the development agenda of member countries. *Good Governance* as part of a development process, refers to among other things, participation, transparency and accountability. Within the framework of good governance, political, social and economic priorities are based on a *broad consensus in society*, and that the *voices of the poorest and most vulnerable* are heard in the decision-making processes regarding the allocation of resources. In addition, *good governance* has major implications for equity, poverty and quality of life. In a nutshell, good governance may be defined as comprising the processes and structures that guide political and socio-economic relationships, with particular reference to commitment to democratic values, norms & practices, trusted services and just and honest business (W' O Okot-Uma, 2002: 1). The purpose for good governance according to celebrated authors, statesman and international organizations are as follows. Amartya Sen, John Rawls and George Soros have looked upon "Development of freedom", "Social justice and fairness" and "Global open society" respectively. Mahathir Mohammad has envisaged "Global civilized society". Commonwealth's commitment to the democratic process and institutions, the rule of law and the independence of the judiciary, just and honest government, and fundamental human rights, and UNDP's "Human Development" meticulous measurement reflect relative achievements of its members towards good governance.

II. Conceptual Framework

Electronic Governance[2] (e-Governance also known as Digital Governance) is the effective use of Information and Communication Technology (ICT) to improve the system of governance that is in place, and thus provide better services to the Citizens. Good Governance rests on the pillars of knowledge and recognition of this set of knowledge by the decision-makers. Digitization of this entire set of knowledge within a network which links every individual including the decision-makers and gives democratic freedom to everyone to access and make use of this knowledge paves the way for e-Governance. The widening use of ICT is leading to distributed Knowledge and Power structures. It is changing the political scenes as it is reshaping democracy and the way citizens interact with the Government. With the emergence of pro-active Knowledge Societies, Governments will have no choice but to constantly improvise to bring in greater efficiency, accountability and transparency in their functioning. e-Governance is part of the Government's policy for social inclusion, part of its strategy is to enhance information technology and to help enhance peoples' lives, and this is carried out through the use of: (a) Web publishing, (b) Intranet Development, (c) Promoting citizen access and (d) Email.

e-Governance entails the use of ICTs to improve the efficiency, effectiveness, transparency and accountability of government. e-Government refers to the use by government agencies of ICTs[3] (such as Wide Area Networks, the Internet, and mobile computing) that have the ability to transform relations with citizens/ communities/ businesses, and other components of government. These technologies can serve a variety of different ends: better delivery of government services to citizens / communities, improved interactions with business and industry, citizen empowerment through access to information, or more efficient government management. The resulting benefits may be less corruption, increased transparency, greater convenience, revenue growth, and/ or cost reductions, greater participation, more development of freedom, better social justice and human development. Traditionally, the interaction between a citizen/ communities or business and a government agency took place in a government office. With emerging ICTs, it is possible to locate service centers closer to the clients. Such centers may consist of a service kiosk located close to the client, or the use of a personal computer in the home or office. Thus, e-Governance is the effective use of ICT to improve the system of governance that is in place and provide better services to the community. While e-Government is defined as a mere delivery of government services and information to the public using electronic means. e-governance allows direct participation of constituents in government activities. e-Governance is not just about government web site and e-mail. It is not just about service delivery over the Internet. It is not just about digital access to government information or electronic payments. It is how citizens relate to governments as well as how citizens relate to each other. It will bring forth new concepts of citizenship, both in terms of needs and responsibilities. e-Governance will truly allow citizens to participate in the government decision-making process, reflect their true needs and welfare by utilizing e-Government as a tool. e-Governance will allow ordinary people to constantly interface with the government in both local and central level on various matters. e-Governance may be a high priority for developing countries, as it is the only means of taking IT to the masses.

Thus, e-Governance refers to the processes and structures pertinent to the electronic delivery of government services to the public. It is functionally dependent on the assertion that Government "is branches", namely, comprising Administration, Political, Civil Service, Parliament and Judiciary functions; Government "is levels", namely, comprising Central, Provincial / State / County or Local functionality; and information sharing as a service can be effectuated within and between Governments and between Governments, the Public Sector and the Private Sector. e-Governance may be summarized as providing citizens / communities the choice of when and where they access government information and services. While e-Governance entails the processes used to provide services to the public, e-Government is the tool to accomplish e-Governance. The conceptual framework discussed above has been outlined in figure-1.

Figure 1 : Conceptual Framework for e-Governance

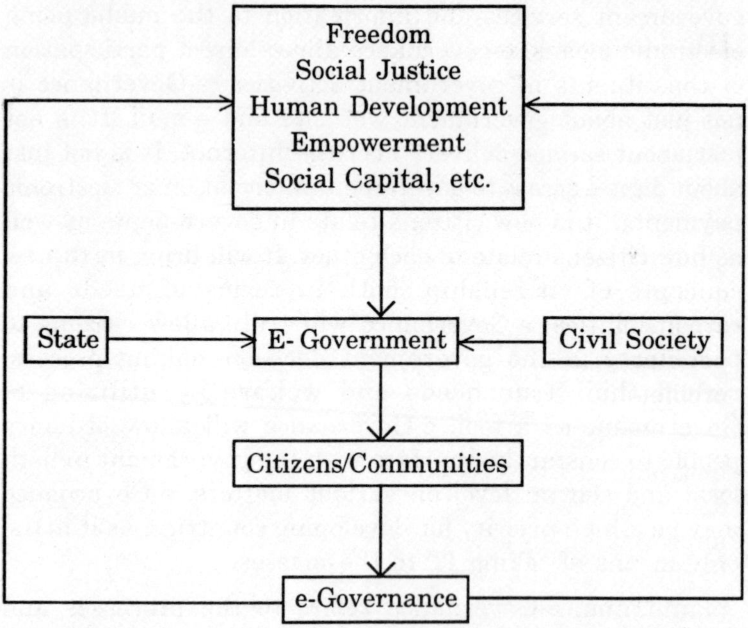

Developments in e-Governance provide opportunities to harness the power of ICT to make the business of governance inexpensive, qualitatively responsive, and truly encompassing. Research studies in the 1990s confirm that "while the full economic impact of ICT cannot be precisely evaluated, its impact has been significant", and also establish the fact that a complementarity relationship exists between ICT and Productivity (i.e. good communication system and information system reinforces commitments to productivity). Davenport (1997) recommends an ecological approach to master information and knowledge environment, as technology alone is not enough for success in information age and depends on information ecology which is the entire information environment of the firm including culture, behaviour and work process, politics, and the technology that is in place. "Trickle-down" and "Trickle-up" processes facilitate development of IT applications for productivity improvement in government.

III. e-Governance in India

Introduction of e-Governance is considered as a high priority agenda in India, as it is considered to be the only means of taking ICT to the "Common Public". Developments in e-Governance provide opportunities to harness the power of ICT to make the business of governance inexpensive, qualitatively responsive, and truly encompassing. Introduction of e-governance is a key to make ICT relevant to ordinary citizens in India where a large number of population are poor and a digital divide is a significant problem[4].

National Informatics Centre (NIC) has been instrumental in steering ICT applications in government departments at Central, State and Districts, facilitating improvement in government services, wider transparency in government functions, and improvement in decentralized planning and management. NIC has played an important role of an "active" catalyst and "facilitator" in informatics development program in Governments at the national, state and district levels, during the last 25 years, and has "reached out into India" during 1985-90 through its NICNET, even before the arrival of "Internet" Technology, to 550 districts of the Country, which is a land of diversity with different types of terrain, various Agro-climatic conditions, different levels of socio-economic conditions, and varied levels of regional development, etc. In 1975, the Government of India strategically decided to take effective steps for development of information systems and utilization of information resources, and also to introduce computer-based decision support system in government ministries and departments to facilitate planning and program implementation to further the growth of economic development and social development. The Central Government was of the view that "development within the government administration" may be used as a "lever for technical development in society" (i.e. Informatics-led Development) as a whole. As a result of this, the Central Government nucleated a high priority plan project NIC under the Electronics Commission / Department of Electronics, in 1976, with the assistance of the UNDP. This strategic decision to overcome "Digital Divide" in Central Government Departments and Ministries, taken during the Fifth Plan Period (i.e. 1972-77), resulted in launching of the Central Government Informatics Development Programme in various Departments and Ministries through NIC. In view of its relevance for all round socio-economic growth (i.e. employment generation and hence poverty reduction), and also to get benefit of the emerging digital economy, the Central Government has created a new Ministry of Information Technology (MIT) by merging the DOE, NIC and Electronics and Software Export Promotion Council in 1999. The NIC is the nodal S&T organization in the Ministry of Information Technology (MIT), for informatics development and networking in government, corporate and cooperative sectors for decision support. NIC has been instrumental in steering ICT applications in Government Departments at Central, State and Districts, facilitating improvement in government services, wider transparency in government functions, and improvement in decentralized planning and management. To facilitate this, NIC has established a nationwide ICT Network - NICNET - with gateway nodes at about 55 Central Government Departments, 35 State/UT Secretariats, and 550 District Collectorates, for IT services. In view of its cost effectiveness, NIC had taken a leading step in establishing "Hub based Wireless Data Network" in many state capitals (Agarthala, Bangalore, Bhuvaneshwar, Calcutta, Chandigarh, Chennai, Delhi, Hyderabad, Jaipur, Lucknow,

Mumbai, and Shillong) in 1997-99 to facilitate high-speed access, ranging from 64 Kbps to 2 Mbps through NICNET (Moni and Vijayaditya, n.d.). In view of the "propensity" for IT-led development in Government, the NIC plays its catalytic role in the area of "informatics for development", which include: (a) e-Governance & e-Commerce, (b) IT Training for Government Employees – IT empowerment, (c) Geographical Information System (GIS), (d) Application of Remote Sensing Data, (e) Network services (Internet, Intranet, & Extranet), (f) Multi-media Information System, (g) Sectoral IT Plans, (h) NICNET Video Conferencing, and (i) Total-IT solution.

The Internet (i.e. network of networks based on TCP/IP communication protocol) is the driving force of convergence of technologies and services industries. Emergence of Information Technology on the national agenda and the announcement of IT policies by various State Governments have recognized the "Convergence of core technologies and e-Governance" as the tool for sustainable development and globalization of economy. In view of its impact on socio-economic development of the Country, the Planning Commission has constituted a Working Group on "Convergence and E-governance". With a purpose to formulate proposals for the Tenth Five Year Plan (2002-07), including the following term of reference: "measures for promotion of e-Governance at various levels of Government".

The Tenth Plan Approach Paper of the Planning Commission calls for an economic growth target of 8% during the Plan Period, with emphasis on second generation reforms, reduction in subsidies and hard economic decisions to raise resources for increased investment and prune non-plan expenditure. The Approach Paper reiterates faster growth is necessary in order to maintain India's position in the World Economy and build upon, in the context of the changing global circumstances and growing aspirations of the People. Public Investment for creation of basic informatics infrastructure with universal access and consequent creation of employment, has been recommended to be realized by allowing every Central Sector Scheme projects and Centrally Sponsored Scheme projects, to utilize up to 2-3% of their annual budget outlay for Information Technology applications for ushering in e-Governance as well as increasing productivity. As compared with the costs faced in building a variety of other infrastructures, the information infrastructure is a remarkably inexpensive way to enhance the productivity of India's economy. A National Information Infrastructure (NII) is evolving as a "network of networks" including such nationwide networks as NICNET, ERNET, HVNet & I-Net, in addition to an extensive Fibre Optic Telecommunication Backbone being set up by Department of Telecommunication (DOT), Railways, and the Private Sector. In order to empower the Common Public, the Government of India (MIT, 2000) envisioned: (a) Internet based Information facilitation for "the Common Public" by various Government Agencies at all levels to be made available by 2005 (IT enabled services). (b) Establishment of about 100 million Internet connections and one million Information Kiosks (i.e. 1-2 connection per village) by 2008 with the participation of private sector and un-organized Sector (self-employed). (c) Promotion of development of Indian Languages Content over Internet. (d) Re-engineering of the Government processes leading to "electronic governance", and (e) Launching of "Mass Compaign on IT Awareness (IT-Yatras)". Impact of IT would be predominant in the social sectors like health, education, judiciary and rural development. Investment in Knowledge based industries is expected to determine India's dominance in this millenium (Moni and Vijayaditya, n.d.).

Public Administration is concerned with the activities of the three branches of Government *viz*. Legislature, Executive and Judiciary, at national level, state level and Grass-root levels (district/sub-district levels) in the Country. Good Governance means providing opportunities and proper delivery of goods and services to the people in a fair, just, effective, responsible and open way. Transparency means openness in the laws, rules and procedures, and the decision-making processes of government and its public institutions. The concept of accountability means government and its institutions must be duty bound to honestly account to the public and the media, in relation to their performance in carrying out their responsibilities.

Information is a vital resource and has its applications in rural, agricultural, social, and industrial development. The extent of the use and application of scientific, technical and social information to advance development determines the progress of a nation. ICT and Informatics Networks are increasingly considered as development tools. Traditionally, the Government is the "major generator" of socio-economic information in India, for their own use as well as for public use. Information collection process in the government departments is a decentralized activity between the Central and various State Governments, as laid down in the Constitution. Transfer of information is considered as a basic requisite for determining the future activities of economic and social development of a country.

As a major step in bringing in e-Governance, NIC implements the following "minimum agenda" of e-Governance, as announced by the Central Government. (1) Internet / Intranet Infrastructure (PCs, Office Productivity Tools, Portals/Vortals on Business of Allocation and Office Procedures) up-to Section Officers level; (2) IT Empowerment of Officers /officials (Training); (3) IT enabled Services; (4) G2G: Government -to-Government Portal; (5) G2B: Government-to-Business Portal; (6) G2C: Government-to-Citizen Portal: Community Information Centre, AGMARKNET Nodes, Passports, Courts, Central Excise & Customs, Land Records, Property Registration, etc.; (7) IT Plans for Sectoral Development; (8) Business Process Re-engineering; (9) Video-Conferencing; (10) Replication of ICT Application: G2C operational at District: Fatehgarh

Sahib (Punjab), Collectorate-2000, ZillaParishad-2001, STAR / CARD / PRISM / PEARL, Ruralsoft, in other States; (11) "India-Image" Portal: G2C Portal to be a state-of-the-art-portal of the Country; (12) G2G Portal, G2B Portal and G2C Portal in Central Government Departments and its Apex Organizations to begin with: (a) Central Excise and Customs, (b) Registrar of Companies, (c) Courts - Supreme Courts, High Courts and District Courts, (d) Passports, (e) Road Transport, (f) Banks and Financial Institutions, (g) Agriculture, (h) Water Resources, (i) Women and Child Development, (j) Health and Family Welfare, (k) Rural Development, (l) Higher Educational Institutions, (m) Industry and Commerce, (n) Energy and (o) Parliament.

Development of an Informatics Model based on "business process re-engineering methodology" and the features of the Information Technology Act 2000 are geared towards getting maximum ROI (Return On Investment). It will increase in productivity and delivery of services in government (i.e. Design and development of an "IT Governance" Model in Government) in the Central Government, State Government and District Administrations. Expansion of NICNET to cover all developmental blocks (6500) is to facilitate G2C access through CIC, in the country.

Major recommendations for the Tenth Plan are as follows. (a) Implementation of minimum agenda on e-Governance at various levels of government by 2005; (b) Implementation of the action plans formulated by the sub-group on "e-Governance" of the main Working Group on "IT for the Masses" (2000) constituted by the Ministry of Information Technology; (c) Allocation of 2-3% of the Non-Plan Expenditure of the Central Government and out of this amount, allocation of 1% as an R&D budget component for S&T projects in ICT applications to facilitate strengthening "e-Governance" ; (d) Identification of National Informatics Centre as the Nodal Agency to implement "e-governance", in view of its expertise in 'e-Government" at various levels of government, since 1975; (e) Strengthening NIC as central Certification Agency (CA) for Government organizations to Issue Digital Certificates for ensuring security, integrity, authenticity and non-repudiation of Information Transactions and prevent impersonification and other frauds. (f) Strengthening of NICNET, which has its nodes in all 550 district administration, 35 state secretariats and about 55 central government departments, with Metaframe System Server based on the emerging IP-anywhere (thereby solving the "last mile" problem) and Open GIS architecture, so as to make the Government Informatics Network (NICNET) delivering services using the state-of-the-art ICT network; (g) Expansion of NICNET infrastructure to sub-district levels (6500 development blocks) for promoting "e-Governance" at various levels of government; (h) Securing a high rate of investment in ICT industries & applications leading to e-Commerce and e-Governance, as the impact of IT would be predominant in the social sectors like health, education, judiciary and rural development, and the primary sector - agriculture (Moni and Vijayaditya, n.d.).

IV. Case Studies

It is evident from the above discussion that e-Government for e-Governance in India have already been initiated. It is too early to comment on the social impact of these developments on the basis of ongoing projects. However, the following case studies are indications of initiatives undertaken in Andhra Pradesh, Rajasthan and Maharasthra. The purpose of the following very brief description of projects is barely to draw attention towards ICT as a reality even in a developing country like India. Because of the space constraint, even necessary details of these projects have been curtailed. Immovable property in rural and urban areas and agricultural land in rural areas are crucial determinants in one's socio-economic background. The system of recording and documenting the changes in land ownership is quite old system. In modern India, the

Registration Act of 1908 and the Indian Stamp Act of 1899 have been regulating the system of recording and documenting the transactions and changes in land ownership in rural and urban areas. The gross revenue derived from stamp duties in Andhra Pradesh in 1997-98 was approximately Rs. 22.11 crores. In this conventional system, the procedure of registration is complex, time consuming and incomprehensible to the majority of the citizens. In the conventional system, the procedure of registration entails 13 odd steps (Satyanarayana, 2000: 78). Sellers /buyers have to undergo the cumbersome procedure and avail the services of the (a) stamp vendors, (b) Document writers, (c) Registration agents and (d) Registration offices. Completion of the entire complex procedures takes 3 days to over 2 weeks time. e-Government in Andhra Pradesh has addressed this issue and the successful implementation of the CARD project has reduced total time to about 3 hour. CARD (Computer-aided Administration of Registration Department) project was launched on 4 November 1998 in Andhra Pradesh with the following seven primary objectives. (a) Demystify the registration process; (b) introduce a transparent system of valuation of properties easily accessible to citizens; (c) bring in speed, efficiency, consistency and reliability; (d) replace the manual system of copying and filing of documents with a sophisticated document management system that uses imaging technology; (e) replace the manual system of indexing, accounting and reporting; (f) introduce electronic document writing; and (g) substantially improve the citizen interface. The CARD project was entirely funded by the Government of Andhra Pradesh. The cost of the project at the time of completion was about 18.5 crores. Two pilot projects were inaugrated on 8 August 1997 and 9 September 1997 respectively in 2 out of the total 214 SROs (Sub-registrar office) with a sanctioned amount of Rs. 23.7 lakhs (Satyanarayana, 2000: 76-93).

India's healthcare system includes a substantial rural system admininstered by the Government of India

(GoI). The system is hierarchical, starting from the health Minister down to community health workers or Auxiliary Nurse Midwives (ANMs). ANMs are the system's direct point of contact with the people. Each ANM is responsible for administering 5,000 persons spread in several villages. ANMs are exclusively women, operating from a sub-Centre, located in or near one of the villages under her charge. The sub-Centre includes her office, with registers and other items required for paper work, dispensing materials, first-aid-materials and other medical supplies. She is not provided with any transportation facility by the government. Her duty is to collect basic demographic data, administer immunization, advise on family welfare and educate people on mother-child health programs. The Indian Healthcare Project began in 1994 as a collaborative effort between the GoI, Apple Computer Inc. and CMC Ltd., India. A study site was selected near Ajmer city in Rajasthan with the following objectives. (a) To provide support tools that would allow ANMs to reduce time spent doing paper work. (b) To increase the accuracy of the data supplied by the ANMs through the healthcare reporting structure. (c) To provide a means for getting healthcare data at the village level into an electronic form, and (d) To provide the ANM with information that helps her to provide more effective service to the villages within her responsibility. The findings of the pilot study are as follows. (a) To provide support tools that would allow ANMs to reduce time spent in paper work. The Newton-based electronic system would help in expediting work. This would not only save hours of tedious labor but also leave her with ample time and energy to devote to the people she serves. (b) To increase the accuracy of data flowing up from the ANMs through the healthcare reporting structure. Although quantitative measures are required, the initial results seem to be promising. Elimination of redundancy and consistency checking would reduce data into the electronic device will actually fit into her daily routine. Maximum time would be saved if she carried the device with her on her rounds and entered the data directly. However, not all ANMs do this even with the paper register system. They often take notes in a diary, which are later transferred to registers in their sub-centre office. The automated report will not only save time and effort for the ANM but also for the supervisor and computer by eliminating laborious hand compilation and calculation, and (d) to provide a means for getting healthcare data at the village level into electronic form. This goal is well served by existing proto-type. The questions need to be addressed are how the solutions will scale over other regions of India? and what efforts the electronic medium will have on roles and relationships within the reporting structure and on significant changes it may make possible for ad hoc analysis, generation of timely information and empowerment of the ANMs for more directed healthcare activities? (Reddy and Graves, 2000: 35-49).

"Warana Wired Village", which is an Joint-venture project of NIC with the Government of Maharashtra and Warana Vibhag Shikshan Mandal, is a "technology solution" of NIC to overcome "last-mile" and "digital divide" problem at the grass-roots levels in India. It is also intended for empowering citizens through "access to information and knowledge (Vijayaditya, 2000: 132-140).

Srinivas (2001) has pointed out in a case study in administrative innovation in Akola district (Maharashtra) that has helped in controlling of black-marketing of the various essential commodities meant for the poor. It has been observed that e-Governance in Public Distribution Outlets (ration shops) in Akola district alone, has saved at least Rs. 50-60 million per annum by making it feasible to cancel about 48 to 50 thousand bogus and duplicate ration cards.

V. Conclusion

It is evident from the above discussion that e-Governance is evolving in India like rest of the world. It is in response to the process of globalization in general and in pursuit of good governance and development in particular. Participation, transparency, accountability, empowerment, freedom, social justice, human development, human rights, social capital have become touchstones for good governance. e-Governance is evolving in response to address these issues. The present state of the art in ICT has made e-Governance feasible where citizens and communities may participate in an unprecedental manner. How far it will succeed depends upon the "political will" of the concerned government and the ideology society evolves for human action and development.

Endnotes

1. Both have been published in this book.
2. At first glance e-government appears to be the application of electronic business concepts and methods to the delivery of government services (e.g., information, benefits, licenses, etc.). However, the literature and other authoritative sources reveal differing definitions. The Deputy Director for the Management, Office of Management and Budget (Clinton administration), defined e-government as follows during recent congressional testimony: E-government involves access to government information and services 24 hours a day, 7 days a week, in a way that is focused on the needs of our citizens and businesses. E-Government relies heavily on agency use of the Internet and other emerging technologies to receive and deliver information and services easily, quickly, efficiently, and inexpensively. The Bush administration provided a broader definition of e-government in its recent strategic budget document, *A Blueprint For New Beginnings: A Responsible Budget for America's Priorities:* By enabling individuals to penetrate the Federal bureaucracy to access information and transact business, the Internet

promises to shift power from a handful of leaders in Washington to individual citizens.The President believes that providing access to information and services is only the first step in e-Government. In order to make Government truly "citizen-centered," agencies will have to work together to consolidate similar functions around the needs of citizens and businesses. The current administration sees e-government as more than just "receiving and delivering information and services." President Bush believes that e-government will provide a capability to restructure the federal bureaucracy and to decentralize power. Looking at the definition provided in the blueprint document one could interpret e-government to be a mix of service information and service delivery coupled with a new form of governance, perhaps e-democracy. The fundamental question then becomes, is e-government narrowly focused on information collection, dissemination and service delivery or is it broader to include traditional forms of western democratic governance (e.g., communication, participation)? Is it useful to distinguish between e-government and e-democracy? Rogers W'O Okot-Uma believes that is worthwhile to make such a distinction: Broadly, Electronic Democracy (eDemocracy) refers to the processes and structures that encompass all forms of electronic communication between Government and the Citizen. In a narrower perspective, e-Democracy refers principally to the processes and structures that encompass all forms of electronic communication between the Electorate and the Elected.

3. For example, in India, the National Task Force on Information Technology & Software Development (1998) recommended the "last mile" linkage either by "fibre optics" or by "radio communication" for IT Applications Services Providers (ASPs), Internet

Services Providers (ISPs), and IT Promotional Organisations, with the aim to "boost efficiency and enhance market integration", through Internet/ Intranet, for sustainable regional development. The logical way to network ever increasing no of housholds is to use the already existing telephone lines, television cables, the electric power lines and the Globally available 2.4 Ghz wireless ISM Band. Using existing telephone wires, Digital Subscriber Lines (DSL) offer speeds upto 8MBPS or more, depending upon the protocol and the distance. Symmetric DSL and Asymmetric DSL are the leading contenders. The CableTV line provides asymmetric bandwidth 2MBPS uplink and 50MBPS downlink on a single TV channel of 6MHz. The U.S. based Media Fusion's Power Line Technology – Advanced Sub Carrier ModulationTM- expects to deliver the signal - at speeds of upto 2.5 gigabits per second (GBPS). With the implementation of IPv6 (IP anywhere), the Bluetooth Technology (2.4GHz ISM Band) may be the mostly used technology of the current decade – to the SOHO (Small Office Home Office) segment.

The Communication Convergence Bill 2000 (CCB-2000) of the Indian Central Government envisages to establish a unified regulatory regime to address the growing technological convergence of tele-communications, datacommunications, internet, satellite and terrestrial broadcasting, cable television, audio broadcasting, and software and content creation. The CCB-2000 defines that "convergence" commonly refers to the provision of different kind of services over the existing infrastructure and the enhancement of existing technologies so as to provide a wide variety of new services viz. Web-casting, Internet Telephony, etc. The CCB-2000 envisages four different service providers namely: (a) Network Infrastructure Facility Provider (NIFP),

(b) Network Service Provider (NSP), (c) Application Service Provider (ASP) and (d) Content ASP. The CCB-2000 facilitates that in the era of convergence, an ASP/Content ASP can utilize the services of any NSP for carrying their application/content.

4. Development economy has witnessed industrial revolution, agricultural revolutions (green–foodgrain, white-milk, yellow-edible oil, blue-fish, and now rainbow), information technology revolution, and bio-technology revolution. Information Technology and Bio-Technology have now become the "drivers" of globalisation of the economy, with their complementarities of liberalisation, privatisation and tighter intellectual property rights[32]. The Tenth Plan Approach Paper of the Planning Commission calls for an economic growth target of 8% during the Plan Period, with emphasis on second generation reforms, reduction in subsidies, and hard economic decisions to raise resources for increased investment and prune non-plan expenditure. The Approach Paper reiterates faster growth is necessary in order to maintain India's position in the World Economy and build upon, in the context of the changing global circumstances and growing aspirations of the People of India.

References and Select Bibliography

Agere, Sam (ed.). 2000. Promoting Good Governance: Principles, Practices and Perspectives. London: Commonwealth Secretariat.

Alam, Aftab. (2002). 'Preface', in Aftab Alam. (ed.) *Crisis of Governance*. Delhi: Raj Publications.

Baark, E. & Heeks, R.B. 1999. 'Donor-funded information technology transfer projects', *Information Technology for Development*, 8(4), 185-197.

Bhatnagar, S. and Robert Schware. (eds.). 2000. *Information and Communication Technology in Development: Cases From India*. New Delhi: Sage Publications.

Bhatnagar, S.C. & Vyas, N. 2001. *Gyandoot: Community-Owned Rural Internet Kiosks*. Washington DC : World Bank. *http://www1.worldbank.org/publicsector/egov/gyandootcs.htm*

British Council. 1999. *Developments in Electronic Governance*. Manchester: British Council.

Cabinet Office. 2000. *e-Government: A Strategic Framework for Public Services in the Information Age*. London: Central IT Unit, Cabinet Office. *http://www. iagchampions.gov.uk/Strategy.htm*

Caffrey, Larry. 1996. (ed.). *Electronic Government in the Information Society*. London: ICA.

Caffrey, Larry. 1998. (ed.). *ICA Information: General Issue*.

Hague, Barry N. and Brian D. Loader (eds.). 1999. *Digital Democracy: Discourse and Decision Making in the Information Age*. London: Routlege.

Heeks, R. 1996. *India's Software Industry*. London: Sage.

Heeks, R. 1999. *Software Strategies in Developing Countries, i-Development*. Working paper no.6, IDPM, University of Manchester. *http://www.man.ac.uk/idpm/di_wp6.htm*

Heeks, R. Forthcoming. 'Public sector information systems management issues', in: *e-Government: An International Text for Public Sector Information Systems*. London: Sage.

Heeks, R.B. 1999. *ICTs, Poverty and Development, i-Development*. Paper no.5, IDPM, University of Manchester. *http://www.man.ac.uk/idpm/idpm_dp.htm*

Heeks, R.B. 2001a. *Reinventing Government in the Information Age*. London: Routledge.

Heeks, R.B. 2001b. *Building e-Governance for Development, i-Government*. Paper no.12, IDPM, University of Manchester. *http://www.man.ac.uk/idpm/idpm_dp.htm*

Heeks, R.B. 2001c. *Understanding e-Governance for Development, i-Government*. Paper no.11, IDPM, University of Manchester. *http://www.man.ac.uk/idpm/idpm_dp.htm*

Heeks, R.B. forthcoming. *e-Government: An International Text on Public Sector Information Systems*. London: Sage.

Matin, A. and P.K.Mathur. (2002). 'Social Stratification in a Crisis: *Conflict, Change and Prospects for Governance in India'*, in Aftab Alam. (ed.) *Crisis of Governance*. New Delhi: Raj Publishers.

Moni, M. and N. Vijayaditya. (n.d.). "Convergence and E-Governance: National Informatics Centre-An Active Catalyst and Facilitator in India". Submitted to the Planning Commission's Working Group on "Convergence and E-Governance" for the formulation of Tenth Five Year Plan (2002-2007). (mimeographed).

Moore, M. 2000. *What Causes Bad Governance?*, Development Studies seminar, University of Manchester, 12 December.

NITC. 2000. *Access, Empowerment and Governance in the Information Age*. Kuala Lumpur: NITC Malaysia Publication.

NITC. 2000. *Governance in an Internetworked World: Towards a Global Civilised Society*. Kuala Lumpur: NITC Malaysia Publication.

Prins, J.E.J. (ed.). 2001. *Designing E-Government: On the Crossroads of Technological Innovation and Institutional Change*. The Hague: Kluwer Law International.

Reddy, Naresh Kumar and Mike Graves. 2000. 'Electronic Support for Rural Healthcare Workers', in S. Bhatnagar and Robert Schware. (eds.). 2000. *Information and Communication Technology in Development: Cases From India*. New Delhi: Sage Publications.

Satyanarayana, J. 2000. 'Computer-aided Registration of Deeds and Stamp Duties', in S. Bhatnagar and Robert Schware. (eds.). 2000. *Information and Communication*

Technology in Development: Cases From India. New Delhi: Sage Publications.

SDNP 2000a. SDNP China Helps to Implement Agenda 21, UNDP, New York. *http://www.sdnp.undp.org/it4dev/stories/china.html*

SDNP (2000b) SDNP Honduras: Civil Society's Information System, UNDP, New York *http://www.sdnp.undp.org/it4dev/stories/honduras.html*

Srinivas, S.V.R. 2001. 'E-Governance in Public Distributive System - The Akola Pattern: A Case Study in Administrative Innovation", *The Indian Journal of Public Administration*, Vol. XLVII, No. 4, pp. 780-783.

Vijayayaditya, N. 2000. 'A Wired Village: The Warana Experiment' in S. Bhatnagar and Robert Schware. (eds.). 2000. *Information and Communication Technology in Development: Cases From India*. New Delhi: Sage Publications.

W'O Okot-Uma, Rogers and Larry Caffrey. (eds.). 2000. *Trusted Services and Public Key Infrastructure*. London: Commonwealth Secretariat. , London.

World Bank (1993) *Turkey: Informatics and Economic Modernization*. Washington DC: World Bank.

DOCUMENT

Action Plan For an Effective and Responsive Government*

Introduction

The Government, both at the Centre and the State, share the concern for ensuring responsive, accountable, transparent, decentralised and people-friendly administration at all levels. There is, however, considerable frustration and dissatisfaction amongst the people, especially the weaker sections of society, about the apathy, irresponsiveness and lack of accountability of public servants, even as the expenditure on staff continues to increase. There is increasing anxiety about growing instances of corruption and criminalisation in public life and administration. The people, particularly the vulnerable, groups, are also greatly concerned about the deterioration in the performance of agencies concerned with law and order and the investigation of offences. Their faith in the registration of offences, their timely investigation and the delivery of prompt justice has been eroded.

* Prepared by Department of Administrative Reforms and Public Grievances, Ministry of Personnel, Public Grievances, New Delhi, Government of India.

Time has come for a strong message to be conveyed that administration is for the people and not for the public servants themseleves. There has to be a change of attitudes, and public servants should realise that efficiency will be measured not in terms of what the services purport to offer, but in terms of public satisfaction. Simultaneously, there has also to be a cleansing of the services and codification of the ethics, value systems and the interface with the politicians.

Necessary corrective steps must be taken to arrest the presen drift in Government and public services, and take urgent measures to restore the faith of the people in the fairness and capacity of administration. With this objective, the Prime Minister had inaugurated a Conference of Chief Secretaries in November, 1996 on 'An Agenda for an Effective and Responsive Administration.' In the Conference, a number of issues were raised which emphasised the need for bringing about a transformation in the public services to make them more efficient, clean, accountable and citizen-friendly. The conclusions of the Conference, which were sent to the State Governments for implementation, are given in Annexure I.

Following the Conference, national debate has been generated throughout the country to elicit views from a wide crossection of people. Responses have been received from retreats organised in Mussoorie and Hyderabad, and number of leading academic institutions in Delhi and other places. Written communications have been received from officials, experts, voluntary agencies, citizens groups, media, etc. Follow up action has been initiated on some of the priority areas to demonstrate the determination of the Government of India for implementing these reforms and to provide models for adoption by the State Governments.

The focus of these discussions has been to evolve a concrete Action Plan, for gearing up the Government machinery to provide a responsive, transperent and clean administration to the people and to address issues of reform and morale in the civil services. The Action Plan proposed to be discussed in the Conference includes initiatives in the following areas:

1. Making administration accountable and citizen-friendly,
2. Ensuring transparency and the right to information, and
3. Taking measures to cleanse and motivate Civil Services.

The adoption and implementation of the proposed Action Plan for an effective and responsive administration would require a strong political will, and reiteration from both the Central and the State Governments of their commitment to provide an accountable and responsive administration. Instances of responsive administration and initiatives taken by the Central and State Governments already are described in the supplementary notes given in Annexure XI.

ACCOUNTABLE AND CITIZEN-FRIENDLY GOVERNMENT

The citizen's perception of the State and its functionaries is primarily based on its role as a service provider, law enforcer and regulator. Improving the quality of administration and providing a responsive interface between the citizen and the public services require initiatives in following areas:

1. Citizens' Charter

The State Governments and the Ministeries/ Departments at the Centre are all involved in some manner or the other, in providing public services. Apart from an overall lack of transparency and accountability in the System, most delivery systems suffer from ad hocism and delaly. It is, therefore, important to identify and publicise the standards of services and time-limits that the public can reasonably expect, particularly in critical activities with a public interface. Government of India has directed Ministeries/Departments and other agencies with public interface to formulate a Citizens' Charter, lay down time-limits and standards for services, avenues of grievance redressal, and put in place monitoring systems and independent scrutiny to ensure implementation of the Charter. A number of Departments have already formulated such Charters. Though the Charter is not proposed to be made justiciable, it would carry a moral commitment of the Government and would provide a framework under which public services can be evaluated. The principles of the Citizens' Charter have been enunciated at Annexure II which the State Government can use to formulate their own charter according to their needs. Some model Citizens' Charters are given in Annexure II for information.

2. Redressal of Public Grievances

The poor record of most public agencies in the area of prompt and effective redressal of public grievances is a major cause of public dissatisfaction and a subject of criticism by the elected representatives. Public grievances primarily arise out of the inaccessibility of officials, failure to even acknowledge applications, non-enforcement of any kind of time-limits, and unsympathetic attitude of officials at various levels. A note highlighting the areas of action is given in Annexure III to enable Central and State Governments to review their existing system of redressal of public grievances, and institute measures not only for streamlining these, but also to monitor the steps taken to improve their efficacy.

3. Decentralisation and Devolution of Powers

Responsive Government would also require complete decentralization of delivery of services through fully empowered elected local Government bodies, both in rural and urban areas, consistent with the spirit of the 73rd and 74th Constitutional Amendments. The Central/State Government need to take steps to strengthen the financial and administrative capacity of the local bodies and vest them with adequate resources and power. A note on the subject is given in Annexure IV.

4. Review of Laws, Regulations and Procedures

In the changing administrative scenario, particularly in the context of economic liberalisation a number of existing laws and regulations have lost their relevance. The laws and regulations militating against the interest of the weaker sections of the society and the poor are required to be urgently amended. Similarly, existing procedures also need to be changed to make the whole process of approvals, sanctions, etc., simpler and transparent. Government of India has initiated a comprehensive exercise for amending the Civil Procedure Code, Company Law and a number of other laws, as well as to reduce the time taken in disposal of cases in civil and criminal courts. It is necessary the State Governments undertake similar exercises in this regard and effect necessary changes in the laws and regulations. A note on the need to review existing laws, regulations and procedures is given in Annexure V.

Transparency and Right to Information

It has been noticed that secrecy and lack of openness in transactions is responsible for corruption in official dealings, apart from being contrary to the spirit of an accountable and democratic Government. Consequently, there is a demand for introductiong greater transparency in the functioning of Government departments and public bodies. There is also a need to ensure to the people an easy access to all information relating to Government operations and Government decisions, as well as that on the performance of the Government, except to the extent specifically excluded by law. It is increasingly realised that, more the effort at secrecy, the greater the chances of abuse of authority by the public functionaries. Therefore, the following two areas/issues need to addressed in this regard:

1. **Transparency in Government and Right to Information**

   There is a widespread consensus on the need to assure freedom of information to the public and to amend such laws that stipulate unnecessary restrictions on free access of the public to information. Government decisions need not be clouded in secrecy, except in the interest of national secrutity. Based on the discussion of an Inter-Ministerial Working Group, a statutory scheme to ensure freedom of information subject to certain safeguards, and to amend a number of central legislations, has been formulated. Details of these are given in the Annexure VI. State Governments could undertake a similar legal exercise, while endorsing the Central initiative, and ensure greater openness in the working of the Government departments, public agencies and elected local bodies, and provide information on procedures for various statutory approvals.

2. **Access to Information**

It is also important to improve the access of the public to information from public offices, through streamlining of internal procedures, computerisation, and by setting up public facilitation counters in offices. It is proposed that all the offices under the Government of India and the Public Sector undertakings will have computerised facilitation/ information counter so that information and assistances is available to the public on various essential services and approvals. The State Governments may consider setting up of similar facilitation counters not only at the municipal and district levels, but also in the various State Directorates. A note on the subject is given in Annexure VII.

Improving the Performance of the Public Services

The civil services in India have played a significant, indeed a critical, role in maintining the integrity of the country and in bringing about major developments in post-independent India. However, in recent times, the services have been facing a grave crisis of identity and role definition. People now believe that public services are meant to benefit government servants and politicians and not the public. The emphasis here is on all publics services which subsume all technical, professional law enforcement and administrative personnel. Though issues relating to efficiency and effectiveness of the administrative personnel. Though issues relating to efficiency and effectiveness of the administrative machinery have been discussed from time to time, the reforms initiated have only dealt with minor procedural changes, without really addressing the issue of improvement in the quality of services. The Government had initiated an exercise to discuss the specific reforms that could be undertaken to improve the image of the services and enhance their effectiveness. The following proposals had emerged in this regard:

1. **Code of Ethics**

   Adoption of the Code of Ethics of public services based on Constitutional principles and values, with appropriate amendments in the existing codes of conduct. Such a code, given in Annexure VIII, not only seeks to regulate the role of the civil servants, but also specifies the relationship between employees in public services and politicians, so that the basic commitment of the civil servants towards the welfare of the public and the principles enshrined in the Constitution is reiterated.

2. **Cleansing the Administration**

   Though the rationale for the civil service in promoting the progress and integrity of the country is as vaild today as before, their is an urgent need to tackle corruption and the increasing erosion of moral values in public life. The recommendations which have emerged in this regard have been collated in the note given in Annexure IX. These, measures, once adopted, would need to be widely publicised to instil public confidence, both in the probity of all political and administrative functionaries, and in prosecution of the corrupt without exception.

3. **Stability of Tenures and Constitution of Civil Services Board**

Frequent and arbitrary transfers of public servants affect the ability of the system to deliver services effectively to the people. It has been seen that implementation of area development programmes and poverty alleviation schemes suffer where the officials are shifted frequently. Since the success of such schemes depends on having officials with sufficient local knowledge and understanding to execute the schemes. Hence, it is felt that arbitrary transfers really operate against the interest of the people. In this context, the note given in Annexure X propose a schemes for state government to constitute high-powered Civil Services Boards to decide on transfers and postings of senior officials, on the same lines as the one already followed by Civil Services Board at the Centre.

Future Action

The above-mentioned package of measures, propesed as a part of the Action Plan on a responsive and accountable administration, would include both a number of one-time actions for immediate consideration, such as the Freedom of Information Act, Citizens' Charter, measures to tackle corruption and grievances redressal; as well as long term and ongoing reforms, such as inculcation of ethical values, objective criteria for transfers and placements, judicial and legal reforms, computerisation, building employees morale and orientation of public functionaries. However, there can be little doubt that any Action Plan is only as good and credible as its level of implementation and monitoring. It is proposed that the Plan itself can be elaborated and operationalised in concrete terms and then pursued individually by the Central and State Governments. The progress under various items of Action plan, would continuously be monitored by the Cabinet Secretary in close consultation with the Chief Secretaries of he various States and Union Territories. The Action Plan would need to be well publicised, not only to secure widespread acceptance and feedback from all the stakeholders, but also to enlist the cooperation of the people in the implementation of the Plan and in its evaluation.

Action Plan

1. Citizens' Charter and an accountable administration,
2. Effective and speedy public grievance redressal system,
3. Empowering elected local bodies in rural and urban areas and decentralised delivery of services,
4. Review of laws, regulations and procedures,
5. Transparency and Right to Information,
6. Access of the public to information from public offices and creation of facilitation counters,
7. Code of Ethics for public services,
8. Tackling corruption and cleansing the administration, and
9. Stability of tenure and scheme for Civil Services Boards.

Annexure-1

Opperative Recommendations of the Conference of Chief Secretaries

The Recommendations of the Conference grouped under three headings: (1) responsive administration, (2) cleansing civil services, and (3) commitment to principles in the Constitution are given in the following paras.

Responsive Administration

1. The crisis in administration calls for a redefinition of the role of government and its function and its real focus to serve the public effectively as much as to ensure efficient and cost-effective administration. Accountability, transparency and cleansing public service are all interconnected issues for ensuring a clean and responsive administration. It is necessary to converge the efforts of various public agencies for delivery of basic services in rural and urban areas and for single-level dealings with the public. This calls for steps to reorganize work procedures, for delegation down the line and an effective management information system accessible to all. Simultaneous steps to address the right-sizing of public services, value for money on public expenditure, restoring, effective audit, monitoring and evaluation, good financial managment system, etc., are needed.

2. It is necessary to introduce greater transparency and openness in the functioning of Government and public bodies. This would cover, for example, movement towards a Right to Information Act, Transparent and well-publicised procedures for approvals by the general public and entrepreneurs under various statutes and regulations for allotment of land and immovable property; systems of assessment, levy and collection of various taxes and charges; award of work tenders for construction and provision of Services; procurement of goods and services; and various arrangements for involvement of private sector in contracting of services; an infrastructure projects by suitable amendment of relevant laws. The aim should be to move towards a citizen-centred administration.

3. The citizens in urban and rural areas should be provided with widespread and easy access—through

the media, posters and various forms of neighbourhood-level communications—to all information relating to Government operations and reverse the undue emphasis on secrecy, details of various Government and local schemes, information on award of tenders and procurement, procedures for identification of beneficiaries under various Government schemes, and for receipt of benefits thereunder, publication of scores for all cases of admission to colleges and for recruitment, delivery of various civil services, etc. The progressive computerisation of information on public operations and work procedures will be of benefit to the government and the people.

4. Accountability should be interpreted in a larger sense in relation to public satisfaction and responsive delivery of services. We may consider the phased introduction of Citizens' Charter for as many service institutions as possible by way of citizens' entitlement to public services, collaboration of consumer organisations and citizen groups-wide publicity to standards of performance, quality, timeliness, cost, etc., for public services, and the provision for periodic and independent scrutiny of performance of the agencies as per set standards.

5. Immediate measures are needed for strengthening the machinery for grievance redressal at all levels, increased thrust on the needs of disadvantaged and vulnerable sections, attention to systemic reforms, meaningful efforts to reach the unserved public-spirited citizen panels to assess service organisations, gender sensitive approach at all levels, and well-understood systems of filing complaints relating to poor services and malfeasance and prompt action thereon, accompanied by close monitoring of delays and punishment of the delinquent while devising ways to filter frivolous complaints. The good examples in different states should be widey

publicised and scaled up along with due recognition for innovation and citizen-friendly attitudes.

6. The fullest possible decentralisation of service delivery and the administration of income support schemes, and effective utilisation of available resources, through the elected urban and rural local bodies, accompanied by the required devolution of powers and resources.

7. Encouragement to the widest possible awareness and participation of citizens and various representative groups in local decision-making, and the implementation of schemes affecting their livelihood and quality of life. The media has an important role to play in this regard.

8. Urgent steps for legal reforms, for access of the citizens to quick and cheap justice, while initiating steps for amendment and simplification of the concern laws and obsolute legislations for introducing simple and speedy procedures. A number of laws and regulations militating against the interest of the poor need to be quickly amended.

Cleansing the Civil Service

1. It is recognised that responsive administration depends on reforms in civil service at all levels, adherence to ethical standards, and basic principles of the Constitution, and a clear understanding of the relationship regulating the civil servants and the politicians. It has to be clearly appreciated that the political executive should concentrate on policy formulation while implementation is left to public services at various levels.

2. The approach to eliminate corruption in public service needs to address prevention, surveillance and deterrent prosecution, and deal ruthlessly with the nexus between criminals and unscrupulous elements. It requires concerted efforts of politicians,

public services and all stakeholders in civil society. The existing procedures for departmental enquiries and vigilance proceeding should be revamped. Rules and legal provisions should be amended to enable immediate and examplary prosecution and removal of corrupt officers without giving them recourse to any political protection. It is necessary to remove the scope for any interference in the prompt prosecution and punishment of corrupt officials. It is necessary to devise systems to break the nexus between politicians, bureaucrats and criminals which has developed in a number of places.

3. The numerous service and conduct rules should be reviewed in order to arrange for the review of the integrity and efficiency of officers at any stage druring the career, and the compulsory retirement of officers of doubtful integrity.

4. Simultaneous with the measures given above, the preventive steps would include not only regulatory reforms to reduce scope for discretion and secrecy at all levels, developmental schemes and approvals.

5. Other in-built steps should include improvment in servivce conditions and right-sizing public services, improving the system of performance appraisal and promotions through transparent procedures, recognised systems of rewards and penalties, consistent action of senior management to support the subordinates in sincere performance of duty according to law and procedures, and in resisting illegal directions. Equal attention in needed to review recruitment procedures, training at induction and subsequent levels, and development of personnel at the operating levels.

Commitment to Principles of the Constitution

1. The Government of India and State Government should draw up a Charter of Ethics and Civil Service

Code for the service, based on fundamental principles of the Indian Constitution such as secularism, equality, impartiality, social justic, attention to the needs of the Weaker sections, rule of law, etc. This code would regulate the role of the legislators and the relationship between civil servants and politicians.

2. It should be agreed that the loyalty of public servants should be only to the service for the public and the rule of law. This is particularly relevant in the context of the permanent character of civil service.

3. State Governments will be requested to devise suitable mechanisms, including a high-powered Civil Service Board, and amend relevant rules for transparent decisions on postings, promotions and transfers of senior officials on the lines of Central Government. Similar Boards should be set up to govern functionaries at lower levels and in elected local bodies. These boards could be strengthened in their apolitical functioning by the oppointment of Civil Servicves Ombudsaman to deal with grievances of officials. It should be recognised that the public suffer equally from frequent trequent transfers of heads of departments. Appropriate legislations may be considered to incorporate some of these suggestions.

Annexure-II

Citizens' Charter and Accountable Administration Scheme

One of the important means of ensuring accountability and transparency in the agencies engaged in providing services to the people, or enforcing laws and regulations, is to organise their actions around the concept of Citizens' Charter. This part of a national movement in countries, like the UK and Malaysia, where it lays out the citizen's entitlement to public services and responsive administration of regulations. It places the citizen at the centre of administration instead of making him a passive recipient of services rendered indifferently with no concern for quality, timeliness or cost. It is to be seen as a visible symbol of accountable government. The Government of India has directed all Ministries, Departments, and agencies under them with a public interface to publish Citizens' Charter, starting with services. The object is to bring all the service rendered by these agencies under the charter over a period of two years.

Citizens' Charter is based on the principles of: (1) wide publicity of standards of performance of public agencies and local bodies; (2) assured quality of service; (3) access to information and courtesy and helpfulness of staff; (4) choice and consultation with the citizens; (5) simplified and convenient procedure for receipt and acknowledgement of complaints, and time-bound redressal of grievances; and (6) the provision for independent scrutiny of performance with the involvement of citizen groups.

While it is not justiciable, it represents the moral and democratic commitment of the government to service of the public.

In order to accomplish this task, it has been directed that each Central Government Department and its public agencies should work out its own Citizens' Charter and related actions in terms of the nature of work and, more importantly, the groups of clients of members of the public, geographical concept, nature of regulatory function and paid-for services. It should also evolve a plan containing both long-term and short-term/moving targets for improved public satisfaction and efficient performance through systems improvement, technological and information inputs, staff orientation, work place changes, use of alternate providers, partnership with citizen groups, voluntary agencies and the corporate sector, etc. An in-built machinery will be set up in each Ministry/Department for independent system auditing and periodic monitoring of performance with reference to the Charter principles and to attend to the capacity-building and orientation of the staff. It is envisaged that consumer organisations, citizen groups, experts, retired public servants, elected representatives and others are involved in this process of formulation and scrutiny of performance so as to ensure that the commitments made actually meet the needs of the people. Once the areas of activities sought to be improved are streamlined, adequate publicity will be given so that the people are made aware of the proposed changes. The entire process will be monitored periodically by a core group under the Cabinet Secretary.

Many Central agencies, such as the Railways, Post, Health, Central Board of Direct Taxes, Central Board of Excise and Customs, Petroleum, Industry, Delhi Development Authority and Passport Office and others have annunced a series of citizen-friendly initiatives. The Ministry of Home Affairs have set up a Task Force to formulate specific steps for a citizen-friendly law enforcement system and crime prevention. It has also announced setting up of a Police Complaints Authority for Delhi. The Central Health Ministry has requested all the State Governments to set up emergency care services in bigger hospitals on the pattern of what has been considered for Delhi, as also a system of registration and rating of nursing homes. State Governments, like Himachal Pradesh, have announced a Citizens' Charter for revenue functionaries.

Proposed Action

The State Governments could consider formulation of Citizens' Charter on the lines indicated above of services provided by various State and local agencies with public interface, such as the Offices of the Collector, Superintendent of Police, Municipal bodies, Zilla Panchayat,

Tehsil and Block Office, Transport Department, Electricity Offices, water supply and sanitation services, etc. Monitoring system similar to those proposed in Government India could be installed to ensure availability of sustained benefits to citizens. The concept of the model office based on computerised counter services will be an important means of implementing the Charter. The close association of citizen groups, elected representatives and media could be considered for success of the venture, and for continuous feedback on performance through independent citizens' panels.

Annexure-III

Effective and Speedy Public Grievance Redressal System

THE POOR record of most public agencies in the area of prompt and effective redressal of public grievances is a major course of public dissatisfaction, and the subject of criticism by elected repesentatives. It is noticed that many of the Government Departments and their subordinate offices, which have substantial public interface/and where large numbers of public are required to go daily, do not display the required orientation to the needs and circumstances of the public, especially the weaker section of society, women and the handicapped.

It is also found that adequate facilities are often not available in the public offices for reception of the public seeking various types of information or with various queries and demands of services, and arrangements for seating the waiting of the public, water supply and sanitation, protection from rain, sun, etc., are insufficient or non-existent in police stations and other public offices which the citizens are required to visit. There are often no display boards relating to information generally desired by the public on the location of offices and facilities, various procedures involved, fees, submission of forms, time taken in disposal, etc. The names of grievance redressal officers are not often widely published, and these officers are also not accessible as stipulated to meet the public.

Apart from lack of facilities and friendly reception, the public grievances primarily arise out of inaccessibility of officials, failure to even acknowledge applications, unwarranted delays and non-enforcement of time limits, lack of information, harassment and activities of middlemen, demand for speed money, ignorance of procedures and forms, and the unsympathetic attitudes of officials at all levels. In big cities, citizens are often required to travel long distances to visit different offices due to lack of decentralised locations at the ward level for providing information on dealing with complaints. The methods for payments of various taxes and service charges are often inconvenient, not suited to the working hours of such members of the public who do not have access to servants. As regards the villagers in dispersed villages throughout the district, they face great problems in approaching the tehsil and district offices for getting copies of records, licenses, payments, applications under various Government schemes, etc.

State Government have instituted systems of time-bound redressal of citizens' grievances, which are often monitored through computers and programmes like Administration to the People in Andhra Pradesh. The district officials are required in many States, like Tripura to visit villages and blocks together periodically in order to listen to the grievances of the people, and redress them on the spot. Janta Darbars are also convened by Ministers.

The progress in respect of disposal of public grievances is being monitored in the Central Governments by the Department of Administrative Reforms and Public Grievances. The Directorate of Public Grievances in the Cabinet Secretariat deals with cases of Individual grievances for Central agencies with a large public interface, and has the power to call officials and the concerned files to give a binding order. Central Ministries like Railways, Posts and Telecommunications have set up Lok Adalats to deal with complaints in the presence of the consumers. There are social audit panels of emminent citizens which look into the quality of services of the Postal and Telecommunications Department. There is an Ombudsman of the commercial banks. The Central Manual of Office Procedure provides for the fixation of time limits for dealing with public grievances, while the Code of Conduct Rules provide for disciplinary action in case of discourteous behaviour or negligence in grievance redressal.

Similar arrangements can be considered at the state level. Apart from cells located in the office of Chief Ministers, as in fact is being done in states like Tamil Nadu, Karnataka and Haryana. This will help in high-level attention to systemic causes of grievances through delegation, decentralisation, flexible norms, simplified procedures, review of forms, etc. The performance review of officials could incorporate attention to grievance redressal and public perception of the services of the agency.

A number of measures could be considered for immediate improvement in the situation. The language and tone of various application forms should be user-friendly, and the forms be widely available in various outlets, including post offices. Every office should display at a prominent place its organisational structure, indicating names of officers and their functions, and location of their rooms. Every public servant should normally by available during working hours to respond to the public in person or on phone. Every application or petition should be acknowledged through standard acknowledgement slips. Time-limits should be fixed for approval or rejection of applications for permits, quotas, certificates and approvals, on the basis of well-publicise and uniformly applied critieria. This should be accompanied by delegation of financial and administratives powers at the operational level and well-enforced standards of accountability. The District Administration should set up mechanisms to contact the people at the local level periodically, specially for remote and inaccessible areas. Senior officials, like Collector and

Superintendent of Police, should not get so overloaded with work or committees that they are unable to devote enough time to meet people regularly and deal with their problems.

The number and periodicity of contact for the people with Government offices would be minimised, and the officers should allow for the flexible needs of the working population. Every department should choose a few priority areas from the citizen's viewpoint for computerisation and allow free access of the citizens to this information in this computer. Finally, every public body should have a well-defined mission statement spelling out standards of service provided to the public, such as garbage removal, water supply to power supply. The officials responsible for good work should be given recognition and reward, and the innovative practices should be widely disseminated.

The real issue, however, is the need to bring about a total change in the attitude of public servants towards redressal of public grievances at all levels and to pin-point responsibility for action on grievance of the people. This is dependent internally on measures to improve their levels of motivation and morale through rewards for good work and punishment for deliberate negligence and through awards for suggestions. The senior officers should constantly supervise the staff at the cutting edge level in police stations, sub-divisions, etc. Every official in public offices should wear name badge.

A demonstrable and effective way of ensuring prompt redressal of public grievances would be through establishment of independent Public Grievances Committees, consisting of eminent citizens. Such Committees can be authorised to inspect the adequacy and functioning of grievance redressal system in various public offices, and report to the Cabinet Secretary (for Central Government) and Chief Secretary of State Government, on actions to remedy the system, and to take firm steps against negligent officials. It is also possible to set up independent watch dog committees at district level to report to State Government on the working of grievance redressal systems. The

Himachal Pradesh Specific Corrupt Practices Act makes the omission on the Part of an officer to discharge his statutory or *bona fide* duty a corrupt practice. Similar enactments or the provisions of draft Karnataka Administrative Procedure Bill could be considered to oblige officials to respond to requests of the public.

Proposed Action

The State Government could consider an urgent review of the system of redressal of public grievances at the State, district, city, block and village levels, and devise arrangements for their sensitive and prompt redressal, and ensure regular independent review of these system. Steps could be taken to fix responsibility in each office for dealing with grievances, for attitudional orientation of officials at all levels, and for continuous monitoring of these redressal systems. This could be integrated with the overall package of measures for responsive administration. The State Government could consider dettong upindependent watchdog committees at the district and city levels to report to high-powered cells in the State Government on the functioning of the local grievance redressal systems, as well as cases of negligence and delay.

Annexure IV

Empowering Elected Local Bodies in Rural and Urban Areas and Decentralised Delivery of Services Context

Responsive administration requires that service delivery and administration of income support schemes are decentralised through the elected local bodies in rural urban areas. This alone make for meaningful democracy, as atriculated in the 73rd and 74th Constitutional Amendments. These Amendments contain the provisions for: regular elections, constituting District Planning Committees, drawing up illustrative list of functions, and establishment of State Finance Commission for assigning commensurate resources to local bodies. The Central and State Governments envisage implementation of all the poverty alleviation schemes and integrated rural development through the panchayats and nagarpalikas. States like Kerala and Andhra Pradesh have made a success of bottom-up planning by providing the help of resource persons to enable Gram Sabhas to prioritise their needs and prepare development plants. Examples abound of support to the widest possible participation of people, women and NGOs in the planning and delivery of services, which also eliminates the delay and costs of bureaucratic intermediation.

At the same time, the agenda of real empowerment of elected local bodies, has largely not gone beyond conforming legislation in most States. Centralised system for Planning and service delivery often through functional agencies, still persist, and the local self-government bodies and the elected functionaries are not enabled to function with adequate control over local functions and resources. The functions for each tier of Panchayati Raj need to be demarcated and commensurate resources provided on the basis of recommendations of State Finance Commission.

The transfer of local function to the elected local bodies will also help in the right-sizing of State Governments, pervaded the former are giving adequate personnel and administrative support. The constitution of District Planning Committees to prepare plans for economic development and social justice, as already done by Kerala, will help to consolidate village and city level plans, based on local priorities and people's contribution. The NDC has already recommended that 41 per cent of the plan resources be set apart for decentralised planning.

The Panchayati Raj Institutions and the Nagarpalikas would also provide an umbrella for the convergence of various sectoral, poverty alleviation and area development programmes at each tier, including schemes focused on women, disadvantaged groups, children, etc. Their involvement in the selection of beneficiaries for various welfare and income support schemes would help to cut down corruption and leakages in these schemes. Madhya

Pradesh and Rajasthan provide examples of the benefits of tranparency in public distribution system, development works, public hearing, etc., with the oversight of Panchayat bodies and local volunteers. As the Approach Paper for the Ninth Plan asserts social audit and transparency in the functioning of Panchayati Raj Institution's is crucial for their growth.

Proposed Action

The Central and State Governments could move purposefully to ensure the effective empowerment of elected local bodies in urban and rural areas, as envisaged in the 73rd and 74th Amendments, through the assignment of all local functions and planning according to the illustrative Lists in the Constitution, accompanied by steps to strengthen their implementation and financial capacity, and the vesting of executive powers in these bodies. The State Government could also take early steps to devolve adequate resources, commensurate with the assigned tasks and decentralised delivery of services, based on the recommendation of State Finance Commissions. The Central and State Governments could encourage and sustain voluntary agencies and people's participation in all the schemes for the delivery of basic services identified in the Conference of Chief Ministers in July, 1996 and in all local development schemes. All village-level schemes could be reoriented and integrated under the Panchayati Raj, and bottom up participatory planning could be encouraged. Cooperatives and similar self-governing systems could be encouraged in all spheres of economy and resource management.

Annexure - V

Review of Laws, Regulations and Procedures

Background

In the course of review of the experience with implementation of various policy changes annouced by the

Government in the context of economic reform and liberalisation of procedures for inflow of foreign investment, it has been found that foreign investors and small and big industrialists alike cite administrative red tape, requirement of multiple approvals, and cumbersome rules and regulations causes of delays and cost escalation, and less than commensurate benefits flowing from policy initiatives attitude of the Government. The effective delivery of services and benefits under various welfare schemes to the public are also frustrated by rigid procedures and archaic laws, apart from insensitive of the officials and unwarranted transaction costs.

It has pointed out that many of the old laws, rules, regulations and procedures in the Central and State Governments have lost their relevance considerably. Many of them not only stand in the way of a responsive administration, but are found to be often operating against the interest of the poor and the marginalised groups. Laws on the subject operated by one or more departments often overlap or conflict with each other, leading to fruitless parallel proceedings. They also increase the cost of transaction and litigation tremendously for the average citizen and subject him to corruption at every stage. The opaqua regulations, however, allow the unscrupulous builders and middleman to break the rules with impunity, sometimes in collusion with the officials.

It is recognised that various State Governments have undertaken detailed exercises to simplify and liberalise various rules and regulations. Many Central Ministeries have also been addressing the issue seriously and a major exercrise for amending various laws affecting economic reform, industries and urban developmennt is under way. The Law Ministery has taken up an exercise for legal reform, having regard to the recommendation of expert committees, to reduce the time taken for disposal of cases in courts, to provide for alternate systems of dispute resolution, to reduce the scope for unnecessary adjournments, facilitate pre-trial conciliation, etc. The

Finance Minister has also announced a series of legal initiatives and review of present laws in the Budget speech.

Central and State Governments could review the regulatory and legal framework in different economic and social sectors to see-whether the objectives for which the regulations were put in place are properly defined, after consultation with affected groups, whether these objectives could be better achieved in any other manner or made more citizen-friendly, whether it is necessary to continue the existing regulations at all, whether the machinery for their implementation is adequate and cost effective, and whether the presumed social and economic benefits of the regulations warrant their continuance. Where there are a number of orders of government on the subject, every Department should bring out a comprehensive government order on the subject every five years. It should also bring out lists of Acts and Regulations implemented by it every five years, along with informative notes in the local language for wide (dissemination).

The review by the States, in turn, could cover the multiplicity of forms and return, and the design of the forms itself, as well as the possibility of making transactions paper-less, as have been tried out by the Central Excise Department in Delhi. It should be possible to receive the applications to various agencies required from an investor or the applicant at one point and help him to secure the clearance of all the agencies. The number of required clearances could be cut down, and the process of approval itself can based much more on self-regulation. Building commencement certificates could be issued by architects, and various certificates could be issued by accredited persons or agencies with severe penalties on the issuing persons for any violation.

Some of the suggested requirements for effective decision making included:

1. Reduction in number of levels and stages (including calling for a number of certificates) through which

decision-making process goes through, so that the Government progressively reposes more faith in the citizens in matters like issue of licences.

2. Delegation of financial power should be in relation to the currect price levels and should be reviewed every three years.

3. It is necessary to review the present provisions of audit and place more emphasis on systems audit to reduce enormous delays due it fear of audit even in trivial matters, disproportionate to the expenditure involved.

4. All public officers should publish handouts in simple local language, the procedures to be followed, the method of filling forms, fees and other requirements, and make them available to the public on demand.

It is possible for the Central and State Governments to work together in this important exercise since it is the essence of more citizen-friendly administration, access to swift justice, reduced corruption, and success of the economic reform process. It will also help to effect savings in the huge time, manpower, and legal costs incurred by central and state governments, and their agencies, in pursuing litigation without any hope of a final result for many years.

Proposed Action

The Central and State Governments could draw upon agenda for priority reform of the legal system and procedures to fracilitate economic reform, reduce obstacles to economic and social activity of the poor and marginalised groups, to enable speedy now of services to target groups in various schemes, to facilitate early approvals under various statues, to provide the people access to swift and inexpensive justice, and to cut down the tendency of cases in criminal and civil courts. A core group of central and state officials and legal experts could be set up to review efforts already taken/under way in this regard, and suggest areas of legal and regulatory amendment/reform to the next meeting of the Chief Minister after wide consultation. Meanwhile, the Central and State Governments could proceed expeditiously with amendments to restrictive laws and procedures, where the proposals are finalised.

Annexure - VI

Transparency and right to Information

Context

There is a political consensus and popular demand for introduction of greater transparency in the functioning of government and public bodies, and widespread and easy access of people to all information relating to Government operations and Government decisions, as well as performance of the Government, except to the extent specifically excluded by law. A new culture of information and helpful attitude, as opposed to secrecy and mystification should pervade all government offices.

It is increasingly realised that, more the effort at secrecy, the greater the chances of abuse of authority by the public functionaries. At the same time, the provisions of Official Secrets Act, 1923, and the Code of Conduct Rules for Government employees prevent most of the information about affairs of Government from being disclosed to the public. The most damaging consequence of the legislation and the Code of Conduct is the generally secretive behaviour which it has encouraged in the civil service, and the denial of items of unclassified information, and the details of development expenditure, to the citizens. The Budget speech of the Chief Minister, Tamil Nadu, mentions that one major reason for occurrence of irregularities is that information leading to decision taken by the officers at various levels do not reach the public.

There have been efforts since 1990 to introduce legislation to ensure Freedom of Information, and to amend the Official Secrets Act. The call for greater transparency and Right to information has been given in a number of States. Some States have issued circulars to ensure the availability to the people of details of development expenditure and inspection of revenue records in public offices, apart from the provision for public hearing. Chief Minister, Andhra Pradesh has announced that a White Paper will soon be issued on giving information to the people. Bilaspur, in Madhya Pradesh, is implementing a transparent public distribution system and recruitment for jobs. The budget speech of the Chief Minister, Tamil Nadu, referes to the proposal of the State Government to enact a law to provide the public Right to Information. According to the Chief Minister, this will enable the public to get details about the schemes of the Government, the works executed by various Departments, the essential commodities supplied to each of the shop under Public Distribution System and pave the way for the people to question the irregularities in the system.

The Government of India set up a working group under the Chairmanship of Shri H.D. Shourie to formulate a Bill for Freedom of Information and amendments to relevant laws for this purpose. Based on the discussions of this Group, a statutory scheme has been formulated to ensure freedom of information subject to certain safeguards in public interest. These are outlined in the Appendix at the end of this Annexure.

Amendments to other Enactments and Rules

Simultaneous with the proposals for enactment of the Freedom of Information Bill, the Government of India is also formulating amendments to Section 5 to the Official Secrets Act, and Sections 123, 124 and 125 of the Indian Evidence Act to bring them in line with the provisions of the new legislation. It is also proposed to amend the relevant sections of the Central Code of Conduct Rules in order to enable Government employees to release information to the public consistent with the provisions of the new legislation. The rules relating to classification of official documents and records are also proposed to be amended suitably.

A detailed exercise could be carried out by an Expert Group to identify various central and State Laws which contain provisions relating to release of information, and propose amendments to bring them in line with the Freedom of Information Act.

Pending action to pass these legislations, detailed instructions could be issued to all the Central Ministeries/ Departments, and agencies and PSUs under them, to introduce greater transparency in their operations, and to ensure widespread and easy access of the public to all unclassified information. This can be followed up by department, specific instructions to be issued and enforced by each department.

Proposed Action

The Central and State Governments could endorse immediate formulation of the Legislation for Freedom of Information on the lines of the statutory scheme, amendments to the relevant provisions of the Official Secrets Act, 1923 and the Indian Evidence Act and other relevant laws. They could process consequential changes in Code of Conduct Rules, Classification of official records, etc. The legislation for Freedom of Information may be introduced in Parliament at the earliest. The administrative arrangements for its implementation may be worked out in three months by a group of Central and State officals and legal experts to be constituted by the Government of India.

In the meantime, the Central and State Government could issue instructions for greater openness in the working of Government departments, public agencies and elected local bodies, and providing information widely on procedures for various statutory approvals, details of allotment of land and property, criteria for assessment and levy of texes, criteria for, and information on, award of work tenders and procurement of goods and services, criteria for and selected lists of, beneficiaries under various Government schemes, building approvals, development expenditure and works, etc. Counters could be set up in public offices of easy and prompt avilability of such information to the public. The employees at all levels could be oriented and directed to be courteous and open in dealing with the public and in the provision of information not prohibited by law.

Appendix

A Statutory scheme for Freedom of Information

Purpose: The statute may be called Freedom of Information Act. It may be enacted by Parliament and shall come into force from a date to be notified in the Gazette. Its purpose would be to progressively provide greater access to information under the control of Government of India, State Government, Union Territories and other governmental agencies and organisations substaintially controlled or funded by the Government (hereafter referred to as public authorities), in order: (a) to promote openness and transparency in administration; (b) to enable fuller and more meaningful participation of the people in making and implementation of policies and programmes affecting the public; and (c) to promote accountability and responsibility in administration.

To fulfil these purposes, the right of access to information would be provided to citizens on the broad principles that: (a) access to information should be the rule and denial of access the exeception; (b) the grounds for denial may be clearly and specifically defined; and (c) there should be a provision for an independent mechanism which provides remedy to applicants against decisions to withhold information.

Scope

The scheme should apply to all Ministries/ Departments of Central/State Governments and their attached and subordinate offices and other bodies, including PSUs and autonomous bodies, substantially funded or controlled by the Government, and local bodies excepting bodies/oganisations, such as intelligence services, that may be specifically exempted from it. So far as the judiciary, Tribunals and such other judicial/quasi-judicial bodies and Parliament/State Legislatures are concerned, the scheme would only cover their administrative/support services with the concurrence of the Chief Justice or the Speaker, as the case may be.

Obligations on Public Authorities

Each public authority should publish periodically, and keep updated information indicating: (1) particulars of its organisation, functions and responsibilities; (2) description of its decision making processes in terms of procedures and powers and responsibilities of its officers and employees; (3) Norms of performance of activities, such as prescribed periods for their processing and completion, physical and financial targets, etc., and the actual achievement with reference to such norm; (4) Classes of records under its control, including the rules, regulations, instructions and lists of manuals, etc., used by its employees for carrying out activities; (5) The facilities provided for access to information; and (6) The name, designation and other relevant particulars of the officer, to be called the Public Information Officer, to whom requests for information may be addressed.

It shall also be the duty of the concerned officers of a public authority to give reasons for decisions—whether administrative or adjudicative—to those affected and to disclose the relevant facts and analyses when major policies or decisions are announced.

Grounds for Refusal of Access in Certain Cases

Access to information may be refused where:

1. The request is too general or of such a nature, that

having regard to the volume of information required to be retrieved or processed for fulfilling it, it would involve disproportionate diversion of the resources of a public authority or would adversely interfere with normal functioning of such authority; provided that, where access is being refused on the ground that the request is too general, it would be the duty of the Public Information Officer in a public authority, to help the requester as far as possible to reframe me this request in such a manner as would facilitate compliance with it;

2. The request relates to information that is required by law or convention to be published at a particular time; and

3. The request relates to information which is already contained in published material available for sale.

Procedure and forms of Access

Each public authority shall appoint officers to be called Public Information Officers in its offices, who should be vested with adequate administrative authority to obtain relevant information within their organisations. While appointing th.se officers, the public authority concerned shall keep in mind the overriding need to provide access to information as conveniently, cheaply and effectively and as close as possible to a citizen's place of residence or business.

It will be the responsibility of the Public Information Officers to deal with requests for access to information and to ensure timely compliance with such requestes where the information being requested for is not being withheld or access is not being refused. The decision whether to accede to requests or not would also be taken by him.

A request under this Scheme should be made in writing and should, as clearly as possible, specify the particulars of the document or record to which access is being sought. Where a citizen cannot, for a valid reason, make a request in writing, the Public Information Officer may either accept an oral request or assist the requester in making a written request.

The Public Information officer shall endeavour to provide access as expeditiously as possible and a decision in the matter should be taken within the maximum period of 30 days from the date of receipt of the request. In case the decision is to refuse access, the grounds for refusal should be clearly indicated, along with a description of the review procedure open to the requester.

In the event it is not possible to respond to a request within the period of 30 days, the period may be extended up to a maximum of another 30 days for reasons to be recorded and communicated to the requester, in writing.

Lack of response from a public authority, within the above mentioned period, shall be deemed to amount to a refusal of request for access to information and the requester shall be entitled to seek recourse to the review procedure.

Access may be provided in one or more of the following forms: (1) A resonable opportunity to inspect records/documents; (2) Supply of copies of documents; or (3) Where the information requested for is stored in computers, a provision of access through terminals or supply of print-outs, etc.

Access should ordinarily be provided in the form it is requested for unless: (1) it would disproportionately divert the resources of a public authority; or (2) would be detrimental to safety or preservation of the record document in question.

Fee

Fees may be charged for access to information and may include an application fee and an additional fee based on the cost of supplying the information, such as cost of research involved in compiling the information and cost of copying, etc. The fee may be waived in the cases where the disclosure can be said to be in the larger public interest.

Exemptions from Disclosure

Disclosure of information may be refused if the information is covered by any of the following categories:

1. Information disclosure of which would prejudicially affect the sovereignty and integrity of India, security of the State, conduct of international relations, including information received in confidence from foreign governments, their agencies or international organisation;
2. Information disclosure of which would prejudically affect the conduct of Centre-State relations, including information received in confidences from a State Government or any of its authorities/ agencies;
3. Information in the nature of Cabinet papers, including papers prepared for submission to Cabinet or submitted to Cabinet, other than the documents whereby such decision are published;
4. Information, other than exelusively factual information, in the nature of internal working papers, such as inter-departmental/intra-departmental notes and correspondence, papers containing advice, opinion, or recommendation for the purpose of deliberative processes in a public authority;
5. Information, disclosure of which would prejudically affect the enforcement of any law, including detection, prevention, investigation or suppression of crime or contravention of any law; or would lead to incitement to an offence; or would prejudically affect the operations of any intelligence organisation to be specified by the Government, or would prejudically effect public safety or the safety of an individual; or would prejudically affect fair trial or adjudication of a pending case; or would reveal the

existence or identity of a confidential record or source of information, or would prejudice future supply of information relating to violation in or contravention of any law;

6. Information, the disclosure of which would prejudically affect the Government's ability to manage the economy or would prejudically affect the legitimate economic and commercial interest of the public authority, or would cause unfair gain or loss to any individual or organisation;

7. Information, the disclosure of which would prejudically affect the management of services under, and operations of public authorities.

8. Information in the nature of trade or commercial secrets or any information having a commercial value, which is likely to prejudically affect the competitive position of a third party provided that, excepting in the case of trade or commercial secrets protected by law, disclosure may be allowed if public interest in such disclosure, outweighs in importance any possible harm or injury to the interest of any such third party;

9. Information, the disclosure of which would not subserve any public interest;

10. Information, the disclosure of which would cause unwarranted invasion of the privileges of an individual; and

11. Information, the disclosure of which may result in the breach of Parlimentary privileges or would amount to violation of an order of a Compctent Court,

Severability

If a request for access to information is refused on the ground that it is in relation to information which is exempted from disclosure, then notwithstanding anything contained in this Act, access may be given to the part of the document which does not contain any information that is exempted from disclosure under this Act and which can reasonably be severed from any part that contains any such information.

Third Party Intervention

Where a public authority intends to disclose information has been supplied in confidence by a third party, or which might contain trade or commercial secrets of a third party, and such disclosure can reasonably be expected to harm the interest of such third party, a notice may be given to it of the intended disclosure and it may be permitted to make a representation within 14 days of the receipt of the above notice, stating reasons why the information should not be disclosed. The public authority shall take such representation into account while taking a decision on the request for information. In the case of information other than trade or commercial secrets protected by law, disclosure may be permitted if public interest outweighs in importanc any possible harm or injury to the interests of the third party.

Internal Review

A requester, whose request for access to information has been rejected by an Information Facilitation Officer, may make an application for review of that decision, to the Head of Department having jurisdiction over the concerned office of the public authority to which the request had been addressed.

The review application shall be disposed of by the concerned Head of Department within 30 days of its receipt. In case the request relates to information in the nature of third party information, the disclosure of which can reasonably expected to cause harm to such third party, the Head of Department shall also send an appropriate notice to such third party affording it the opportunity to make a representation, and shall take into consideration any such representation, if made, while taking a final decision on the review application; provided that, excepting in case of trade or commercial secrets protected by law, disclosure may be permitted if public interest outweighs the expected harm or injury to the interests to any such third party.

A review application may also be made as regards the fee proposed to be charged by the Information Facilitation Officer.

Appeal

The Machinery under the Consumer Protection Act, 1986 may be used as an appellate mechanism with an appeal under the Freedom of Information Act being dealt within the same manner as a complaint under the Consumer Protection Act.

Rules and Regulations

Rules and regulations may be made to carry out the purposes of the Act. They may deal with matters, such as fees and waiver of fees, forms of application for access, review and appeals against decisions to deny access, procedures for review, appeal and other similar matters.

Annual Reports of Public Authorities

All public authorities shall, in their annual reports, include a separte chapter detailing the operation of the Act. The reports may mention, *inter alia,* statistical data including the number of requests for access to information received during the year, the number of refusals along with broad reasons for refusals, the costs incurred in providing access and the fees recovered, details of review applications and appeals and their disposal, etc.

Councial for Freedom of Information

Councils may be set up at National as well as State levels, under the chairmanship of the Ministers in charge of Department of Administrative Reforms with a suitable number of members representing such interests as may be specified, for reviewing the operation of the Act and to advise the Government on making the Act effective, including training and orientation of employees, streamlining procedures, etc.

Review of Other Laws and Rules/ Regulations

There are a number of laws containing provisions which may impinge on disclosure of information which would need to be reviewed and amended to make them consistent with the proposed Freedom of Information Act. For example, the provision of Section 5 of the Official Secrets Act will have to be amended suitably, keeping in view the principles underlying the proposed Freedom of Information Act. Similarly, Sections 123, 124 and 125 of Indian Evidence Act may need to be reviewed. Rule 11 of the Central Civil Services (Conduct) Rules, 1964, and its corresponding provision, *i.e.,* Rule 9 of the All-India Services (Conduct) Rules, 1968 would also need to be amended. Similar action would need to be taken in respect of the relevant rules for the State Civil Services. The Working group on Right to Information and promotion of open and transparent government is looking into some of these aspects. However, a detailed study is required to identify all laws which may have to be revised.

Annexure - VII

Computerised Access of the People to Information from Public Offices and Facilitation Counters

Scheme

An intergral aspect of administrative reforms, both in the short term and in the longer perspective, in related to the speedy and easy access of information to the public on the services and activities of Government and the development of appropriate Management Informations

Systems in Government. There are considerable delays in redressal of grievances and securing access to information, since government department with a public service interface do not have a mechanism to provide information to the citizens across the counter or to deal with their queries and complaints at single point.

This would necessarily involve two areas. The first is related to the development of an appropriate computerised network of information to internally link all offices of Central Government, Telecom or Railways, as well as to integrate Central or State offices for effective information sharing in the cause of services to investors and the public, and more intelligent government. The second aspect would be linked to the need to ensure widespread and easy access of citizens to information at various levels in the Government, and its agencies, as well as the issue of revenue records and certificates, simplified and speedy systems of securing approvals and permits, redressal of grievances, etc., with the help of computers.

The Expert Group set-up by the Government of India is examining these issues. Meanwhile, the Government is studying the legislative amendments or new laws necessary to ensure the legal and transactional acceptability of computerised data transfer and print outs.

It is evident that a significant infrastructure to create a computerised public interface is already available through National Informatics Centre (NIC), which is working closely with the state governments. The district NICNETs are fully operational, and district level NIC coordination Committees have been setup to supplement the Committees at the State Level. NIC has already setup 6,000 data bases and the GISTNIC is providing information on various aspects of the economy and functioning of Government, to which a new section on public services is now proposed to be added. All the districts are proposed to be computerised with NIC help over the next few years, to provide up-to-date information on judgements and the stage of cases, with 150 courts covered already. Many state governments are taking full advantage of the facilities provided by NIC, including the Central Assistance for the computerisation of land records, and have also devised their own systems to computerise procedure information to public, etc. States like Andhra Pradesh are monitoring the movement of files, and implementation of schemes through computres.

As part of the programme to disseminate information on public services to the public, it is proposed to set up citizen information centres on a pilot basis (starting with all State Capitals) through the efforts of the Department of Consumer Affairs and Public Distribution and the involvement of state government. These centres would be run by volutary agencies with assistance from the Consumer Welfare Fund. However, the real help needed by the citizens in terms of securing various services or getting their complaints promptly attended to, besides information on procedures and forms, can be provided only through counters set up in public offices.

The Government of India has decided that all officers of the Government and agencies under it should have a computerise public interface, aimed at dissemination of information to the public for a fee or free of charge. The Central Government Ministries and their agencies would take steps to ensure provision of all unclassified information on procedures and decisions to the public through facilitation counters which should be set up near the reception hall of the Ministeries or offices, similar to the Lakhina model in Maharashtra. These counters would be operated continuously during the day by trained officials with courteous approach, with the capacity to converse in English and the local language, and capable of using computers. The salient features of the facilitation centre are given at the end of this annexure. These counters can be provided with computer counsels to provide instant information on the status of pending cases, waiting lists, etc., and also print out permits and licences across the counter wherever possible.

The State Government could consider similar steps to identify services most frequently required by the people, and set up people facilitation counters in all offices with a public interface in the districts and towns, State Departments, Directorate and Public Utilities. The Central Government could consider supporting the establishment of these counters through help from the NIC training of staff, etc., and ensure delegation of powers and procedural changes for this purpose. The Central and State Governments can jointly work towards providing the people of India in all tehsils, districts and towns so that, over the Ninth Plan period, all the public offices have at least one information and facilitation outlet for the harassed consumers or the applicant. The facility could be extended to the police stations at the same time.

Proposed Action

The State Governments could consider steps to promote widespread and easy access of the people in rural and urban areas to information on public services, details of Government schemes, status of applications, allotments and permits, etc. They could ensure this through a systematic and phased computerisation of administrative operations with the help of NIC, and the emphasis on providing quick information and assistance to the people across the counter for priority services in all offices with public interface. This could be linked with the scheme for public facilitation counters in all government offices.

Appendix

Public Facilitation Centre: Salient Features

— Provide information regarding services, schemes and procedures through brochures, booklets, reports, etc.

— Provide information regarding position of waiting list and applications through computer, screens updated every day, and through computerised query to departmental data base.

— Provide information regarding matters, such as bill payment, registration, land/house allotment, payments, etc., on phone or personally to the public.

— Forms which are to be utilised for various procedures should be available at the Facilitation Centre, even if the processing is to be done elsewhere.

— Receive complaints, issue acknowledgement slips, indication the section dealing with the complaints.

— A sufficiently senior officer is to man the Faciliation Centres with appropriate orientation, capable of speaking English and local language for handling customers, and knowledge of use of computers.

— Time limits and other details be notified through display boards at the Facilitation Centres for completion of various procedures and for disposal of cases.

— Ensure easy accessibility to Facilitation Centres for the customer and average citizen, and publicity regarding the location and hours of access.

— Utilising Interactive Voice System where feasible for enquiry response.

— Benches and fans for the waiting public, especially the old and the handicapped.

Annexure-VIII

Code of Ethics for Public Services

Responsive and clean administration depends, *interalia,* on adherence of the employees in public services to ethical standards and the basic principles of the Constitution, such as secularism, social justice, attention to the needs of weaker sections and vulnerable groups, equality and rule of law.

Both Central and State Governments no doubt have notified regulations governing the conduct of employees in various services which address these issues. However, they are more in the nature of formulations of do's and don'ts, and do not represent a positive statement of values and beliefs that should govern the public and private conduct of civil servants.

Nor do they provide clear directions to the employees on certain issues effecting their morals, motivation, sensitivity, and professional skills, This is relevant at the present juncture, when there is much confusion regarding the desirable service norms for these services, and the rewards from adherence to the highest standards of probity and integrity. There has been support for such a code from both officials and members of the public.

It is in this context that the enclosed Code of Ethics has been formulated. It spells out the employee's obligation to the Government and the Constitution, the right of public comment, conflict of interest, accountability to the public, concern for the value of public assets, release of information, integrative role, professionalism, and teamwork. It clearly brings out the expected behaviour of the employee in case of illegal directions of superiors, the need to refrain than seeking favour from politicians, the principles of responsive administration, supportive role of senior officers, and the role of public services in a secular Constitution wedded to the Rule of Law and Directive Principles of Policy. The Code would apply to all services, generalist and technical. The Government of India proposes to give a legal shape to this code by incorporation it in the Code of Conduct rules for the All India Services and Central Government employees.

Proposed Action

This initiative of the Central Government for assuring values in the public services could be endorsed by the State Government and they could consider enforcing the Code of Ethics as an integral part of the Code of Conduct Regulations for State Services, after appropriate changes to suit local circumstances.

Appendix

Code of Ethics for the Public Services in India

Objective

The objective of Code is to prescribe standards of integrity and conduct that are to apply in the public services. The principles stated below underlie and supplement the rules and laws regulation the public and private conduct of various public services.

Obligation to Government and the Constitution

The Constitutional and administrative role of the Public services is to assist the duly constitued Government, of whatever political colour, in formulating and implementing policies of the Government and in administering the public services under the Central of the Government in the most effective and efficient manner, within the framework of the Indian Constitution.

It is the obligation of every employee in the public services to uphold the Rule of Law and respect for human rights, and to act solely in the public interest while making recommendations or exercising administrative authority. He or she must maintain the highest standards of probity and integrity.

In relation to the general public, employees in the public services should conduct themselves in such a manner that the public feels that the decisions taken or the recommendations made by them are objective and transparent, and are not calculated to promote improper gains for the political party in power, for themselves or for any third party.

Employees in the public services should not seek to frustrate or undermine the policies, decisions and actions taken in the public interest by a duly constituted Government, be declining or abstaining from action which flows from ministerial decision or statutory obligations, Where, following the instruction of the superior authority implementation of such decisions or action would appear to conflict with the exercise of impartial professional judgement, or affect the efficient administration of the department or undertaking, the employee should set out the points of disagreement clearly and courteously in writing to the superior authority, and seek explicit written instruction thereon.

Where an employee in public services has reasonable grounds to believe that he or she is being required by the superior authority to act in a manner which is illegal or against prescribed rules and regulations, or if any legal infringment comes to his or her notice, he or she should decline to implement the instruction. He or she would also have a right to bring the facts to the notice of the Head of Department or the Chief Secretary (Cabinet Secretary in the Central Government) or the Minister. It shall be incumbent on the Chief Secretary (Cabinet Secretary in the Case of Central Government) to examine the issue carefully and advise the Chief Minister) Prime Minister in the case of Central Government) appropriately.

Right of Public Comment

Generally, employees in public services have the same rights of free speech and independence in the conduct of their private affairs as other members of the public. However, they also have a duty not to compromise the Government by public criticism of, or comment on, policies. They should, therefore, ensure that their contribution to any public debate or discussion on such matters maintains the discretion appropriate to the position they hold, and is compatible with the need to maintain a politically neutral Public Service.

Conflict of Interest and Peer Pressure

Employees in public services should refrain from decision in respect of which they have reason to believe that they are calculated to benefit any particular person or party at the expense of the public interest.

Every employee in the public services shall disclose any clash of interest when there is conflict between public interest and private interest, or he or she is likely to benefit from any act of omission or commission while discharging his or her functions.

Employees in public services should be alert to any actual or potential conflict of interest, financial or otherwise, and should disclose this to their superiors, whether the conflict covers them or their family members.

Employees in public services should maintain their independence, dignity and impartiality by not approaching politicians and outsiders in respect of service matters or private benefit, and exercise peer pressure to dissuade those within their own cadre who do so, and to set in motion disciplinary proceedings against such persons. Any such approach on his or her behalf in such matters would be deemed to be at the instance of the employee.

Accountability and Responsiveness to the Public

Consistent with accountability to the superior officers and the Ministers in accordance with Constitutional provisions, employees in the public services should be accessible to the people and practice accountability to them in terms of quality of service, timeliness, courtesy, people orientation, and readiness to encourage participation of, and from partnerships with, citizen groups, for responsive Government.

Employees in the public services should be consistent, equitable and honest in their treatment of the members of the public, with particular care for the weaker sections of society, and should not ever be, or appear to be, unfair or discriminatory. Decisions in pursuit of discretionary powers should be justifiable on the basis of non-arbitrary and objective criteria.

Employees in the public services should accept the obligation to recognise and enforce the citizen's right for speedy redressal of grievances and commit themeslves to provide service of declared quality and standards to the citizens.

Employees in public services should respect the right of the public to information on all Government activities and transactions except where they are debarred from releasing information by provisions of law or valid instructions.

Concern for Value of Public Assets and Funds

Employees in public services should avoid wastage and extravagance, ensure effective and efficient use of public money within their control, and endeavour that the benefits of schemes for disadvantaged and poor sections of society are not wasted or diverted for the benefit of others. They should avoid ostentation and set examples of austerity for others.

Non-Abuse of Official Position

Since employees in public services have a responsibility to take decisions on merits, and they are in a position of trust, they must not use their official position to influence any person to enter into financial or other arrangements with them, or with anyone else. They must not abuse official position to obtain a benefit for themselves or for someone else, in financial or other forms.

Safeguards in Release of Information

Employees in the Public services should not unauthorisedly release information which is not permitted by law, or compromise private or business interests, or the privacy of an individual when such information has been received in confidence. They should not take improper advantage of official information acquired in the course of their work, for unwarranted gain themselves or others.

Integrative Role

Every employee in public services should recognise the integrative role of public services in national development, and resist internal and external attempts to fragment public services and society on caste, communal or religious lines. He or she should cultivate national outlook to rise above sectarian, service, cadre or departmental loyalties.

Continuous Improvement Through Professionalism and Teamwork

It shall be the duty of every employee in the public services to continuously upgrade his or her skills and knowledge, strive for creativity and innovation and nurture values of team working and harmony.

All employees in public services should promote and exhibit public and private conduct in keeping with the appropriate behaviour and standards of excellence and integrity. They should support the juniors in the latter's efforts to resist wrong or illegal directives and in abiding by the Code of Ethics. At the same time, they should reward good work and punish any dereliction of duty or obligations, based on objective and transparent criteria.

Annexure - IX

Tackling Corruption and Cleansing Administration

The Context and Consequence

It is not an exaggeration to talk about corruption in terms of a crisis or a cancer endangering India's society, polity and economy. There has been a distinct increase in transactions in Central and State Governments, where the presence of corruption has been substantiated. Evidence points to an increase of corruption in higher bureaucracy and elected political functionaries, often in collusion or in nexus with criminal elements. Corruption is rampant in administration of welfare schemes, public distribution system, police, revenue and irrigation departments, and several other sectors where people come into contact daily with administration. Corruption at lower levels takes the form of speed money for expediting approvals or providing legitimate services, or bribes for twisting rules. A matter of grave concern in the vertical integration of corruption at various levels of government between officials and politicians and the inability of top functionaries to check the prevalence and growth of corruption. Corruption in public life is of course part of the malaise of black money and erosion of the moral fibre of Indian Society.

The effect of corruption of the economy and public administration in terms of waste, distorted resource allocation, reduced revenues, unfavourable perceptions of foreign inverstors, etc., is obvious. More insidious from the point of view of responsive government and the welfare of the poor, is diluted standards of goods, services and construction, hazards to life and safety of the public from spurious goods, leakage of benefits and subsidies meant for the poor and the denial of fair treatment and justice to people other than those able to access money and influence. That is why there is a strong demand by the public for effective punitive and corrective measures to tackle the problem. This concern is reflected in the manifestoes of all political parties in the 1996 General Election.

The Scheme

The Government of India is committed to integrity and impartiality in public life and clean administration, and to take effective steps to eradicate the evil of corruption. It is determined to pass the legislation for Lok Pal in the current session of Parliament. Along with similar statutory steps by the States, it should be possible to proceed vigorously in cases of allegations against ministers and public functionaries through an independent institution with credibility and assured powers.

Along with this following steps can be considered for investigation and prosecution quickly all cases of corruption and misconduct of officials at all levels and for ensuring swift and exemplary punishment of the guilty:

1. Elimination of corruption in public services should address preventive, surveillance and deterrent punishment, and deal ruthlessly with the nexus of officials with criminal elements and venal political functionaries.

2. Rules and legal provisions should be amended to enable immediate and exemplary prosecution and removal of corrupt officials without recourse to any political protection.

3. There should be no scope in the rules for any interference in prompt prosectuion and punishment of corrupt public servants, and permission for such prosecution should be given within a prescribed period to investigating agencies, like the CBI, where prior approval has been stipulated. At the same time clear norms should be laid down to prevent demoralisation of public servants on account of frivolous complaints or inquiries.

4. The Investigating agencies and vigilance machinery should be strengthened by provision of adequate staff, power, resources and independence, accompanied by proper accountability for results. The preventive aspect of corruption in government or the public sector depends on an independent and well-staffed vigilance set-up.

5. Amendments should be formulated to the relevant rules on the lines of those proposed in the rules relating to All India and central services to provide for the premature retirement of officials at a

reasonably early stage of employees' careers to weed out elements which are either inefficient or of doubtful integrity. It is further necessary to amend the relevant Service Rules to enable the review of integrity and efficiency of officials at any stage during their carreer, and to provide for premature retirement of officers of doubtful integrity in public interest.

6. The existing procedures for departmental enquiries and vigilance proceedings for Central and State Government employees should be revamped in order to ensure their completion within a year. The proposed steps in Central Government include:

(a) Prescribing firm time limits for all the stages from preliminary investigation to issue of chargesheet, to actual enquiry and the issue of final orders of exoneration or punishment.

(b) Ensuring, through training, compliance with all legal requirements of enquiry and opportunity to the defendant so as to avoid procedural infirmities that lead to legal challenge;

(c) Agreeing with Public Service Commission and Chief Vigilance Commissioner on time limits for consultation and advice;

(d) Ensuring adequate number of full-time or part-time inquiry officers, and providing them with adequate incentive and training;

(e) Suspending or transferring to non-sensitive posts those personnel who are being prosecuted or proceeded against departmentally on charges of corruption;

(f) Providing for summary procedures in cases where charges relate to penalties other than removal, dismissal and reduction in rank;

(g) Dealing with deficiencies pointed out by the Courts of Law; and

(h) Making a careful distinction between petty procedural irregularities and substantive misconduct to eliminate the former from detailed inquiries and close such case after recording adverse remaks in the CR, issue of warning or counselling the officer.

7. Attachment and forfeiture of properties (Movable or immovable) acquired by public servants by corrupt or illegal means not only in their own names but also in the names of their relatives and others under their control can be considered, through provision modeled on the Smugglers and Foreign Exchange Manipulators (Forfeiture of Property Act, 1976); and prompt penal action in respect of proven holding of assets disproportionate to known sources of income.

8. Areas of discretion available to various levels of administration should be curtailed to the minimum, along with steps to prevent their arbitrary use. Equally urgent are steps for deregulation, procedural simplification, elimination of unnecessary controls, decentralisation and delegation, monitoring of service delivery through citizen groups, greater transparency in all areas of public interface and corruption prove agencies, and the review of the rules and procedures governing procurements, contracts and extortion, as these would bring down the incidence of speed money on the one hand and extrusions at the decision-making level.

9. Objective and transparent criteria for the transfer and promotion of officials in order to insulate them from political influence in action taken according to law and in public interest.

10. Strengthening role and powers of Audit in the identification of financial and procedural irregularities to be followed by investigation for possible corruption.

11. Close networking of different agencies like Lokpal/ Lok Ayukta, CBI/CVO, Income Tax Authorities, Enforcement Directorate and CAG in terms of sharing of information and intelligence, and coordinated investigations.
12. Encouraging adoption of Code of Ethics not only by civil servants but also all public functionaries, media, professionals, and the corporate sector based on constitutional principles and moral values.
13. Assuring adequate remuneration, congenial working conditions and access to housing and health care for the employees.
14. Mobilising public opinion against corruption, increasing awareness of avenues of complains and investigation, and supporting efforts of citizen groups, media and NGOs in this respect.
15. Encouraging officials at all levels to bring irregularities or suspected corruption to the notice of the Chief Secretary, and to reward such officials in cases where the fraud reported by them are established.

Points for Decision

The Central and State Governments could draw up, adopt and implement the measures suggested above consistently and effectively, with an agenda of long-term and short-term actions, and based on total coordination of Central and State agencies and the CAG. The Lok Ayuktas could be adequately empowered and resourced to deal effectively with all cases or allegation of corruption. The efforts could be centred on immediate and exemplary prosecution and removal of corrupt officials without any political protection, while supporting honest and competent employees. The agenda could be monitored regularly by the Prime Minister/Chief Minister, Cabinet Secretary/ Chief Secretary and the results would be widely publicised so as to instil public confidence in the probity of all political and administrative functionaries.

Annexure - X

Stability of Tenure and a Scheme for Civil Services Boards

Background

It is not sufficiently realised that the effective and people-friendly administration of various policies and schemes of the Government, and the responsive delivery of services; depend critically on the stability of tenure of senior officials incharge of the programmes, and enforcement of laws. The responsivencess of a civil servant, and his capacity for evenhanded treatment of all sections of the public, depends to a substantial extent, on the degree to which he or she has a sense of continuity in the official position and does not feel threatened by the risk of premature transfer or any punishment for even-handed administration. The effectiveness of public administration in the states suffers from the ease with which tenures of officials serving in the field either in the regulatory or development field are cut short, leaving the officials demoralised, the public dissatisfied, and with the credibility of the Government seriously eroded. The public in fact perceives such actions as reflective of an unholy nexus between undesirable elements among politicians and civil servants. To impart stability to tenures of officers at the cutting edge of field administration, like District Magistrates, Superintendents of Police, Heads of Departments, etc., would not only help the officers to deepen their knowledge and experience, but also help the public to receive the services expected of the civil services with expedition and efficiency. The consequences of irrational and abrupt transfers are manifold. Most importantly, they result in unstable, short tenures, leading to frustration and demoralisation; the 'partiality' and 'objectivity' of the officer comes under strain; building up of experience-based expertise is prevented; and ultimately, the task or the job is prevented from being performed and thereby, the Government's objectivities are to that extent, not attained. Different individuals react differently to the situation described above. A few resist firmly and pay the price; some offer passive resistance and try to do their best; what is worrisome is that an increasingly large number give in and reap the rewards of compliance. The major casualty is, of course, the total system.

While the conduct Rules provide for various opportunities to the officials in respect of proceedings of suspension, demotion, dismissal and minor penalties, they do not enjoy such safeguards as regards unjustified transfers. It is quite commonplace in several states to see mass transfers of senior officials at the district and secretarial level wherever there is a change of Government or leadership. It is often the case that the legitimate hierarchy for effecting the transfer and promotion of various officials is marginalised in favour of extra Constitutional systems based on extraneous influences. Consequently, not only is the ability and authority of the superior officials in enforcing complaint action in the public interest by subordinate officials eroded, they become incapable of ensuring effective and responsive administration through lower level functionaries. At the same time, the sytem should provide for weeding out the non-performers on the basis of objective criteria.

The demand for stability of tenure and objective criteria for transfers and promotions is not only an element of motivation and efficient performance of civil servants, but is a matter of great concern for the public at large. It is seen that, when an official with sufficient knowledge of the district or city or the department is available for a sufficiently long time to formulate policies, and implement schemes of poverty alleviation and the seven basic services in response to people's needs, effective governance is visible, especially in the context of the decentralisation of powers at the local level. This is seen from examples of excellent initiatives in this regard in districts or cities from officers with a long tenure and rapport with the citizens and their representatives, and the low level of development and utilisation of funds in districts or cities witnessing frequent rotation of officers. Further, the people can expect to receive fair, equitable treatment, unaffected by considerations of speed money or other benefits, only if the official is encouraged to have the courage and confidence to take decision without fear or favour, or the penalty of premature transfer. These considerations are equally valid for the police and law enforcement agencies.

There has been a long-felt need for creation of an institutional arrangement for better personnel management at the state level. The Administrative Reform Commission in its report on State Administration in November 1969 had also felt the need for setting up an Establishment Board in each state for proper management of selection and posting for posts of the level of Under Secretary and above in the State Secretariats and field organisation. The matter has also been taken up in the Conference of Chief Secretaries held on the November 20, 1996. It had been concluded that the State Government could be requested to devise suitable mechanisms, including establishment of a high powered civil services board, and amend relevant rules for enabling transparent decisions on postings, promotions and transfers of senior officials on the lines of Central Government.

Such an institutional arrangement already exists in Government of India in the form of the Central Staffing Scheme. Under the Central Staffing Scheme of the Government of India, the Appointments Committee of the Cabinet (ACC) is empowered to take decision in respect of selection and appointments of officers to Secretarial posts of and above the rank of Under Secretary to Government of India and certain important non-secretarial posts as also on various other related issue of personnel management. In this respect, ACC is assisted and advised by the Civil Services Board and the Central Establishment Board constituted therefor.

Though a complete transplant of the Central Staffing Scheme to the states is neither feasible nor desirable, it is suggested that the State Governments could consider initiating similar institutional arrangement. The true potential of the senior officials can be properly utilised for better management and development of the State. In this respect, guidelines for setting up the proposed Civil Services Board and its functions are enclosed herewith as Appendix.

These guidelines can become truly operative and generate credibility and morale in the civil services and the public only if Government employees are not permitted to bring political or other extraneous pressure to bear on the Government or on the transferring authorities for transfers and promotions. This issue is addressed in the Code of Ethics. Any employee, who brings such pressures should be liable for disciplinary action and in such cases strict punishment should be awarded. Such action should be initiated also in cases where references are received by Heads of Departments from outside agencies including political functionaries and members of the public as well as bureaucrats for effecting transfers. It could be ensured that these guidelines are seen as carrying the authority of the Chief Minister so that a proper message goes down the entire system.

Proposed Action

The State Governments could consider adoption of the above mentioned scheme for setting up Civil Services Board with the proposed functions, for recommending to the Chief Minister proposals on the transfer, promotion and placement of senior officials other than the Chief Secretary, DG of Police, and Chief Conservator of Forests, and for recommending action on grievances of officers, such as premature transfers or undue political pressure.

Appendix

Scheme for Civil Services Board

The proposed scheme will not apply to top functionaries like the Chief Secretary, Director General of

Police and Chief Conservator of Forests who shall be apoointed by the Chief Minister as at persent.

The State Government may set up a Civil Services Board, charged with the responsibility of recommending to the Government transfers and postings of all officers of and above the rank of Joint Secretary in the State Secretariat, apart from Heads of Departments, Additional Heads of Departments, Divisional Commissioners, Financial Commissioners, Collectors/District Magistrates and District Superintendents of Police. The Board could comprise the following: (1) Chief Secretary—Chairman: (2) One officer of the rank and status of Additional Chief Secretary (preferably the seniormost) or Chairman of the Board of Revenue or the senior-most Financial Commissioner as the case may be in a State—Member: and (3) Secretary DOPT or Secretary, Appointments, GAD, as the case may be in State—Member-Secretary.

The Home Secretary and DG of Police could be associated while considering matters relating to appointments at the level of DIG and above in the Home Department. The Secretary, Forest Department and the Principal CCF could be associated in connection with matters relating to the Conservator of Forests and above. Similarly, the Secretary of the Administrative Department concerned could be associated, as a special invitee, when a proposal concerning the Head of the Department or an Additional Head of that Department is being considered by the Board.

The Board's functions could be as under: (1) To recommend a panel of name for appointments to all posts mentioned in second paragraph above; (2) to recommend All India Services officers and State service officers for their promotions as well as short and long-term training within and outside the country; (3) to advise the Government on personnel policy, especially career management of AIS officers and other State Civil Service officers; (4) To make proposals on transfers of such Officers; and (5) To entertain appeals of officers against premature transfers and other grievances and submit the same with the Board's views to the Chief Minister.

The Board should meet on a pre-determined day of the week.

The merits of the suggested system would be: (1) Ensure more responsive and citizen-friendly administration, and effective execution of development schemes and programmes of poverty alleviation and welfare of weaker sections; (2) Appointments and promotions would be made after due consideration of all relevant factors and would be governed by the collective wisdom of the Board, while leaving the final decision to the political executive; (3) It would, over a period of time, make possible much greater accountability of officers in terms of performance and service to the people as, in the envisaged system, minimum tenures, say of two to five years or as per the norm prescribed by the Government; (4) Over time, with experience of the working of this system, more attention would begin to be paid to cadre management and career planning; and (5) The civil service and the public would benefit from the presence of officials who are impartial and committed to the values enshrined in the Constitution.

Any premature transfer before completion of prescribed tenure should be based on sound administrative grounds to be spelt out in the transfer order itself. Such premature transfer may be deemed to be a minor penalty, so that the officers have a right to appeal against such orders if they feel aggrieved, and summary procedures can deal with the situation.

In view of the importance of ensuring public confidence in the integrity and impartiality of the process of recruitment of candidates for public service, the selection of Chairman/Members of Public Service Commissions and Service Selection Boards should be done on the basis of recommendations of a similar committee.

Above all, there needs to be an agreement at the level of both the political executive and the top officials that the instrument of transfer should not be allowed to be misused by the civil servants or the politicians in power; nor should the power be vested in persons other than the constituted authorities of Government. As a matter of policy, extension of service should not be given to any employee.

With the increasing numbers of district development and municipal cadres, institutionalised and transparent systems of placement and career planning appear to be necessary to supplement this. The Government should continue the present practice of rotation in sensitive posts. Consideration for posting at the place of posting of the spouse, attention to the needs of women and the handicapped, etc.

Annexure-XI

Supplementary Notes on Initatives Taken on Action Plan and Responsive Administration Government of India on Action Plan

The Government of India has taken following initiatives on Action Plan:

1. Constitution of Working Group on Right to Information and Transparency to draft legislative proposals.
2. Steps to initiate formulation of Citizen's Charter by a number of Central Ministries and Departments with public interface, and introduction of various citizen-friendly procedures and decentralised services by Railways, Posts, Telecom, Petrolem Ministry, Customs and Excise, Income Tax, etc.
3. Constitution of an Expert Group for Drawing up short-term and long-term plans for computerisation of Government operations and provision of services to the public, and steps already taken for computerisation in many Ministries.
4. Central scheme for computerisation for land records, digitisation of village cadastral maps, and

consolidation of land holdings, with substantial benefits to cultivators, revenue administration, agricultural operations, etc.

5. Announcement of constitution of an independent Public Grievance Commission, as well as Police Complaints Authority for Delhi, speedy redressal of grievances relating to the Police on the one hand, and all the public utilities and departments of the Government of National Capital Territory of Delhi on the other. The Ministry of Home Affairs has set up a High-Level Committee with state representatives to examine various aspects relating to a more responsive administration, citizen awareness of their rights, modification to existing laws, etc., and to make recommendations in three months.

6. Operation of the Directorate of Public Grievances in the Cabinet Secretariat to entertain and decide finally on grievances relating to Central departments and agencies with a large public interface, such as telecommunications, passports, and insurance.

7. Introduction of a pilot scheme by the Department of Consumer Affairs and PDS to set up citizen information centres in selected cities, to be run by voluntary agencies, with links to the Public Services menu on the GISTNIC.

8. Support to national and state training institutions for training of officials at various levels in the emerging areas of economic reform, decentralisation, delivery of basic services, gender development, health care, primary education. AIDS contol, nutrition, etc.

9. Operation of Staff Adalats in Railways, Posts and Telecom for continuous attention to the problems and grievances of the staff.

10. Operation of Lok Adalats in Telecom, Posts, etc., for satisfactory settlement of the problems of the people

and consumers by face-to-face interaction; and working of Social Audit panels, composed of eminent citizens, to listen to people's views and suggest improvement in the Posts and Telecom.

11. Approval for the use of the Local Development Fund with M.P.'s for the installation of citizen Radio in village Panchayats, public transport, etc., to provide emergency communication and two-way messages to the public.

12. Initiatives of the Ministry of Health and Family Welfare for upgradation of emergency facilities in major Central Government Hospitals in Delhi, a system for regulation of private nursing homes through peer groups; the mobilisation of community participation and consumer awareness for safe food and drugs; and linkage of PHC's to extend secondary health-care services to the people in rural areas.

13. Formulation of a Code of Ethics for employees in public services.

14. Formulation of specific steps for streamlining the system of departmental enquiries and vigilance proceedings.

15. Steps for strict action against corruption and for integrity in public servants at all levels as, signified by the introduction of Lok Pal Bill in Parliament.

16. Constitution of an Efficiency Unit in the Cabinet Secretariat to undertake continuous exercise for delineation of Government functions, departmental re-structuring, procedural reforms, etc.

Initiatives on Responsive Administration

A number of initiatives have been taken by the State Governments and Central Government agencies in respect of responsive administration in recent years. These deserve to be studied and scaled up in the Central and State Governments as a whole, utilising wherever possible available funds in sectoral programmes. These need to be linked to the decentralised delivery of services through elected local bodies on the following lines:

1. Improved sanitation and garbage collection with people's involvement in a number of cities like Surat, Pune and Chennai;
2. Taking grievance redressal to the people through mass contact and Lok Adalats at the village and neighbourhood levels;
3. Mass mobilisation schemes, such as *Janmabhoomi* and "Administration Going to the People" in Andhra Pradesh, bottom-up planning in Kerala, mass literacy compaigns etc.;
4. Computerisation land records and other information, and people-friendly revenue administration in a number of districts;
5. Giving one life-time certificate to the people as done in Andhra Pradesh by incorporating birth, nativity and caste certificates;
6. Setting up service counters for instant information and relief to the citizens in a number of Central Government Departments, like the Passport, Railways, Posts as well as the offices of Collectors;
7. Ensuring transparency and Right to Information to the people including making a provision for public hearings as done in States like Rajasthan and Madhya Pradesh, association of neighbourhood groups and citizen bodies in the planning and implementation of welfare schemes, planning and implementation of poverty alleviation and housing schemes, and empowerment of resident welfare groups as done in cities like Bangalore and Pune;
8. Establishing partnerships with voluntary agancies for health, nutrition and other schemes, and setting examples of inducting support from corporate sector;
9. Developing an innovative role of the AIR for grievance redressal as done in UP.

The Central and State Government may take concerted measures for improved quality of administration and responsive services and schemes for the citizens through a package of multifaceted initiatives all of which will together help to promote accountable and people-friendly government. These may include the following:

1. Wider accountability of all public servants for people-satisfaction and delivery of services according to a Citizens' Charter similar public statement of departmental goals.
2. Fullest possible decentralisation of service delivery, income support schemes and welfare activities through empowerment of elected rural and urban local bodies, accompanied by appropriate devolution of powers and resources in terms of the spirit and provisions of the 73rd and 74th Constitutional Amendments.
3. Encouragement to the widest possible awareness and participation of citizens and representative groups and voluntary agencies in the formation and implementation of schemes as already envisaged in ongoing sectoral schemes and in the Five Years Plan document.
4. Simplification and clarity in forms and procedures, with arrangements for setting up citizen information centres in all the districts and towns.
5. Transparent procedures and criteria for beneficial identification in the provision of services and subsidies, the operation of the public distribution system, etc., to ensure that the benefits fully reach the poor and the disadvantaged, alongwith a system of public hearings to facilitate consultation by the pubilc at the local level.
6. Giving the citizens widespread and easy access to all information relating to Government operations and laws, and reversing the undue emphasis on

secrecy surrounding award of tenders and procurement, identification of beneficiaries, allotment of various assets, admission to colleges and schools, etc.

7. Steps to enact legislation for Freedom of Information, amendments to the Official Secrets Act, Codes of Conduct, rules for classification of records, etc.

8. Training and orientation of both officials and elected representatives at all levels, steps to upgrade their skills, access to technological and computerised aids for information processing and storage, top-level support by delegation of powers and workplace improvement and rewards for good performance.

9. Equipping and orienting all public offices and delivery centres to provide quick and responsive delivery of public services, grievance redressal and information to the public, alongwith convergent services for target groups in areas of basic services identified by the Conference of Chief Ministers in July, 1996.

Contributors

1. **Abdul Matin** - Reader in Sociology, Aligarh Muslim University Aligarh.
2. **Aftab Alam** - Teaches Political Science at the Aligarh Muslim University, Aligarh.
3. **Akhtar Majeed** - Director, Centre for Federal Studies, Jamia Hamdard, New Delhi.
4. **Ambrose Pinto, S J** - Director, Indian Social Institute, New Delhi.
5. **Arshi Khan** - Lecturer in Federal Studies, Jamia Hamdard, New Delhi.
6. **M.A. Kishore** - Coordinator, Human Rights Programme, Aligarh Muslim University, Aligarh.
7. **Md. Zafar Mahfooz Nomani** - Lecturer in Law, Aligarh Muslim University, Aligarh.
8. **M.M. Sankdher** - Professor in Political Science (Retd.) Delhi University, Delhi.

9. **P.K. Mathur** - Lecturer in Sociology, Aligarh Muslim University, Aligarh.

10. **P.M. Bakshi** - Former Director, Indian Law Institute and Member Law Commission of India, New Delhi.

11. **Ravi. P. Bhatia** - Delhi University, Delhi.

12. **S.S.H. Azmi** - Former Chairman & Dean Faculty of Law, Aligarh Muslim University, Aligarh.

Index